CATHOLIC RECORD SOCIETY
PUBLICATIONS

RECORDS SERIES
VOLUME 82

Bishop Herbert Vaughan and the Jesuits

Education and Authority

Edited by
MARTIN JOHN BROADLEY

PUBLISHED FOR
THE CATHOLIC RECORD SOCIETY
BY
THE BOYDELL PRESS
2010

First published 2010

ISBN 978–0–902832–25–1

A Catholic Record Society publication
published by The Boydell Press
an imprint of Boydell & Brewer Ltd
PO Box 9, Woodbridge, Suffolk IP12 3DF, UK
and of Boydell & Brewer Inc.
668 Mt Hope Avenue, Rochester, NY 14620, USA
website: www.boydellandbrewer.com

A CIP catalogue record for this book is available
from the British Library

Information about the Catholic Record Society
and its publications may be obtained from the Hon. Secretary,
c/o 114 Mount St, London W1X 6AH

This publication is printed on acid-free paper

Printed in Great Britain by
CPI Antony Rowe, Chippenham and Eastbourne

CONTENTS

ILLUSTRATIONS

ACKNOWLEDGEMENTS

During the course of collecting and editing the correspondence and the diary contained in this Records Volume I have received the kind help and generous support of numerous people who have provided documents, deciphered handwriting, translated letters, offered advice, proof-read scripts and answered innumerable enquiries with unfailing courtesy. I wish to thank Br James Hodkinson SJ, Fr Thomas McCoog SJ, Anna Edwards and Mihaela Repina at the Jesuit Archives, Mount Street, London; the staff at the Archives of Propaganda Fide, Rome; the Archivist and staff at the Jesuit Archives, Rome; Iris Jones, The English College Archives, Rome; Tamara Thornhill, Westminster Archdiocesan Archives; Fr David Lannon, Salford Diocesan Archives; Fr Peter L'Estrange for kindly allowing me to quote from his thesis; Emma Maglione, the Portico Library, Manchester; Vincent Morrison, The Xaverian College, Manchester; Dr David Laven, the University of Manchester; the staff of Manchester Central Reference Library; Br Richard Bailey, Julie Bloomer, Peter Conroy, Fr Anthony Dykes, Robert Galassi, Stella Halkyard, Christine Hill, Dr Peter Nockles.

I would also like to thank Professor Alan McClelland for encouraging me to publish this research and for reading drafts and making suggestions as to how it might be improved. I owe special gratitude to Dr Peter Doyle; throughout this project he has been a source of ever-patient and courteous help and advice.

ABBREVIATIONS

AAW	Archives of the Archbishop of Westminster
ABSI	Archivum Britannicum Societatis Iesu
APF	Archives of the Sacred Congregation for the Propagation of the Faith, Rome
ARSI	Archivum Romanum Societatis Iesu
SDA	Salford Diocesan Archives

Herbert Vaughan, Bishop of Salford

1832–1903; consecrated at the age of forty as the second Bishop of Salford. This photograph was probably taken at the time of the Fourth Westminster Synod, 1873. (Reproduced by kind permission of the Archives of the Mill Hill Missionaries)

Peter Gallwey SJ

1820–1906; educated at Stonyhurst, ordained 1852. Provincial of the English Province 1873–1876. (Reproduced by kind permission of Archivum Britannicum Societatis Iesu)

Cardinal Alessandro Franchi

1819–1878; Prefect of Propaganda Fide; one time professor of diplomacy at the Pontifical Academy of Ecclesiastical Nobles. [Taken from *Lives of the Cardinals*, no date]

Rmo Padre

Profittando del ritorno del Rmo P. Weld non voglio omettere di scriverle queste mie righe per manifestare tutta la soddisfazione che ho provato nel conferire col detto Religioso sopra gli affari religiosi d'Inghilterra. La fortunata combinazione del prossimo arrivo di Mgr. Manning mi permetterà, lo spero, di poter soddisfare il meglio possibile alle giuste e ragionevoli indicazioni che il medesimo mi fece in rapporto alla nuova Università Cattolica. Intanto io debbo ringraziarla per tutto ciò che V. P. ha fatto col concorso degli altri suoi Religiosi, a vantaggio di quelle missioni; pregandola ad un tempo a favorire sempre più l'insegnamento nelle grandi città, e particolarmente a Londra e Manchester.

Letter of Cardinal Franchi to Peter Beckx SJ

This letter, dated 13 November 1874, would become the singular and most vital piece of evidence in the Jesuits' argument that they were being encouraged – and in opening their Manchester school thus carrying out the wish of Propaganda – to do all they possibly could for education, especially in Manchester. (Reproduced by kind permission of Archivum Romanum Societatis Iesu.) See p. 10 below for a translation.

Nel prevenirla poi che in questi giorni si darà corso all'invito, di già fra noi concertato, da farsi al P. Cabos d'condursi qua in Roma per somministrare gli opportuni schiarimenti sulle Religiose del Madure; su di chè mi metterò d'accordo col P. Armellini; passo a confermarle i sensi della mia più distinta e affettuosa stima.

Roma li 13 Novembre 1874

Suo Affmo Servitore
Alessandro Card. Franchi

Benedicat *f* of Deus et dirigat gressos vestros in semith[?] *[?]*

Pius PP. IX

The above was written June 3rd 1875 by the Holy Father for the Xaverian
Brothers to encourage them in the work of Education which they are prosecuting
with great devotedness & fidelity in Manchester, especially having in
view the development of the Collegiate Institute

+ Herbert. Bishop of Salford.

June 17. 1875

Portrait of Pope Blessed Pius IX *opposite*

This portrait was presented by Herbert Vaughan to the Xaverian College on his return to England after the conclusion of the dispute with the Jesuits. In his own hand Vaughan had added the following inscription: 'The above [referring to the Pope's message written underneath the photograph: 'May God Bless you and guide your way in holiness'] was written June 3 1875 by the Holy Father for the Xaverian Brothers to encourage them in the work of education which they are prosecuting with great devotedness and fidelity in Manchester, especially having in view the development of the Collegiate Institute.' The inscription is dated 17 June 1875. (Reproduced by kind permission of the Xaverian College, Manchester)

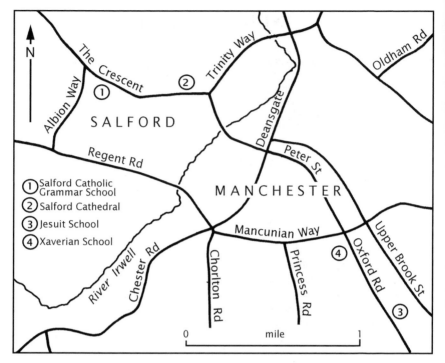

Location of the Schools

During the course of the dispute both parties made use of maps to reinforce their own arguments and to illustrate the distance between the Salford Catholic Grammar School and the Jesuit College in Ackers Street, Manchester. Vaughan saw the distance between the two schools in terms of proximity; in contradistinction the Jesuits considered the distance to be sufficient to warrant the establishing of their school in Ackers Street. The modern map illustrates the positions of: the Salford Catholic Grammar School, Salford Cathedral, the Xaverian College or Catholic Collegiate Institute in Grosvenor Square, the Jesuit College in Ackers Street (near to the Jesuit church of the Holy Name).

INTRODUCTION

It would be mistaken to dismiss the dispute of the regulars and the seculars as matters of petty jealousy, born of unnecessary rivalries. Some important principles were at issue between the contending parties which, in general, each believed crucial for the furtherance of Catholic truth in England. Motivation was usually inspired by religious principles rather than personal aggrandisement, by the rights of institutions to propagate Catholicism in their own tradition.[1]

Edward Norman sees how, viewed from certain perspectives, one may conclude that the history of the nineteenth century English Catholic Church consists of disputes. Among the disputants he specifically names Herbert Vaughan, the Bishop of Salford, and Fr Peter Gallwey, the Jesuit Provincial. This present volume concerns itself with the dispute that existed between these two men in the middle of the 1870s.[2]

William Turner,[3] the first Bishop of Salford, died suddenly in July 1872. Herbert Vaughan[4] was only forty years of age when he was chosen to succeed to the geographically small yet industrially important diocese of Salford, encompassing as it did the twin cities of Salford and Manchester. Among the clergy of the diocese he was not considered the heir apparent. Canon Peter Benoit[5] probably seemed the most obvious contender; he had acted as Vicar-General to the late bishop, "and during the last seven or eight years of the Bishop's life practically governed the Diocese."[6] However, a reputation for being strict and demanding debarred him from universal popularity.[7] As far as Henry Edward Manning, Archbishop of Westminster, was concerned, Herbert Vaughan was the most suitable candidate; he determined to ensure that he was also the most obvious choice.

[1] Edward Norman, *The English Catholic Church in the Nineteenth Century* (Oxford, 1984), pp. 88–89.
[2] For an overview of the dispute see Oliver P. Rafferty, 'The Jesuit College in Manchester, 1875,' *Recusant History* 20 (2) (1990), pp. 291–304.
[3] William Turner, 1799–1872, first Bishop of Salford 1851–1872: see John O'Dea, *The Story of the Old Faith in Manchester* (London, 1910), pp. 157–160.
[4] Herbert Vaughan, 1832–1903, second Bishop of Salford 1872–1892. For biographies of Vaughan see J. G. Snead-Cox, *The Life of Cardinal Vaughan* (2 vols., London, 1910); Robert O'Neil, *Cardinal Herbert Vaughan* (Tunbridge Wells, 1995).
[5] Peter Louis Benoit, 1820–1892; became Vicar-General in 1855; he was involved in the bringing of the Xaverian Brothers to Manchester.
[6] Herbert Vaughan, *The Bishop of Salford's Reply: Uncanonical Reopening of the Jesuit College and Summary of the Whole Case* (1875), p. 4.
[7] O'Neil, *Cardinal Herbert Vaughan*, p. 198.

Manning took the opportunity of Turner's funeral to assess Benoit's reaction to the possibility of Vaughan's nomination to Salford. Vaughan's first biographer, J. G. Snead-Cox, observes:

> Doubtless Manning tried his powers of persuasion on other members of the Chapter, but in Canon Benoit, who had himself been pointed to as a probable successor to Bishop Turner, he had gained an effective apostle.[8]

According to Robert O'Neil, Manning had to remove "formidable obstacles" in order to promote his preferred candidate.[9] One such obstacle was Benoit himself; Manning later arranged for him to become the administrator of the missionary college founded by Vaughan at Mill Hill. Of what nature the other obstacles consisted we cannot know; other than, during his speech at the luncheon to celebrate the new bishop's consecration, the Provost, Canon Croskell, referred to a rumour that Vaughan "had been forced upon the diocese against the wishes of the Chapter. 'That was false,' he said."[10]

When the Diocesan Chapter met on 7 August 1872 to draw up the *terna* – the names of three candidates who might succeed Turner – Peter Benoit's name was not among them. After six scrutinies the names, in alphabetical order, were:

Robert Croskell (Vicar Capitular)

John Rimmer

Herbert Vaughan

Manning, in consultation with the rest of the English Hierarchy, and prior to the *terna* being submitted to Rome, had Vaughan's name put first. At the Hierarchy's meeting concern was raised about Vaughan's nomination on account of how his zeal for defending the truth could sometimes lack prudence.[11] This was dismissed by Manning as nothing more than a slight complaint and possibly a result of the wounded pride of those who had opposed Vaughan over Catholic Education, the Temporal Power of the Papacy, and Papal Infallibility. His laudatory letter, strongly recommending the nomination of Vaughan and reassuring Propaganda Fide that he, Manning, had not forced his choice on the Salford Chapter, ends with his insisting on the need for Vaughan's presence among the English Hierarchy as a means of bringing to it intelligence and energy.[12]

The nomination of Herbert Vaughan as the second Bishop of Salford was made known to the Diocesan Chapter in a letter written by Manning,

---

[8]   Snead-Cox, *Life of Cardinal Vaughan*, vol. 1, p. 240.

[9]   O'Neil, *Cardinal Herbert Vaughan*, p. 198.

[10] Snead-Cox, *Life of Cardinal Vaughan*, p. 245.

[11] APF, Anglia 19, 1871–1874.

[12] APF, Anglia 19, 1871–1874.

dated 2 October 1872.[13] Shortly before his episcopal consecration, 28 October 1872, he received a congratulatory letter from the Jesuits, to which he replied:

> It is a consolation to me to know that there is a strong body of the Society in the Diocese of Salford. I hope I need hardly say that I shall always endeavour to cooperate with you in all your good works and that on the other hand I shall count upon your support in the public duties in which I may be engaged. I hope to be able at an early date in Nov. to pay a visit to my old *alma mater*.[14]

The details briefly outlined above provide two important points to be borne in mind when considering the issues represented by this present volume. First, the influential role played by Manning in securing Herbert Vaughan's nomination as bishop is most clear. Second, reference to Vaughan's energy and zeal, which at times suffered from a notable lack of prudence, and Manning's influence upon the young bishop, whose zeal and determination in pursuing his aims, and those of Manning, are also evident.

Peter Gallwey,[15] too, the Jesuit Provincial, was possessed of a nature no less zealous than that of the bishop-elect of Salford. His obituary in the Jesuit in-house journal, *Letters and Notices*, bears witness to a "combative instinct"[16] and ability to "act with an unyielding decision;"[17] it carefully passes over the Manchester college case with a cautionary word – "it would be injudicious to enter into details concerning them here, the more so as the full history of these incidents has not yet been attempted."[18] A biography, written in 1913, described him as being: "naturally a man of strong character, and with definite views and strong will;"[19] of his years as Provincial, the silence is maintained – "any reference to Father Gallwey's actions in his Provincialate would be out of place in these Memoirs."[20] Oliver Rafferty draws attention to Gallwey's

---

[13] "I have today received a letter from the Propaganda announcing that the Holy Father has named Fr Herbert Vaughan to the See of Salford. I make this announcement first to you as Vicar Capitular [Robert Croskell]; and that I may express the edification you have given me in this election. You will find Fr Vaughan full of respect and affection for you personally; and I believe you will soon know what I am losing in him, and what you have gained." Salford Diocesan Chapter Minutes, p. 78, Manning to Croskell, 2 October 1872.

[14] ABSI, CL/5, Vaughan to ? [letter begins 'My dear Fr Rector], 12 October 1872. Vaughan attended Stonyhurst College 1841–1845.

[15] 1820–1906, Provincial 1873–76. See M. Gavin, *Memoirs of Father P. Gallwey S.J.* (London, 1913).

[16] *Letters and Notices*, vol. 29, p. 45

[17] *Ibid.*, p. 52.

[18] *Ibid.*, p. 52.

[19] Gavin, *Memoirs of Father Gallwey*, p. 17.

[20] *Ibid.*, p. xi.

time as Provincial: "Somewhat unusually, his term of office lasted only three years, from 1873 to 1876: a term of six years is more usual."[21]

The protagonists personify the view of the historian Dom Cuthbert Butler: "For better or for worse, Church History is in great measure made up of the differences and quarrels of good men."[22] The differences and the quarrels in which Vaughan and Gallwey became embroiled were largely inherited, rather than something they themselves created. Vaughan described the whole issue as a "little episode;"[23] Pius IX was more forthright in his description – *Quell' affare dei Gesuiti é una vera porcheria.*[24] Whichever description one prefers, no doubt remains that this 'little local difficulty' would lead to a resolution which in turn would have an effect on the whole Catholic missionary world.

The immediate problem consisted essentially on the one hand, of Gallwey's wish to exercise in Manchester a privilege granted by the Holy See, whereby the Society of Jesus could open a school, without necessarily securing the permission of the local bishop, in areas where it already had a house or church; on the other hand, Vaughan contested this right; he too wanted to establish in Manchester a commercial college under his own jurisdiction. Below the surface of this problem lay deeper, unresolved issues. Where did the root of the problem lie?

Suspicion between the Jesuits and the secular clergy had a long history. It began, in the first instance, with a dispute over Church leadership following the death in 1584 of the last Catholic bishop in England – William Watson, Bishop of Lincoln. This dispute – the 'Archpriest Controversy' – may be summarised as follows. After Watson's death, the Catholic community in England had no head or guide; this had effectively been the case since Watson's imprisonment at Wisbech Castle in 1559. A partial and temporary Church government was supplied by William Allen[25] until his death in 1594; however, he held no episcopal authority. At the death of Allen the community became divided. One party, mostly

---

[21] Rafferty, 'The Jesuit College in Manchester,' p. 300.

[22] Cuthbert Butler, *The Life and Times of Bishop Ullathorne*, vol. 1, quoted in Norman, *English Catholic Church in the Nineteenth Century*, p. 4.

[23] Shane Leslie, *Letters of Herbert Cardinal Vaughan to Lady Herbert of Lea 1867 to 1903* (London, 1942), p. 268. However dismissive Vaughan's description might appear and so make light of the matter, the strain of the whole affair told on his health, see below, Correspondence, 16 October 1875 and fnn.

[24] Vaughan Diary, below, 3 May. Among several possible translations of this phrase, it can be translated as: "this affair with the Jesuits is a real pig's ear."

[25] 1531–1594, Cardinal; Fellow of Oriel College, Oxford; forced to flee England; concentrated his efforts on the training of priests for the conversion of England. He founded colleges at Douai and Rome and was instrumental in the founding of Valladolid. In his support of Philip II's invasion of England in 1588 he incurred the anger of many English Catholics.

Jesuit, known as 'the Exiles,' wished to destroy Elizabeth I's government; the other – 'the Appellants' – remained politically loyal and "blamed the Jesuits for exciting Elizabeth to take action against Catholics."[26] The appointment in 1598 of George Blackwell as Archpriest, with partial episcopal jurisdiction yet without episcopal consecration, made matters worse. John Bossy observes how "the archpriest's office was without precedence in the English Church, he did not exercise his functions within the framework of canon law ...; he had a kind of propulsive power, but no real jurisdiction, over the seminary clergy; and none whatever over the regulars or the laity."[27] The secular clergy accused Blackwell of pro-Jesuit policies detrimental to the Catholic cause in England, and of failing to stand up to the Jesuits. Several appeals were made for his removal. The controversy was formally resolved in 1602 by a papal brief of Clement VIII which tried to settle the seculars' main grievances by requesting Blackwell not to consult the Jesuits about secular clergy affairs. However, this did not remove the potential influence the Jesuits might have over the Archpriest and thus in turn over the secular clergy; the dispute remained unresolved. George Birkhead succeeded Blackwell as Archpriest in 1608. Birkhead petitioned the Pope and members of the Roman Curia to inaugurate a series of reforms among English Catholics, as the seculars considered the archpresbyterate to be an inadequate form of governing the Church in England. They preferred the establishment of a self-sufficient means of governance that would both stimulate the growth of Catholicism and yet not be perceived as a political challenge to state authority. Not all the secular clergy were in favour of the appointment of a bishop, on the grounds that it might prove antagonistic and thus reduce tolerance toward Catholics in England. The Jesuits' reservations about such an appointment were based on the fierce nature of persecution at the time. They considered such a move to be inopportune. John Vidmar notes the polemical nature of how the controversy has been related:

> Though the controversy over leadership died with the arrival of Birkett, [*sic*] the scars remained and would be re-opened periodically, not only in the writings of Charles Dodd[28] and Joseph Berington[29] in the seventeenth and eight-

---

26   John Vidmar, *English Catholic Historians and the English Reformation, 1585–1954* (Brighton, 2005), p. 6.
27   John Bossy, *The English Catholic Community, 1570–1850* (London, 1975), p. 46, quoted in Michael C. Questier (ed.), *Newsletters from the Archpresbyterate of George Birkhead*, Camden Society Fifth Series, vol. 12 (Cambridge, 1998), p. 5.
28   *The Church History of England* (3 vols., Brussels, 1737–42); *The Secret Policy of the English Society of Jesus* (London, 1715).
29   *State and Behaviour of English Catholics* (London, 1780).

eenth centuries, respectively, but even well into the nineteenth century with the writings of Charles Butler, John Lingard, and Mark Tierney.[30]

The histories of the English Reformation written by Butler,[31] Lingard[32] and Tierney[33] reflect the antipathy between seculars and regulars. It is the work of Tierney which is particularly relevant to the question dealt with in these pages, for it was from this source that Manning drew the historical basis of his opposition to the Jesuits.

Mark Tierney[34] played a central role in a campaign of 1840 to prevent regulars being appointed as bishops. His particular concern was the power of the Jesuits, especially the control exercised by them over the English colleges abroad; in his opinion, this made them a recruiting ground for the Society. His major work – a re-edition of Charles Dodd's *Church History of England* – was "an attempt to carry the anti-Jesuit crusade into the arena of history."[35] He hoped a new edition would exalt the secular clergy. He dismissed any thought of how it might open old wounds and agitate bitter feelings, claiming that only someone "whose intrigues have been worse than tempest in the land, and whose spirit, still unchanged, is ready to cry out against the unveiling of its mysteries," would take offence at his work.[36] The Jesuits, and equally so the bishops, found him a nuisance. His work remained unfinished.

Edmund Sheridan Purcell's *Life of Cardinal Manning*[37] omitted certain details, written by Manning in the form of an autobiographical note, of his opposition to the Jesuits. This was done on the grounds "that it might give pain to persons still living, or provoke controversy at home or abroad."[38] Purcell provides sufficient detail of the Cardinal's estimation of the Jesuits, leaving the reader, with the aid of a little imagination, well able to assess its true nature.

Prior to Purcell publishing his biography, Vaughan asked him "to omit from your biography all detailed mention of the Cardinal's strictures

---

[30] Vidmar, *English Catholic Historians and the English Reformation*, p. 17.
[31] *Historical Memoirs Respecting the English, Irish, and Scottish Catholics, From the Reformation to the Present Time* (London, 1819).
[32] *History of England* (8 vols., London, 1819–30).
[33] *Dodd's Church History of England* (ed.) (5 vols., London, 1839–43).
[34] 1795–1862, a secular priest.
[35] Vidmar, *English Catholic Historians and the English Reformation*, p. 78.
[36] *Ibid.*, p. 79.
[37] *The Life of Cardinal Manning, Archbishop of Westminster* (2 vols., London, 1896).
[38] Purcell, *Life of Cardinal Manning*, vol. 1, p. vii. Of the omitted passages, Sheridan Gilley writes: "The note on the Jesuits was omitted, though in a manner more damaging than its inclusion would have been." Sheridan Gilley, 'New Light on an Old Scandal: Purcell's Life of Cardinal Manning,' in Dominic Aidan Bellenger (ed.), *Opening the Scrolls* (Downside Abbey, 1987), p. 188.

upon the Jesuits."[39] The motive for doing this was for "the public good and the Church," rather than any personal feeling for either Manning or the Jesuits. Vaughan believed that it would amply justify Purcell's reputation as an "honest biographer" if he were simply to state how the Cardinal "entertained prejudices or strong opinions against the Society, or against their system." Vaughan pleaded the need for peace, mutual goodwill and the unity of forces – something of which the Church stood in need. Reflecting no doubt on the experience of his own dispute with the Jesuits, now nearly twenty-five years before, Vaughan sounds a word of caution – evidence that he has added prudence to zeal? – "The history of the past – when regulars and seculars fought each other in prisons, and even in the presence of martyrdom – ought to be our warning." He was of the opinion that nothing could be gained by "fighting useless battles over again." Vaughan does not attempt to deny Manning's opinions of the Jesuits. He simply points out how Manning,

> confined [these] to his own private notebook … All that he gave the world to know was that he did not employ the Jesuits, when the choice lay before him; *and I do not see why you should give the world any further information than this.*[40]

The omitted details are to be found in the 'Suppressed Chapter,'[41] in which Manning had spoken of his,

> … firm belief that to the action of the Society of Jesus in Rome from Father Parson's time to 1773 may be traced the loss of the English people … If the Episcopate of England had been renewed, and maintained, millions of English people would have been supported in their faith. The renewal of the Episcopate in England was rendered impossible by the action of the Society. The proof of this is to be seen in Tierney's edition of Dod's [*sic*] *History*, in the documents in the Appendix, and in abundant documentary evidence.[42]

The reading of "Historical documents, such as Dod's [*sic*] *History* with Tierney's Notes and Appendix"[43] had compelled Manning to examine the conditions of the Catholic Church in England. He concludes, "… the action of the Society in England was to divide and discredit the so-called secular clergy; and in Rome to hinder the restoration of bishops in

---

39   ABSI, Vaughan to Purcell, 8 November 1894.
40   *Ibid.*
41   'Cardinal Manning's Judgment on the Society of Jesus.' A copy of this autobiographical note exists in ABSI (no reference other than 'Purcell's Suppressed Chapter').
42   *Ibid.*, pp. 2–3.
43   *Ibid.*, p. 7.

England."[44] Some of the objections raised by Manning would later be echoed by Herbert Vaughan.[45]

Most conflicts during the seventeenth and eighteenth centuries between the regulars and the Vicars Apostolic revolved around the thorny question of what control should/could the latter exercise over the former in the instances where the regulars were ministering as missioners in the districts of the Vicars Apostolic. Peter L'Estrange describes the then existing structures of authority as "frail."[46] Benedict XIV's *Apostolicum Ministerium* (1753) laid down the rules governing the relationship between the two parties: the regular clergy were to be considered subjects of the Vicars in all matters relating to the mission. However, as L'Estrange points out, this instruction was written at a time when the penal laws were still in full force and religious houses did not exist in England.[47]

The privileges and exemptions enjoyed by the Orders to assist in their internal organisation were a source of conflict; they clouded the extent of the bishops' authority over the members of the Orders. The suppression and subsequent restoration of the Jesuits further exacerbated this conflict. Suppressed in 1773, the ex-Jesuits were placed under the control of the Vicars Apostolic; in 1802 the Pope gave permission for the English Jesuits to be linked to the Russian Province (where the bull of suppression had not been enforced). The Society was fully restored in 1814. In England the restoration was delayed until 1829, owing to the fear of the Vicars Apostolic that it would impede Catholic Emancipation. The Jesuits, too, were fearful that they, "like Jonas, must be thrown into the sea to save the ship."[48] At the time of the suppression, the Jesuits made up the highest number of regular clergy working in England. "During the period of suppression and the protracted restoration of the Society, the relationship of the Jesuits with the Secular clergy and Vicars Apostolic was affected by the history of their disputes in previous centuries,

---

[44] *Ibid.*, p. 8.

[45] For example: when the Seminario Romano and the English College, Rome, were in the hands of the Society all the best students became Jesuits; the objection to a Jesuit (Alfred Weld) saying "We hold that whatever is good for the Society is good for the Diocese"; that the Society cannot take the place of the Universal Church, nor the Hierarchy, nor the Holy See; the corporate action of the Jesuits in England has been excessive. See below: Correspondence, Vaughan to Gallwey, 17 August 1874; Diary 12 May, 27 May, 31 May; Appendix 3; also Herbert Vaughan, *The Jesuit Claim to Found a College of the Order in Manchester in Opposition to the Judgment of the Ordinary* (1875), pp. 7 and 15.

[46] Peter L'Estrange, 'The Nineteenth-Century British Jesuits, with special reference to Their Relations with the Vicars Apostolic and the Bishops' (unpublished D.Phil. thesis, University of Oxford, 1990), p. 31.

[47] *Ibid.*, p. 58.

[48] *Ibid.*, p. 59.

and the troubles of these years of restoration and emancipation affected, in turn, that relationship."[49] Amidst the general anti-Catholicism of the nineteenth century the Jesuits were a particular target of public suspicion and dislike.[50]

The history of the Jesuits and the bishops is not one of continual conflict and tension; cooperation did exist and to no small degree. Evidence at least of the desire for this is found in Vaughan's reply to the letter he received from the Jesuits, wishing him well for his consecration.[51] However, suspicion was fuelled by two decrees promulgated on 29 September 1838: one allowing the regulars to attach Indulgences to certain religious observances and to inaugurate pious confraternities in their missions; the other, the granting of permission to build churches without necessary approval of the local bishop.[52]

Resulting from the above decrees, there arose a further disagreement between the seculars and the regulars, this time regarding the building of a church in Liverpool. In 1840, 'The Society of St Francis Xavier' was begun with the aim of facilitating a new church under the care of the Jesuits.[53] This provoked a strong reaction among the secular clergy. One

---

[49] *Ibid.*, p. 47. For examples of such conflict in London, Wigan and Oxford, see pp. 71–90.

[50] Queen Victoria wrote to her daughter in 1872: "The Jesuits are a fearful body – and I am doubtful whether any laws can be severe enough against them. But I really do not know the state of the case abroad sufficiently well; still I know that dear Papa always thought they should be turned out of the country." Quoted in L'Estrange, 'Nineteenth-Century British Jesuits,' p. 12.

[51] See above, p. xix.

[52] For the texts of the decrees see Bernard Ward, *The Sequel to Catholic Emancipation* (2 vols. London, 1915), vol. 1, pp. 258–259. Due to past disputes that had taken place in England, Pope Benedict XIV suppressed all Indulgences and placed them under the administration of the Vicars Apostolic. Ward comments: "the practical result was not very far reaching" p. 143. The second decree, however, had important ramifications; it permitted regulars to establish churches and chapels without the permission of the bishop. Dr Griffiths, Vicar Apostolic of the London District 1836–1847, feared it "would disturb the peace of the Catholics of England ... if churches are built without the consent of the Bishop, flocks divided, and part taken from one church and transferred to another without his consent" p. 144. Given the decree had been issued without any consultation with the bishops, Griffiths wrote to Propaganda Fide asking for the decree to be suspended. When the two decrees were discussed the bishops resolved: "the first, respecting Indulgences, was uncalled for ... and would be a source of discord between the Regular and Secular clergy ... the second was subversive of episcopal jurisdiction, and would give rise to dissensions and scandals" p. 146. As a consequence they asked the Pope to revoke the second of the two decrees. The reply was to the effect that the consent of the Ordinary was needed, but that a refusal could only be made on just grounds. The Holy See reserved to itself the right to examine these grounds. For the formal response by Rome to the Bishop's request see Ward, pp. 259–260.

[53] See Maurice Whitehead, 'The Contribution of the Society of Jesus to Secondary Education in Liverpool: The History of the Development of St. Francis Xavier's College, c. 1840–1902' (unpublished Ph.D. thesis, University of Hull, 1894); also, 'The English

who was especially hostile to the plan was a young widower by the name of Lawrence Toole[54] who had entered Ushaw to study for the priesthood after the death of his wife; after ordination he served in the diocese of Salford.

Toole wrote a twelve-page letter to James Lennon, a member of the Society of St Francis Xavier. The letter rehearsed the effects of the Arch-priest Controversy and claimed that the project of the church "was set on foot to annoy Dr Briggs."[55] Toole spoke of the Jesuits as, "ever intriguing and secretly plotting to overturn the Episcopal Authority in this country." Maurice Whitehead, referring to the later conflict of 1875 and beyond, sees how in this conflict "the seeds of that great storm existed in Liverpool in the early 1840s."[56] Lawrence Toole would reappear in the late 1860s and 1870s when, as a Canon of the Salford diocese and rector of St Wilfrid's, Hulme, – the neighbouring mission to the Jesuits at the Holy Name – he was bitterly opposed, along with the great majority of the Chapter, to both the Jesuits opening a church in Manchester and later trying to establish a College there. The Jesuits considered him largely responsible for the Society being excluded from Manchester for over twenty years.[57]

Following a report submitted to Propaganda Fide by Cardinal Charles Acton,[58] the dispute in Liverpool was finally settled in favour of the Jesuits. What is more, Acton's recommendation was, "that a Jesuit college be established in Liverpool as a first step in an urgently needed national effort to meet the educational needs of the sons of the Catholic middle classes of England."[59] The then Jesuit Provincial, Randal Lythgoe, had already noted that near to the land the Society had bought in Liverpool for their planned church, the future University of Liverpool was under construction. Whitehead comments:

> Doubtless he was worried by the thought that the Anglican middle classes were providing new educational opportunities for the youth of Liverpool while the growing English Province of the Society of Jesus, now able and willing to offer a similar opportunity to the Catholic boys of the town was

Jesuits and Episcopal Authority: The Liverpool Test Case, 1840–43, *Recusant History* 18 (1986), pp. 197–219.

[54] 1807–1892, ordained priest in 1841.

[55] ABSI, College of St Aloysius, District Accounts 1700–1848; Toole to Lennon, [n.d.]. John Briggs 1788–1861; in 1833 he became coadjutor Vicar Apostolic of the Northern District; he succeeded to the Northern District in 1836; from 1840 he was Vicar Apostolic of the new Yorkshire District; in 1850 he became the first Bishop of Beverley.

[56] Whitehead, 'The Contribution of the Jesuits,' p. 43.

[57] See below, Correspondence, 19 April 1875, Weld to Gallwey.

[58] Charles Januarius Acton, 1803–1847; secretary to the Sacred Congregation of Regulars; was instrumental in the division of England into eight apostolic vicariates.

[59] Whitehead, 'The English Jesuits', p. 211.

being hampered in its work by a prelate[60] who should himself have been actively fostering the education of his flock.[61]

The Jesuit College of St Francis Xavier was to become, within the space of a generation, the largest Catholic secondary day-school in England.

There were striking similarities between Manchester and Liverpool. In Manchester, Owens College – later Manchester University – was built across the road from the Jesuit church of the Holy Name; the Society saw how, as it had in Liverpool, this might provide significant opportunities. The Manchester laity saw the College of St Francis Xavier as something desirable and providing for the educational needs of the Catholic middle class.[62] In both Liverpool and Manchester, the respective bishops were not in favour of the Society having a college. In 1842 Bishop Brown declared that he intended to open a boys' school within a mile's distance of the site of the proposed Jesuit church. The Society thus acted swiftly; they did not wish to lose the opportunity of establishing a college. Not wishing to be later accused of setting up a rival school, Lythgoe immediately therefore rented a small house, where he intended to open a day-school for boys.[63] This too would find echo in the Manchester college dispute; the Jesuits here acted swiftly in order to 'seize the day' and so establish a college of their own.[64]

Manning identified the Fourth Provincial Synod of Westminster (1873) as the time when dragons' teeth were sown. It was here that his oft-times difficult relationship with the regulars, especially the Jesuits, came to a head. Purcell observes how Manning found it difficult to balance episcopal authority with the privileges claimed by the regulars. For example, he disputed the Society's claim to open schools wherever they had a house; for this reason he never allowed a grammar school or college of the Society to be founded in Westminster.[65] Manning invited the Synod to draw up a decree regulating the relations between the regulars and the bishops. No decree was drawn up; according to Purcell many of the bishops opposed Manning.

Some years after the Synod, Manning wrote how,

> In that Council the first seeds of the contests of the Bishops and the Regulars were sown by Gallwey's unseemly speech and Father G. Porter's theory that *The Sincere Christian* and the *Catechismus ad Parochos* are the books for the

---

60 Bishop Brown, 1786–1856; Vicar Apostolic of the Lancashire District.
61 Whitehead, 'The English Jesuits', pp. 208–9.
62 See p. 136 below, 'Petition from the Manchester Laity to Propaganda Fide', and Appendix 8.
63 Whitehead, 'The English Jesuits', p. 213.
64 This may be seen particularly in the early part of the Jesuit correspondence.
65 Purcell, *Life of Cardinal Manning*, vol. 2, p. 506.

secular clergy. He did not say, but this means, that all that is higher is not for them.[66]

At the Synod, Gallwey asked Vaughan's permission for the Society to open a school in the district of the Holy Name – the Jesuit church in Chorlton-upon-Medlock, Manchester. The request met with a refusal; Vaughan explained that he had already publicly announced his plans to open a commercial college in the same city. His refusal was also based on the grounds that damage would ensue to the college run by the Xaverian Brothers, situated approximately ten minutes walk away from the church of the Holy Name.[67] Centuries of underlying and unresolved questions were finally about to come to the surface.

The nub of the problem was authority. The Jesuits, subsequent to their restoration, had to rebuild their internal structures and reassert the legitimate authority granted to them by the Holy See in the pursuance of the aims of the Society. This included a certain amount of freedom from episcopal control. L'Estrange observes how it took until 1866 for the English Province to reach the size it had been at the time of the suppression.[68] At the same time it must be borne in mind that the English Hierarchy, too, was only recently restored (1850). The efforts demanded in its reconstruction, and the enormity of the task, were much greater than even those facing the Jesuits. Bishop Ullathorne poignantly wrote: "a new hierarchy is jealous of its rights and guards itself against any interference with those rights, until claims are canonically established."[69]

Added to seemingly unavoidable jealousy was the prevalent, and more important, issue of the ignorance of the bishops regarding the rights enjoyed by regulars. Bishop Ullathorne believed that had the bishops been distinctly informed of the privileges claimed by the Jesuits, a great deal of trouble would have been averted.[70] This was echoed some years later by Bishop Clifford of Clifton in a private memorandum; it merits an extensive quote:

> The ignorance which at this time reigned concerning the privileges of the Jesuits was wonderful. The Jesuits openly made claim in England and elsewhere as if they possessed extraordinary privileges, and quoted the Bulls of Popes granted formerly to the Society, saying that these were revived with the restoration of the Society by Pius VII. These claims met everywhere with tacit acceptance … [English] Bishops, though ignorant of the extent of the privileges claimed, took it for granted that the Jesuits had extraordinary privileges;

---

[66] Purcell, *Life of Cardinal Manning*, vol. 2, p. 507. For the context of Porter's remark see L'Estrange, 'Nineteenth-Century British Jesuits,' p. 254.
[67] For Vaughan's reasons of refusal see Appendices 3 and 11, below.
[68] L'Estrange, 'Nineteenth-Century British Jesuits,' p. i.
[69] See Correspondence below, 8 August 1875, Waterworth to Gallwey.
[70] *Ibid.*

they suspected that they were strained, but nobody knew exactly what they were, and nobody knew how to find them out exactly, as it was supposed that many of them were privately given by the Pope.[71]

A report by the English bishops, submitted to Propaganda Fide in the light of the Manchester dispute, makes it clear that the question of a Jesuit school in Manchester was but part of a much larger question in need of clarification – the authority of the bishops in the light of the privileges claimed.[72] One matter, upon which the authority question was keenly felt, particularly between the bishops and the Jesuits, was education.[73] Manning declared that the real point at issue was: "who is to form the clergy and educate the laity in England;"[74] hence the sub-title of this volume, 'Education and Authority'. It is evident that Vaughan was an instrument in Manning's hands; Snead-Cox claims that Manning had, in the case of Vaughan's dispute with the Jesuits, "made the cause his own."[75] It is perhaps true to say that the cause had really been his from the first.

The major concern of the laity, especially the middle class, was not so much the 'authority struggle', but education itself. They simply wanted the most suitable education for their children and the freedom to choose that. This is evident in the letters written by members of the Catholic laity, contained in this records volume; and most particularly in the preamble of the petition submitted to Propaganda Fide by leading members of the Manchester laity.[76] Education was no less vital an issue for the laity as authority was for the bishops and regulars.

To the above factors we must add the ever-increasing movement away from lay control of the Church, and dependence on the Old Catholic families, toward episcopal control. The fact that Catholicism had survived, especially during the times of persecution, was thanks to the sustenance offered to it by the landed Catholic families. Two members of these families will appear in the pages that follow: William Clifford[77] and Alfred Weld.[78]

---

71 Snead-Cox, *Life of Cardinal Vaughan*, vol.1,pp. 275–276.
72 See below, 19 April 1875, Report of the Archbishop and Bishops on the College in Manchester.
73 For other areas of potential conflict see Snead-Cox, *Life of Cardinal Vaughan*, p. 322.
74 Manning to Bishop Bernard Ullathorne, cited in Shane Leslie, *Henry Edward Manning: His Life and Labours* (London, 1921), p. 312.
75 Snead-Cox, *Life of Cardinal Vaughan*, vol. 1, p. 320.
76 See below, 18 June [1875], Vaughan to Furniss; 2 July 1875, Noble to Vaughan; Noble to Furniss, [n.d.] p. 133; 31 July 1875, Stutter to Furniss; 31 July 1875, Noble to Franchi; 2 September 1875 Stutters to Wilding; Appendix 8.
77 1823–1893, Bishop of Clifton. He, Weld and Vaughan were all related to one another.
78 1823–1890, one-time Provincial of the English Province, later English Assistant to the Jesuit Superior General.

Of pivotal importance in the shift away from seigneurial Catholicism is the authority of the episcopacy as a source of unity. Manning envisaged the restoration of the Hierarchy as the opportunity whereby the Catholic Church in England became a more visible part of the universal Church, which would in turn have a revitalising effect. "Consequently, he argued, every bishop in the hierarchy became a conduit of the spirit and mind of the Holy See to his diocese 'with fullness and minuteness not possible in the vast vicariates of other days.' Manning's day was to be the days of the bishops."[79] Alan McClelland goes on to explain how "Manning's support ... for the episcopacy when in conflict with hitherto largely free-lancing independent religious orders and congregations needs to be seen within such a context."[80]

In the present context the theme of episcopal authority is significant for two reasons. The Jesuits, without naming names, accused some – among whom we may count Manning and Vaughan – of holding an excessive theology of the episcopacy and having too high a view of episcopal authority.[81] *The Case* – the Jesuits' reply to Vaughan's accusations and criticisms made against them – speaks of "an exaggerated idea of the rights and powers of the Bishop, inasmuch as he is bound, like other men, to use those powers and rights with all the fairness and consideration for the interests of others."[82] Vaughan by his threatening to suspend *a divinis* the Jesuit community in Manchester, because they reopened the college, did in fact act beyond the legitimate limits of his authority.

The First Vatican Council (1869–1870) formally defined the doctrine of Papal Infallibility. The desire of some of the Council Fathers for a strong and clear statement on the position, rights, and duties of episcopal authority – which would have constituted the subject matter of a further *Constitutio* – never materialised; the Franco-Prussian War forced the sudden break-up or breaking-off of the Council.[83] An elucidation

---

[79] V. Alan McClelland, 'The Formative Years, 1850–92,' in V. Alan McClelland and Michael Hodgetts (eds.), *From Without the Flaminian Gate. 150 Years of Roman Catholicism in England and Wales 1850–2000* (London, 1999), p. 7.

[80] *Ibid.*, pp. 9–10.

[81] "No one would be tolerated among the Catholics of England who denied, in the abstract, any of the rights or prerogatives of the Holy See. But to oppose the exercise of the rights of Religious Orders, and to give an exaggerated impression of the omnipotence of the Bishops in their dioceses, to speak as if they had in their hands the monopoly, not only of the care of souls, but of the work of education for all grades, the highest as well as the most primary, is, in the ultimate analysis, to question the powers of the successor of St. Peter." Anon., *The Case of the Bishop of Salford and the Society of Jesus* (1879), p. 50. See Appendix 12.

[82] *The Case*, p. 33.

[83] Ullathorne wrote from the Council: "The pope, I believe, is bent on the definition [of infallibility], if he can, as the crowning of his reign, and I think it will in some shape probably pass. What I am anxious most about is to get a balance on the side of the epis-

and thorough treatment of the theology of the episcopate by the Council was therefore made impossible. Evidence from Vaughan's diary speaks of a hope of this being eventually settled.[84] When it was adjourned on 20 October 1870, there was an expectation that the Council would be resumed when the political troubles were settled. This of course never came to be, "The drafts about missions, discipline, and pastoral care disappeared into the archives."[85] Paul VI would later refer to this theological rupture as, "the broken threads of the First Vatican Council."[86]

The Manchester Case demonstrates the tension between papal authority and episcopal authority; not, however, in a 'Gallican' way.[87] Exemptions and privileges, granted by the Holy See to the orders, were by their nature immediate, and thus 'by-passed' episcopal authority.[88]

---

copate, by defining its divine origin as a counter-balance, and by putting landmarks about the *ex cathedra*. If this is not done we shall have a wild enthusiasm, especially on the part of converts, and a disposition amongst the clergy and even laity to lower the power of the episcopate, and a stronger centralization." Cuthbert Butler, *The Life and Times of Bishop Ullathorne* (2 vols., London, 1926), vol. 2, p. 51. Mgr Darboy, Archbishop of Paris, complained that only the duties of bishops were spoken of, and not their status, powers jurisdiction and rights: "It is neither logical, useful, or becoming to speak of the duties of bishops unless their rights have previously been asserted." Cuthbert Butler, *The Vatican Council* (London, 1930), vol. 1, p. 221.

[84] See below, Diary, 26 May.

[85] Owen Chadwick, *A History of the Popes 1830–1914* (Oxford, 1998), p. 221.

[86] Walter M. Abbott, *The Documents of Vatican II* (London, 1966), p. 390.

[87] 'Gallicanism' is a term used to describe certain religious opinions once peculiar to the French Church. Gallicanism, in opposition to 'Ultramontanism,' tended to a restraint of the Pope's authority in the Church in favour of the authority of the bishops and the temporal ruler. "Vatican I rejected extreme papalism by stressing the inherent rights of the Bishops. Because the Council was prematurely broken off, there was no time to work out a more thorough theology of the episcopate." Karl Rahner (ed.), *Sacramentum Mundi: An Encyclopedia of Theology* (London, 1968), vol. 1, p. 223.

[88] Vaughan did not disagree *per se* with these privileges. In his first pamphlet, *The Jesuit Claim*, he acknowledged that, "He gladly and *ex animo* recognises the wisdom of their exemption from the ordinary Episcopal jurisdiction, according to the canons – first, in order that their own unity, peace, and religious observances may be the better maintained; and secondly, in order that by their direct dependency on the Roman Pontiff, the faithful also, among whom they live and minister, may become more closely bound to the centre of unity, which is the Apostolic See." p. 17. However, he goes on to qualify what he means: "At the same time the Bishop respectfully represents if a Religious Order, *under plea of privilege*, be permitted to intrude – and more especially if the intrusion be effected in the manner already described [Vaughan describes the Jesuits' action of opening a school in his diocese as an "invasion … made in the night unknown to the Bishop and in spite of him" p. 15] – between the Bishops and the execution of their matured Diocesan projects, the hands of the Episcopate will become paralysed and the normal organization and government of the Dioceses in England impossible. This is one of the *causarum majorum* and is referable as such to the wisdom and judgement of the Holy See." p. 17. Cardinal Franchi, the Prefect of Propaganda Fide, "… realised that if Vaughan pressed his claim to the superiority of episcopal jurisdiction over Jesuit privileges, the matter would involve an investigation of the whole range of relationships between the bishops and regular clergy. The Cardinal

Some years after the closure of the Manchester school discussion still continued as to the limits of the bishops' authority, in the pages of the *Month*[89] and the *Tablet*.[90] Both parties claimed to represent the authority of the Holy See. The Jesuits insisted on the independence of the religious orders in the work they had been given to do by Rome, for example teaching. *The Case* accused the bishops, in all but name, of encroaching on this freedom.[91] This, and other issues, would finally be resolved in the constitution *Romanos Pontifices*.[92]

Sources

The sources reproduced in the following pages trace the development of the dispute between Vaughan and the Jesuits. The bulk of the material consists of the exchange of letters between various members of the Society; notably, Peter Gallwey the Provincial, and Alfred Weld the English Assistant to the General, based at Fiesole; numerous others are from the Society's Secretary Fr Armellini, and the staff of the Holy Name church, Manchester, to the Provincial. A significant portion consists of letters between Vaughan and Gallwey. A smaller proportion includes letters to, and from, Cardinal Alessandro Franchi and Fr Peter Beckx, the Jesuit Superior General. Vaughan himself kept precious little of his correspondence; the Salford Diocesan Archives holds no correspondence about the dispute; with few exceptions, the same is true of the

---

Prefect hoped to avoid such an investigation. Instead, he arranged for two meetings between the Jesuit General, Fr Beckx and Bishop Vaughan, anxious that they might arrive at some compromise whereby the Jesuits closed the school [which they had opened without Vaughan's permission] and Vaughan did not dispute the Jesuit privileges ... If Vaughan was correct in his view of episcopal power, then it restricted the exercise of Papal power as this was mediated through the operations of the exempt religious orders. Hence Franchi's desire to achieve a settlement without examining the question of privileges." Rafferty, 'The Jesuit College in Manchester,' p. 297.

[89]   The *Month* 15 (1878).

[90]   See the *Tablet*, 14, 21, 28 September 1878; 5, 12 October 1878; 9 November 1878; 7 December 1878. See L'Estrange, 'Nineteenth-Century British Jesuits,' pp. 173–180, for discussion on this debate. See below for correspondence on the matter, 4 October [1878], Vaughan to Jones; 5 October 1878, Jones to Vaughan; 10 October 1878, Jones to Vaughan; 12 October 1878, Jones to Coleridge; 15 October 1878, Jones to Coleridge.

[91]   See *The Case*, pp. 41, 47–52.

[92]   Issued 8 May 1881, it defined the relationship between the regulars and the bishops. The constitution was extended to the United States (1885), to Canada (1911), to South America (1900), to the Philippine Islands (1910) and generally to all missionary countries. The provisions of the constitution are: the exemption of religious from episcopal jurisdiction; relations of religious engaged in parochial duties, and matters pertinent to temporal goods. See 'Romanos Pontifices' in *The Catholic Encyclopaedia* (New York, 1912). For an account of events leading up to *Romanos Pontifices*, see Snead-Cox, *Life of Cardinal Vaughan*, vol. 1, pp. 320–357.

Archives of the Archbishop of Westminster; thankfully, Gallwey made copies of his letters to the bishop.

It will be seen that some letters pre-date the beginning of the actual dispute, while others originate after the closure of the Jesuit College. Both have been included so as to place the immediate conflict in a wider context, to highlight the role of Manning, and to show that the issue remained in some minds unresolved, even after the closure. They are demonstrative also of the depth of feeling felt by members of the Society in regard to Vaughan's accusations, and evidence the need for him to make reparation commensurate with the damage caused.

Wherever possible the original letters have been used. A very few letters, available no longer elsewhere, have been copied from Shane Leslie's biography of Manning, and Snead-Cox's biography of Vaughan. Reference has been made, where applicable, to letters published elsewhere, for example: in either of Vaughan's or Gallwey's pamphlets, *The Case*, or Snead-Cox's biography. Very little editing of any correspondence has taken place. Letters originally written in Latin, Italian, and French have been translated; endeavouring to remain faithful to the original, every effort has been made to avoid a too literal and hence clumsy translation. Abbreviations found in the original have been expanded in the present text in square brackets; underlining appears in italics.

Sources not included are: Vaughan's two privately published pamphlets, representing as they do his points of view, the reasons why he refused permission for the Jesuit College, and his criticism of the Society's behaviour. These pamphlets are: *The Jesuit Claim to Found a College of the Order in Manchester in Opposition to the Judgement of the Ordinary*, which was prepared for the bishops' meeting in Low Week, 1875; and *The Bishop of Salford's Reply: Uncanonical Reopening of the Jesuit College and Summary of the Whole Case*, which was in reply to the Provincial's address[93] to the Hierarchy at their Low Week meeting. The pamphlet by Gallwey, *Facts and Documents Relating to the College of the Society of Jesus in Manchester*, written as a briefing paper and sent to Propaganda Fide to inform the Congregation of the Society's side of the dispute; and the Society's later publication (1879), *The Case of the Bishop of Salford and the Society of Jesus*, have also been excluded. All these documents are available at the Salford Diocesan Archives and the Jesuit archives at Mount Street, London. The pamphlets of Vaughan and Gallwey are not included as they duplicate much of the material provided in the correspondence; also, the narrative of each is implicitly traced in the sequence of the letters. Evidence of the proceedings of the dispute found only in the pamphlets and not in the correspondence

---

[93] See Appendix 5.

has been included as an appendix, along with a précis of *The Case of the Bishop of Salford and the Society of Jesus*. This substantial document contains, like the pamphlets, many of the letters written around the time of the actual opening and closing of the college. It is in large part a response to the 'Brief Summary of the Whole Case,'[94] printed in the second of Vaughan's pamphlets. The précis provides the main objections the Society raised against the assertions and accusations contained in the two pamphlets; these are to be found in the 'Summary of the Bishop's Case, sent to his Agent in Rome' (Appendix 3) and 'Brief Summary of the Whole Case' (Appendix 11).

The sources in the Jesuit archives, Mount Street, London, have previously been used in relation to the Manchester dispute, notably by Snead-Cox, Rafferty, and L'Estrange. Snead-Cox used certain parts of the *corpus* to illustrate Vaughan's desire to be 'ruler in his own diocese;' this included paraphrasing parts of Vaughan's diary kept at the Archives of the Archbishop of Westminster. Rafferty refers only to the material available at Mount Street; in doing so he has given a detailed overall picture of the immediate elements of the conflict. L'Estrange, in his unpublished D.Phil. thesis, drew on sources at both Mount Street and the Jesuit archives in Rome. His study deals with the wider issue of the relationship between the Jesuits and the Vicars Apostolic and the bishops in the nineteenth century. The 'Manchester School Case' forms a central chapter to his study.

The diary that Vaughan kept during his stay in Rome, April–June 1875, is one of six volumes kept at AAW. It was not his custom to keep a full and permanent diary. The diaries are sporadic and, apart from the first two, mostly concern his various trips abroad. The diary reproduced below is more in the nature of a journal. One gets the impression that it was written with the intention of recording Vaughan's version of events. He often quoted in Italian what others had said about the affair; these quotations are given in italics, with English translations in square brackets. In numerous cases the Italian is faulty; this presumably reflects Vaughan's imprecision in writing grammatically correct Italian. Despite these errors the diary is important, for it allows the readers to sense the zeal and urgency with which Vaughan pursued his goal and the delicate nature of the negotiations.

To these archival collections I have added sources from the archives of Propaganda Fide, Rome; never before referred to in the context of the Manchester case, this relatively small cache of documents widens the scope, and in so doing demonstrates the historical import of the dispute which took place in Manchester. The Bishops' Report to Cardinal

---

94   See Appendix 11.

Franchi, the Prefect of the Propaganda,[95] is clear evidence that the deeper issue was the question of authority.

John Hungerford Pollen (1858–1925), the Jesuit historian, wrote a critique of Snead-Cox's chapter dealing with the dispute between Vaughan and Gallwey.[96] A letter of Snead-Cox to Pollen acknowledges that parts of the biography had not met with Pollen's approval.[97] In response, Snead-Cox explains, "the only purpose for which it was written [was] to show how the case presented itself to the Cardinal. My only concern was to see the thing as he saw it."[98] He goes on to distinguish the task of the historian, which is to make oneself "familiar with the truth" from all angles, whereas the role of "a biographer … is simply to ascertain which view of the matters in issue was taken by the man whose life is being written." Pollen suggested that a statement of the Jesuit side of the case should be included in any future edition there might be of the biography. Snead-Cox was agreeable to this, and suggested that perhaps Pollen himself might be the person to do it, "so as to make it authoritative."[99] Pollen's drafted critique was probably written with the intention that, should a second edition of the biography appear, his analysis would be included. It may be concluded that Snead-Cox had no intention of misrepresenting fact[100] when, in his biography, he presented the argument from Vaughan's point of view; he did so, as he put it, "to recapture the mood in which he faced the difficulty and as far as possible let that mood be reflected in this book."[101] This he did in pursuance of his role as a biographer rather than an historian.

Pollen's 'Study of Chapter XII' is written from the perspective of an historian, and fulfils Snead-Cox's criterion – that "in all quarrels there are two sides, and a man writing history ought to make himself familiar with the truth;" in observing this Pollen produced a balanced assessment of the whole case. The foundations for the Society's actions are laid on the fact that, "they were acting at the express desire of the Cardinal Prefect of Propaganda, and were making use of a privilege, which the Pope had given and had sustained for centuries."[102] The Society's Achilles heel was Gallwey – "a man of great and heroic virtues … of a stock for which fighting had no fears … he entered too lightly into a contest, which could

---

95   See below, pp. 76–82.
96   ABSI, RY/2/2, 'A Study of Chapter XII: Notes on the Case of the Jesuits.' The text is marked, 'Not for publication, draft for correction.' The chapter in question was: 'Ruler in His Own Diocese,' Snead-Cox, *op. cit.* pp. 270–305.
97   ABSI, RY/2/1, J. G. Snead-Cox to Pollen, 29 March [n.y.].
98   *Ibid.*
99   ABSI, RY/2/1/, Snead-Cox to Pollen, 6 April [n.y.].
100 Snead-Cox to Pollen, 29 March [n.y.].
101 Snead-Cox to Pollen, 6 April.
102 Pollen, 'A Study of Chapter XII.'

only end in defeat."[103] Gallwey interpreted too narrowly the letter from Cardinal Franchi to the Jesuit General, Peter Beckx, in which the Society was encouraged to do all it could for the education of the middle class.[104] Gallwey, too, later recognised this to have been a fundamental error.[105] Franchi's letter was in reality a broad encouragement, for the benefit of the diocese in general. Gallwey saw it as "imposing a duty, in the execution of which he ought not to look aside to right or to the left, nor allow anything to deter him."[106] Likewise, the arguments put forward by Vaughan were not entirely well-founded throughout.

> The allegation that he *must* start a *commercial college*, in order to secure *priests* for his diocese, needs the support of many other considerations before its validity become apparent.[107]

It was not only the Jesuits who found Vaughan's reasons for refusing them leave to establish a college unconvincing. The Xaverian Brothers, too, were not satisfied by his protestations of being their staunch defender. One of his strongest objections to the Jesuit College and upon which he relied heavily, was that it would harm the "vested interests" of the already established Xaverian School in Grosvenor Square – only ten minutes' walk from where the Jesuits proposed to open their college. On his return from Rome in 1875, after he had successfully won his appeal against the Society, Vaughan presented the Xaverian School with an autographed picture of Pius IX, on the reverse of which the Pope had attached a hand-written note sending special wishes to the Xaverian Brothers in view of the future development of the Collegiate Institute in Manchester.[108] However, within a year of the closing of the Jesuit College Vaughan, despite previous statements that he wished to "develop the Xaverian," opened a new college next door to the Xaverians in Grosvenor Square. This school became St Bede's College; soon after opening it removed to Alexandra Park.

> Hard feelings developed between the two schools, a decision of a subsequent English Provincial Chapter being to send a committee to the authorities of St. Bede's to try to settle the differences. This entire matter with Vaughan remains shrouded in mystery.[109]

103 *Ibid.*
104 See below, Correspondence, 13 November 1874, Franchi to Beckx.
105 See Pollen, 'A Study of Chapter XII.'
106 *Ibid.*
107 *Ibid.*
108 Brother Plunkett, 'Historical Sketch of the English Province,' *The Ryken Quarterly* (1964), p. 14.
109 *Ibid.*

I hope that what follows may throw some light on this mystery. I also hope, by having made these important sources more readily and widely available, further research may be facilitated into the history of the development of Catholic education in the second half of the nineteenth century and the role played by the bishops and other agencies in this development; especially that of Manning and Vaughan, whose part in that story was so central and vital.

In brief, the whole of what follows may be summarised thus: the struggle witnessed in Manchester was fought on the grounds of educational provision; however, it was representative of the last round in a protracted and expansive conflict of authority between the bishops and regulars.[110] Centuries of misunderstanding, conflict and the jealousies of fallen humanity and, no less, ideals and principles, had become distilled into one issue: 'Bishop Herbert Vaughan and the Jesuits: a question of education and authority.'

[110] Pollen wrote: "When we remember that this was the first serious Church legislation on any scale since the *Regulae Missionis* of 1753. There is really no wonder whatever that such a debate should occur, should be necessary. The *Regulae Missionis* took years, so did *Britannia*, so did the decree of 1696 – and the archpriest legislation." Pollen, 'A Study of Chapter XII', ABSI, RY/2/2. Britannia was "a Breve ... which declared that as the regulars had apostolic authority, the leave or approbation of the ordinary 'neither was nor is hereafter needful unto them.'" Ethelred L. Taunton, *The History of the Jesuits in England 1580–1773* (London, 1901), p. 413.

THE CORRESPONDENCE

Weld to Gallwey
Fiesole,[1]
11 March 1874.[2]

My dear Fr [Gallwey],[3]

I do not know if you are aware, but you ought to know, that Dr Manning[4] has petitioned to Rome for the withdrawal of the Constitution 'Apostolicum' of Benedict XIV[5], which would put all our houses which have less than 12 religious under the Bishops. We are getting up a memorial against him in Rome. I have sent them a memorandum to help them and here send you the substance that if there is any thing you think it worth while to send you may do so.

[The rest of the letter consists of eleven points making up the memorial; the tenth point is as follows.]

In Manchester, Bishop required us to have a parish; there and in Glasgow we were limited in the number of Fathers, and both at Manchester[6] and in London[7] we were prevented from having a school for boys.

---

[1] Near Florence. After the destruction of the Papal States in 1873 the Jesuit Curia moved to Via San Gerolamo, Fiesole.

[2] Archivum Britannicum Societatis Iesu (ABSI) C/3, Arthur Weld to Peter Gallwey, 11 March 1874.

[3] Peter Gallwey SJ, 1820–1906; educated at Stonyhurst, ordained 1852. Provincial of the English Province 1873–1876.

[4] Henry Edward Manning, 1808–1892; Archbishop, later Cardinal, of Westminster 1865–1892.

[5] *Apostolicum ministerium*, the Constitution of Benedict XIV, dated 30 May 1750, whereby the four Vicars Apostolic of England and Wales received rules to assist them in the administration of their respective districts.

[6] Gallwey had asked Herbert Vaughan at the Fourth Provincial Synod of Westminster (1873) for permission to open a school in Manchester. The following is taken from the first of Vaughan's pamphlets written in opposition to the idea of a Jesuit college. "The Bishop replied that this would be impossible; that not only had he publicly announced that he was himself going to undertake this work, but that he had actually embarked on the undertaking, that vested interests had to be consulted before the Society could be allowed to begin a College in Manchester; and that the building of a College attached to the Church of the Holy Name would entirely frustrate the plans which the Bishop had made for the educational organization of the Diocese." *The Jesuit Claim to Found a College of the Order in Manchester in Opposition to the Judgement of the Ordinary* (1875) (hereafter, *The Claim*), p. 4.

[7] In the same year that this letter was written (1874) Manning, with the purpose of serving middle-class education, opened St Charles's College, Kensington. V. A. McClelland

Ever yours sincerely in J[esus] C[hrist]
A.Weld[8]

Weld to unknown
Fiesole,[9]
11 May 1874.

My dear Fr,

I have just seen Monsignor Stonor.[10] I told him what you told me about Archbishop Howard's[11] idea that we did not do enough for the middle class etc. And that we were not allowed a school in London or Manchester ... He expressed his sorrow that Archbishop Manning would keep things so in his own hands that he would let nobody do anything (you must not betray him). He was very friendly.

Gallwey to Vaughan
7 August 1874.[12]

My dear Lord,[13]

You will not be angry with me for writing this letter. I think if you will trust us, I can guarantee that neither you nor the Diocese will have reason to repent. If you will permit us to have a Grammar School or College in Manchester: 1) I think you will have more vocations for the

---

identifies the opening of this college as "one of the reasons why Manning would never allow the Society of Jesus to open a Grammar School in London. He could not afford that his magnificent enterprise at Kensington should be ruined by the Society's attracting the best pupils ... His opposition to the Jesuits opening a school in London was also based on a fear that they would seize all the promising youths who wished to be priests for their order and leave the mediocre material for the diocese ... They took only the intellectual cream of aspirants to the priesthood." V. A. McClelland, *Cardinal Manning: His Public Life and Influence 1865–1892* (London, 1962), pp. 53–54. These same reasons would be echoed by Vaughan in his dispute with the Jesuits.

8   Alfred Weld SJ, 1823–1890; Provincial of the English Province 1864–1870, English Assistant in Rome 1873–1883; sometime editor of *Letters and Notices*, the *Month* and the *Messenger*.

9   ABSI, BN/6, fragment of a letter; the handwriting is that of Weld.

10   Mgr Edmund Stonor, 1831–1912; son of Thomas Stonor, 3rd Lord Camoys; Canon of St John Lateran; titular Archbishop of Trebizond; enjoyed a wide acquaintanceship with Roman authorities and was used by the English Hierarchy as an agent in Rome.

11   Archbishop Edward Henry Howard, 1829–1892; titular Archbishop of Neo-Caesarea, specialised in Oriental Rites at Propaganda Fide.

12   ABSI, RX/5, Gallwey to Herbert Vaughan, 7 August 1874. See *The Claim*, pp. 18–19; Anon., *The Case of the Bishop of Salford and the Society of Jesus* (Manresa Press, 1879) (hereafter *The Case*), pp. 80–81.

13   Herbert Vaughan, 1832–1903; Bishop of Salford 1872–1892; Archbishop of Westminster 1892–1903.

secular priesthood and foreign missions than you will get by other means and at much less cost to the Diocese; as a proof – I was teaching in our Liverpool school[14] 30 years ago when it began. In my time (three years,) we never had more than 30 boys, yet out of that lot ten, if I mistake not, became priests: six seculars and four religious. I suspect strongly that the Rev. John Beesley, now at Ashton, was one of my scholars. So was Canon Croft, of Worksop; and his brother, the Rev. Thomas Croft, of Usk; and Rev. W. Hilton. They would be educated up to the end of their classic course, without costing the Diocese anything, or at most, a trifling sum. The foreign missions would also gain. 2) The presence of Owens College[15] would help much for the preparation of young men for Civil Service. 3) We could also have a course of philosophy in English in the evenings. 4) I think also we would improve our own teaching by getting what we could pick up from Owens College. 5) If you choose to establish a boarding-house, you could educate boys from the country for a very small sum.

I have put these thoughts frankly and honestly before you, and I am begging prayers that you may be inspired to do what is best. If you think my suggestion at all worthy of consideration, I would call upon you sometime about the 20th.

This plan would nowise interfere with Mgr. Capel's[16], and would yet provide for many who want to enter the army, etc., without too much expense.

Very truly,
Your Lordship's Servant in Christ,
P. Gallwey.

---

[14] St Francis Xavier's, founded 1842.

[15] Owens College was effectively the first of the civic universities founded in the second half of the nineteenth century. Formed in 1851 from a legacy of £100,000 left by the Manchester merchant John Owens, the college was first housed in Quay Street in the city centre. In 1873 it moved to a purpose-built campus on Oxford Road, opposite the site of the Jesuit church of the Holy Name. It gained university status in 1882, thus becoming the Victoria University of Manchester.

[16] Mgr Thomas John Capel, 1836–1911; rector of the Catholic University at Kensington; the college, established in October 1874 by Archbishop Manning, was envisaged as an organisation under the Hierarchy with examiners drawn from existing Catholic colleges with degree-conferring faculties and complete with a senate. The Religious Orders, including the Jesuits, were excluded from it. For a history of the college and the dispute with the Jesuits see V. A. McClelland, *English Roman Catholics and Higher Education 1830–1903* (Oxford, 1973), pp. 277–322.

Vaughan to Gallwey
Bishop's House,[17]
Salford.
17 Aug. 1874.

My dear Fr Gallwey

I have delayed replying to your note, in order to obtain the benefit of the prayers which you were obtaining for my guidance. I must say that I have no hesitation as to the conclusion which it is my duty to make known to you, now more formally by letter than when we spoke *viva voce* upon this subject, last year.[18]

You will perhaps remember that, some years ago the Society obtained permission from the Bishop of Salford[19] to establish a School or College in Manchester. After having carried it on for some time, you finally, by an act of your own abandoned it.[20] The Bishop to save the enterprise from complete failure then took it up, and it carried on to this day.[21]

---

[17] ABSI, RX/5, Vaughan to Gallwey, 17 August 1874. See *The Claim*, pp. 19–20; *Facts and Documents relating to the College of the Society of Jesus in Manchester* (1875) (hereafter *Facts and Documents*), pp. 3–5; *The Case*, pp. 81–82.

[18] See above, n. 6.

[19] William Turner, 1799–1872; first Bishop of Salford 1851–1872. See John O'Dea, *The Story of the Old Faith in Manchester* (London, 1910), pp. 157–160.

[20] The school, situated near the area known as All Saints, at the Oxford Road end of Rusholme Road, was opened in 1852 by Frs Jerrard Strickland SJ and T. Parkinson SJ; it closed eighteen months later. Vaughan later claimed that the Society had assured Turner that they had £5000 to spend on the school and accused them of not carrying out their promise to do so. See *The Claim*, p. 12. The Society rejected this statement: "The £5000 is a fable and so is the promise to spend that sum on the College." See below, Etheridge to Coleridge, 7 May 1878.

[21] Vaughan refers to the original school as the 'Manchester Catholic Grammar School'. Turner continued to run the school by staffing it with diocesan clergy. In August 1862 it came under the auspices of the Xaverian Brothers and became known as the 'Catholic Collegiate Institute', situated in Grosvenor Square, All Saints. In 1906 it moved to Victoria Park and became the 'Xaverian Grammar School'. David Lannon, in his 'Bishop Turner and Educational Provision within the Salford Diocesan Area, 1840–1870' (unpublished M.Phil. thesis, University of Hull, 1994), notes: "The Xaverian Brothers came to Manchester in 1850. In spring 1852 Fr Benoit suggested they open a middle school. Their founder was not particularly impressed at what he considered interference but agreed that such a middle school would offer the best chance of the financial support he desperately needed. An initial attempt was made by Brother Paul Van Gerwen at their house at 64, Grosvenor Square, All Saints [very near to the Jesuit school]. Opened in 1853 the school closed at the end of that year because the Jesuits had upon invitation just opened another middle school. Ryken wrote in February 1853 to Benoit expressing his shock, reminding Benoit that they had agreed that his Brothers should start such a school. It jeopardised, he believed, all his plans and he felt they should leave Manchester. Turner, deciding Manchester needed a middle school, had turned to the Jesuits. Benoit's negotiations with the Xaverian Brothers had either been too protracted or ineffective, or had been conducted without Turner's knowledge: an unlikely happening" p. 148. This may explain Benoit's antipathy to the Society of Jesus, for Turner admitted to Fr Etheridge SJ, "I am given to

Another Catholic Grammar School or Middle School has been established since then.[22] One of these schools is actually in the neighbourhood of your church.[23] Vested rights have come into existence, and it would hardly be right or considerate to interfere with them, or to put them in jeopardy, as you would do by your proposal. Then again, I have publicly and formally announced my intention of developing one of our Grammar Schools into a Commercial College,[24] upon a sufficient scale and plan to meet the existing requirements as soon as I have completed the work of the Seminary.[25] It is my intention to invite the Society to take a certain part in the undertaking, and I shall be glad to receive from you now an assurance that I may count upon your co-operation in carrying it on when the time comes to make a beginning.

Finally, considering all the circumstances, the present backward condition of our Diocesan[26] and Hierarchical[27] organisations – the

understand ... that, in consequence of introducing the Jesuits in Manchester I had lost the good opinion and popularity of all my clergy. What has caused me real pain is to see the altered views of Mr Benoit himself. On a fitting opportunity I intend to have some serious talk with him." ABSI, Letters to Bishops and Cardinals, Turner to Etheridge, 4 January 1853. If Turner did speak to Benoit it was to no avail; Benoit persisted in his opposition to the Society: twelve years later Turner commented to Thomas Harper SJ, "there is not a member of my Chapter more opposed to your coming here than Canon Benoit." See below, Harper to Coleridge, 23 April 1878.

[22] The Salford Catholic Grammar School opened 1852 in the bishop's house, The Crescent, Salford.

[23] The Catholic Collegiate Institute staffed by the Xaverian Brothers, in Grosvenor Square, All Saints.

[24] See Appendix 1, extract from Vaughan's pastoral letter, 30 November 1872, announcing his intention to establish a Catholic Commercial College in Manchester.

[25] The Seminary of Pastoral Theology, situated adjacent to Salford Cathedral, was intended to be a place of transition between the actual seminary where the newly ordained had studied and parochial life in the parishes of the diocese. See J. G. Snead-Cox, *The Life of Cardinal Vaughan* (2 vols., London, 1910), vol. 1, pp. 252–259.

[26] In his pamphlet, *The Claim*, Vaughan explained that, "The duty of a Bishop is to organise his Diocese and to develop its different sources of strength." Among these duties he envisaged that "there ought to be a first-rate Commercial College" in Manchester. One advantage such a college might confer would be the prospect of it being a means "of recruiting clergy from the better classes of the Diocese." This was considered important, as at the time one-third of diocesan clergy were foreigners, or persons from dioceses outside England. A Jesuit college in Manchester – Vaughan maintained that there was not room for such – would mean surrendering the education of the better classes into the hands of the Jesuits. The Jesuits had "already many educational establishments in England, – two of them in Lancashire. The one in Salford Diocese [Stonyhurst] ... educates the sons of many of the principal Manchester Catholics. Another College in Manchester would give them a complete monopoly of the education of the easy and middle classes in the Diocese." p. 8.

[27] This reference to hierarchical organisation is the real crux of the whole matter. See p. 80 below, 'Report of the Archbishops and Bishops on the College in Manchester.' Also *The Claim*: "the Bishop respectfully represents that if a Religious Order, *under the plea of privilege*, be permitted to intrude – and more especially if the intrusion be effected

vested interests which are at stake – the opportunity which you have already had – the undertaking to which I am pledged – and the fact that you already possess one College in the Diocese, I must beg of you entirely to dismiss the idea that it is possible for the Society to establish another house of education in Manchester.

I do not know whether you are aware of the condition upon which the late Bishop gave leave for a mission of the Society to be founded in Manchester. According to a Memorandum[28] which I have by me, it is said that "it was distinctly agreed between the Bishop and the Provincial, that the Fathers were never to establish any school in Manchester beyond the parochial school needed for the children of the poorer class of this Congregation."[29] I am very sorry not to be able to do what you wish in this matter. I have had to consider the matter in all its bearings and *coram Deo*, and I believe that the decision I have come is A.M.D.G.[30]

---

in the manner already described [Vaughan refers to it as an "invasion [was] made in the night unknown to the Bishop" p. 15] – between the Bishops and the execution of their matured Diocesan projects, the hands of the Episcopate will become paralysed and the normal organization and government of the Diocese in England impossible. This is one of the *causarum majorum* and is referable as such to the wisdom and judgement of the Holy See." p. 17.

28 'Memorandum of the late Bishop's Secretary and Confidential Adviser as to the Agreement Between Bishop Turner and the Provincial S.J., 11 October 1873': see Appendix 2. Vaughan later claimed with regard to Benoit's memorandum that, "A special value attaches to the evidence of Canon Benoit because it was chiefly he who had urged the late Bishop to re-admit the Jesuits into Manchester in charge of a Mission, and had always been very favourable to the Society. His testimony is that of a friendly witness." *The Claim*, p. 4. Compare this view with the evidence above, n. 21.

29 In *The Claim* Vaughan states that this "condition", of the Society not being permitted to open a College, was an intrinsic part of the agreement upon which the Society were re-admitted to Manchester in order to build a church. The agreement "was not drawn up in writing, the Bishop trusted to a verbal agreement, for it was not his habit or the practice of his time to act with the same official precision, and with the use of forms such as are becoming customary now that the Church in this country is gradually assuming its normal condition." p. 11. Vaughan also explained why it could not "be regarded as unnatural or extraordinary that the late Bishop should have imposed such a condition. For it was not the first time that he had admitted the Jesuits into Manchester under a similar restriction. On the first occasion he had limited them to the establishment of a College, on which they assured him they were going to spend £5000," but they withdrew without having spent the promised sum. "In like manner … when the Jesuits in 1867 came again … telling him [the Bishop] that they had a large sum of money to be applied [to building a church] his Lordship … gave his consent … also under a condition – they should not found a College." Turner did this "to protect himself and his successor against the possibility of others coming in to reap where they had not sown, of frustrating his plans before they had come to maturity." pp. 12–13. The inference is that the Jesuits had twice failed to keep their word regarding sums of money. The Society would later contest this agreement, and would speak of it in terms of being "an intimation". See below, Weld to Gallwey, 28 October 1874; Gallwey to Vaughan, 19 December (1874).

30 *Ad Maiorem Dei Gloriam* 'To the greater glory of God', the motto of the Jesuits.

Wishing you every blessing,
I am, your faithful and devoted servant,
+Herbert, Bishop of Salford

Gallwey to Vaughan
20 August 1874[31]
Glasgow

My dear Lord,

I cannot but admit that many of your Lordship's reasons are very valid, – and at the same time I am grateful for the friendly tone of your letter.

With regard to our having given up our school in Manchester, I think I ought to say this much, that we only did so after receiving a very clear and decided answer from the late Bishop, that he saw no probability of our being ever permitted to have a church there.[32] The school unsupported by a church threatened to be a losing concern, and consequently we were forced to retire.[33] Had we any hope left of being allowed a church, we would certainly have held our ground. A good Grammar School near the Cathedral,[34] and another at our end, would not be too much for Manchester, but I most fully agree in all that you say respecting vested rights.

I was not aware of the agreement made with the late Bishop to which you allude.[35] With regard to co-operating in your future College, if any possible plan could be contrived, I would willingly help, but before you commence your work, I shall be found out and turned off, meanwhile a good many vocations will be lost.

---

[31] *The Claim*, pp. 20–21; *The Case*, p. 83.

[32] "I have reconciled the clergy to your commencing a day school in Manchester. They appear to be satisfied when I told them you did not contemplate building a church." ABSI, Letters of Bishops and Cardinals, Turner to James Etheridge, 26 January 1853.

[33] It must not be supposed that Turner was angry with the Jesuits for having, in their own words, "to abandon the school in Manchester." Although he regretted "exceedingly" this decision, he both recognised that the Society had "done a real service to religion" and that he owed "a debt of gratitude to the Society for the kindness and courtesy I have received." He was determined to continue "that cordiality and harmony which ought to exist between a bishop and the Society." ABSI, RX/5, Turner to Joseph Johnson, 20 May 1854.

[34] Salford Catholic Grammar School.

[35] This alleged agreement, made between Bishop Turner and Fr Weld, the then Jesuit Provincial, on the occasion of the Society's second entry into Manchester, was to the effect that the Jesuits "were never to have a school in Manchester other than schools for the poor." See above, Vaughan to Gallwey, 17 August 1874.

Very truly,
Your Lordship's servant in Christ,
P. Gallwey.

Weld to Gallwey
San Gerolamo,[36]
Fiesole.
16 September [1874]

My dear Fr,

In addition to what I said about the Manchester school on Saturday, I would say that though our parish gives us an additional right to a school, it is not to be assumed that boys are to come from our parish only. As long as there is no other school that gives a good Classical education in Manchester, such a school is wanted by all boys capable of profiting from it. How many parents in Glasgow wanted a classical education? But it is very important it should be given them, provided the essentials of commerce are not neglected.

Ever yours sincerely in J[esus] C[hrist]
A. Weld

Weld to Gallwey
San Gerolamo,[37]
Fiesole.
28 October 1874

My dear Fr,

You may rely on my putting what you send me fairly and honestly before Fr General.[38] Only it is rather hard to get time. I have officially only one hour in the week unless there is something immediate, so I have to condense, but I gave him your meaning as well as I can and kept nothing back, of this you may be quite sure.

In your last letter you speak of the Manchester College. I think for me to do anything you should try and send me some facts such as I asked of you before. What Catholics go to Owens College? What can be said to answer the Bishop's argument about vested rights? What are those schools? Where? with a map of Manchester. Also any facts about the middle schools which the Parish Priests are getting up. Get me as much exact information as possible – I must be able to prove what I

---

36 ABSI, C/3, Weld to Gallwey, 16 September [1874].
37 ABSI, C/3, Weld to Gallwey, 28 October 1874.
38 Peter Beckx, 1795–1887; Superior General of the Society of Jesus 1853–1887.

assert – of course as soon as you can. We ought to be able to prove the need and the wishes of the people. They say Cardinal Franchi[39] is well disposed but he is a clear headed straightforward man, and we must be precise in what we advance.

I have nothing to add today except that [*sic*] with respect to the condition Bishop Vaughan speaks of.[40] There was no *condition* whatsoever. I think you will find the Bishop's letter to me in the box I left in Mount Street. I kept them all. Fr Harper[41] had written to me to tell me that the B[isho]p had shewn him a piece of ground which he designed for us, and had told him to tell me.[42] I wrote to the Bishop to ask if this was to be considered as a permission etc. He wrote back almost if not exactly in these words "If either of these two pieces of land suits you, the sooner you begin the good work the better."[43] This was his first letter. This letter I think exists. Afterwards when we refused to build on that ground and preferred Ackers Street he made difficulty till I offered to give some help to Mr Fox,[44] he then wrote immediately giving leave. I think this letter is there too. We gave Mr Fox £25 a year for two years and I believe everybody laughed at us for it.[45] The Bishop was content with this. One day he said to me "We don't want a school." I looked on it as a thing to be got later. I think these facts or most of them are written in a journal which was in that box of which I spoke before. I return the B[isho]p's letter which I have copied.

It would be a good thing to find out how many boys have gone to the Secular Priests from S[aint] F[rancis] Xavier's,[46] Liverpool during these few years. Fr Harris might know. It would show that our schools help the diocese.

---

[39] Alessandro Franchi, 1819–1878; Prefect of Propaganda Fide; one time professor of diplomacy at the Pontifical Academy of Ecclesiastical Nobles.

[40] See above, Vaughan to Gallwey, 17 August 1874.

[41] Thomas Harper SJ, 1821–1893.

[42] This was in December 1865 when Bishop Turner approached the Jesuits with the view of their returning to Manchester and building a church there. See below for Harper's very detailed account of the matter in his letter to Fr Coleridge, 23 April 1878; also Bishop Turner's letters to Fr Weld at ABSI, Letters of Bishops and Cardinals, ff. 336–347.

[43] The exact words were: "If the site or sites mentioned by Fr Harper meet your approval the sooner you commence the good work the better and my blessing be with it." ABSI, Letters of Bishops and Cardinals, f. 339, Turner to Weld, 3 January 1867.

[44] Rev. Thomas Fox, 1827–1881; resigned a canonry of Northampton diocese before moving to Salford diocese; rector of St Edward's, Rusholme, 1863–1873. Fox objected to the proposed site of the Holy Name church, as he believed it would be harmful to his own church of St Edward. The Society offered him £25 per year as a means of compensation for any financial loss he might suffer as a consequence of the Holy Name being built in Ackers Street. See ABSI, Letters to Bishops and Cardinals, Turner to Weld, 31 January 1867; Weld to Turner, 1 February 1867; Turner to Weld, 2 February 1867.

[45] See ABSI, RX/7, Fr Tomas Porter to Weld, 9 and 21 January 1869.

[46] The Jesuit College in Liverpool.

Pray for yours ever sincerely in J[esus] C[hrist],
A. Weld

Franchi to Beckx
Rome,[47]
13 November1874

Most Reverend Father,
   Profiting from the return of the Most Reverend Father Weld, I take the opportunity to write to you these few lines to express the utmost satisfaction that I felt in conferring with him about religious matters in England.
   The fortunate combination of the imminent arrival of Mgr. Manning will allow me I hope to satisfy, in the best possible manner, the just and reasonable considerations that he himself made with regards to the new Catholic University. Meanwhile, I find myself obligated to thank your Reverence for all that you have accomplished, with the support of your excellent Religious, for the advantage of these missions; praying you meanwhile to support evermore education in the big cities, and particularly in London and in Manchester.
   Furthermore, in giving you advance notice that in the next few days, as we have already discussed, an invitation will be made to Father Cabot to come to Rome to provide the necessary explanations about the Sisters of [illegible], upon which I will come to an agreement with Father Armellini, can assure you of my highest and most respectful esteem.

Your most affectionate servant,
Cardinal Alessandro Franchi

Beckx to Gallwey
Fiesole,[48]
15 November 1874.

Rev. Fr Gallwey, Provost Provincial,
   This evening we have begun the Spiritual Exercises, and Fr Weld is returned to us for a few hours. He briefly reported to me his actions: among other things he has spoken to H[is] E[minence] the Cardinal Prefect of Propaganda[49] and to some others, about whether we have the right of erecting Schools where we have houses, and everyone answered

---

[47]   Archivum Romanum Societatis Iesu (ARSI), Anglia 1005.IV.I, Franchi to Beckx, 13 November 1874.
[48]   ABSI, RY/2/2, Beckx to Gallwey, 15 November 1874.
[49]   Cardinal Alessandro Franchi.

unanimously that such is our undoubted right, indeed they displayed the desire that we *should* open schools. The Cardinal Prefect has deigned to write to me to this effect, which I share with Your reverence on the attached sheet.[50] For this reason Fr Weld thinks it would be good if Your Reverence were to speak immediately with the Most Rev. Lord Manning to indicate to him that we intend to open a school in London and that we intend you speak with him to agree a more suitable location, and that everything may be done in good harmony.

Fr Weld thinks the Most Rev. Lord Manning is somewhat obliged in this matter, and that the Eminent Prefect cannot retract his word, given to me in his letter, a copy of which I send.

This idea does not displease me, but I have not been able to mature it sufficiently to define or prescribe anything certain, and so I share it with you, so that you may see and weigh carefully what is to be done, once all the circumstances have been considered; and we shall be able to deal with this matter again once the exercises have been completed. I understand that one must act with caution and prudence regarding this question, especially when dealing with the Most Rev. Lord Manning. To the wise few words are plenty.

Peter Beckx S.J.

Weld to Gallwey
Fiesole,[51]
16 November 1874.

My dear Fr Provincial,

I have been so busy since I wrote last and had so little convenience for writing that I could not tell you of the further progress I had made in your affairs. I returned here this morning and we begin our retreat tonight.

After my first interview with Cardinal Franchi I was strongly advised to get something from him in writing, and also to see some of the other Cardinals of the Propaganda in case the question should go before the Congregation.[52] I accordingly went again to Cardinal Franchi and added some points to my story, then told him it would help very much if he would give me a few lines to give Fr General encouraging him to push on education especially in London and Manchester.[53] He answered that

---

[50] See above, Franchi to Beckx, 13 November 1874. See below, Gallwey to Vaughan, 13 March [1875].

[51] ABSI, C/3, Weld to Gallwey, 16 November 1874.

[52] The Sacred Congregation of Propaganda Fide.

[53] It was probably on this occasion that Weld took the opportunity to speak to Franchi

he would do so willingly and told me to come again on the Friday and he would give me a letter. He added that Arch[bisho]p Manning was coming to Rome, and he would speak to him about it, and he hoped all would be right.

I told him he must take as a basis that we have a right to open schools where we are, and persuade the Arch[bisho]p to agree with you as to a suitable position. This he promised to do. I then went to Cardinals de Luca,[54] Patrizi[55] and Consolini[56] who are the most influential of the Propaganda. They all expressed the same opinion of surprise that we had been excluded from the higher studies,[57] that as we had not been asked we could not be blamed for not taking part; that what we are now doing could not be interfered with, that Manning's College[58] was insufficient for a city of 3½ million of inhabitants, and that we had an undoubted right to open schools where we were already established. Cardinal Bilio[59] was out of Rome or I would have seen him also. The position in which I left the various questions with Cardinal Franchi is this:

1) Lower studies. He will explain to the Arch[bisho]p that we have a right where we are, and persuade him to agree with you as to a suitable site if another is preferred.

2) Higher studies. What we are doing now is not to be interfered with.

3) He quite approved of our programme to transfer the Philosophy and Theology of our scholastics to a place near London when it is convenient to us to do so and after a little delay to transfer to the same place our lay higher studies.

It was necessary to agree to some delay about this last point in order not to appear to act in opposition to Capel, about which they were all anxious and as I had told him that a College of ours not far from London was the best way for us to take part as things now are. They were all

about the matter of Turner's stipulation made to him when he was Provincial, to the effect that the Society was not to open a college in Manchester. In a memorial submitted to the bishops at their Low Week Meeting in 1875, Gallwey, who was then Provincial, stated that Weld, "for the security of his own conscience laid fully before the Cardinal Prefect of Propaganda all that passed between Bishop Turner and himself, and that the Cardinal declared that on this score there was no difficulty." See pp. 59–63 below, Gallwey's Memorial to the Bishops, 7 April 1875. For Vaughan's understanding of this see Gallwey's Memorial, n. 172 below.

54 Antonio de Luca, 1805–1883; Prefect of the Sacred Congregation of the Index 1864–1878.

55 Constantino Patrizi, 1789–1876; Dean of the College of Cardinals.

56 Domenico Consolini, 1806–1884; Prefect of Economy at Propaganda Fide.

57 From taking part in the Catholic University at Kensington College.

58 St Charles's College, Kensington.

59 Luigi Maria Bilio, 1826–1884; played an important role in the preparation of the *Syllabus of Errors* and *Quanta Cura*.

anxious that all should be done peacefully and especially that Protestants should not know any differences that may exist.

Now as Cardinal Franchi is going to speak to Dr Manning, I think we should lose no time in acting upon what we have got so as to keep the Cardinal to his good purposes. I may here say *confidentially* that some of ours have not great confidence in his standing up for us.[60] Though since he has been Prefect of Propaganda we have certainly had nothing to complain of. There is not much fear of his *forbidding* the use of a right which he has acknowledged, but I do fear the Arch[bisho]p may persuade him by his eloquence that a school is not wanted, and induce him to ask Fr General to wait. I think therefore it is best to act at once and write to the Archbishop that Fr General has written to say that the Cardinal Prefect has written to him on the subject of a school in London, and that though his Eminence acknowledges that you can do it by virtue of your establishment at Mount Street, he would be glad if you would agree with the Archbishop upon a suitable site.

It will have to be done with great courtesy, but I am inclined to think there is more danger to be feared from not doing it. If the Arch[bisho]p tells the Cardinal that Fr General has already acted on his letter it will strengthen him very much against any arguments of Dr Manning. In all this Fr General leaves you to follow your own judgement.

It has just occurred to me that it will also be good to get Fr Armellini[61] to say to the Cardinal that Fr General has already taken action in the wish expressed in his letter, but your writing at once will remove any appearance of your choosing his absence for asserting your right.

I have written this after my retreat so excuse delay.

Ever yours in Xt.
A. Weld

Vaughan to Gallwey
Bishop's House,[62]
Salford
7 December [1874]

My dear Fr Gallwey,
I quite enter into your feeling about the new chapel in Grosvenor Square.[63] I should be sorry if it were to be an injury to the interests

---

[60] Weld demonstrates here his shrewdness; as time passed his fears would be proved right.
[61] Torquato Armellini, 1823–1901; Secretary of the Society of Jesus.
[62] ABSI, RY/2/2, Vaughan to Gallwey, 7 December 1874.
[63] The church of the Holy Family, Grosvenor Square, is in the All Saints area of Manchester.

of the Holy Name. It is some yards – not a great many – nearer to your mission than St Alphonsus School, which has for years served as a chapel on Sundays, to the great inconvenience of the school and of the people. I do not think that it will be a permanent public chapel. In any case I will do what I can to see that you suffer no natural injury. I have some experience, from the way S. Edward's, Rusholme, is nearly swamped by the progress of your three decker.[64] You cannot help it, of course.[65]

I am much obliged for your friendly act in mentioning to me the report about our correspondence in France.[66] The circumstances were these; a Jesuit Father returning from Rome made a number of statements concerning my relations with the Society in Manchester, which were not only, as I consider, slanderous but painful and injurious to my character. The lady to whom they were made was shocked, and wrote to me about them. I thereupon sent a copy of our correspondence with permission to show it to the said Father, and with the injunction to return it to me. This she did; but it now appears from what you say that she has retained a copy of it. I shall therefore write to her to destroy it. What may have been said in Rome of course I know not, but I feel quite sure that the words or sentiments expressed by others were not yours. It might be more perfect to bear all imputations in silence, but one ought to remove them, it seems to me, if they are likely to injure some other work or persons, as I thought they might in the present case.

Believe me to be
Your faithful and devoted servant,
+ Herbert Bishop of Salford

Gallwey to Vaughan
8, Salisbury Street,[67]
Liverpool.
11 December 1874,

My dear Lord,
I was very sorry to learn from your Lordship's letter that unpleasant remarks had been made in Rome and in Paris about our correspondence

---

[64] The church of the Holy Name. St Edward's was the neighbouring mission. A 'three decker' was a type of pulpit common during the time of the Evangelical revival.
[65] In *The Claim*, Vaughan is not nearly so understanding: "... the Church and the Mission of St. Edward's have been drained and literally ruined through the great Church of the Holy Name with its staff of Priests having been set down in too close a proximity." p. 10.
[66] See below, n. 68.
[67] ABSI, RX/5 (fragment), full text in *The Claim*, pp. 22–23; *The Case*, pp. 83–85.

respecting a College.[68] The matter is quite new to me. I had to give official information to two or three persons that your Lordship had not thought it possible to grant my petition. What glosses were subsequently added by others I know not, and am really sorry if any unfair and rash comments have been made on the course which your Lordship thought the right one. We shall most certainly be the sufferers, if we in any way propagate or encourage unjust and calumnious misrepresentations. As far as my own thoughts are concerned – I can see quite clearly that there is much to be said for the view which your Lordship has taken – and I should consider it wicked to speak or write any rash condemnation of it. At the same time I very often pray that another view may succeed in its place, and that your mind may revert to its earlier phase. For it seems to me (as I am sure you will allow me to speak frankly) that the zeal which helped you to carry through your bold undertaking for the Foreign Missions will hereafter give you more consolation that the cautious policy which you think the best at present.

Just at this moment, we have very earnest petitions for Missioners from the Bishop of Grahamstown, from Madras, from Jamaica, and from Malta. The demand for English Missioners is ever increasing, as your Lordship knows. Now it seems to me that in Manchester and the manufacturing towns around there is an ample nursery of priests, not only for your Lordship's Diocese, but for other poor souls besides – provided the chance is given by early education. I have known pretty intimately many of your Lordship's family. I cannot think that the grace which has been given to you will permit you to limit your pastoral charity only to those institutions in which the Diocese is decidedly concerned.[69] I think

---

[68] The copy of this letter as reproduced in Vaughan's pamphlet, *The Claim*, p. 21, is prefaced with the following explanatory paragraph. "In the month of September, the Bishop of Salford received a letter from an influential friend in France informing him of a visit received from a Jesuit Father returning from Rome and of the account which that Father had given of the Bishop's hostility to the Society, and of his want of zeal for souls, as exemplified in his refusal to allow the Society to open a College in Manchester according to their Rule, while his people were crying out for Jesuit education and suffering for the want of it. The retention of the goodwill and friendship of the Bishop's informant appeared to him to be sufficient to justify him sending a copy of the correspondence between himself and the Provincial S.J. in the preceding month, with a request that it should be returned. It was returned; – with the expression that it was entirely satisfactory. Father Gallwey, in a letter (which has not been kept) at the beginning of December, called the Bishop's attention to a report he had received from a Jesuit that a letter of his to the Bishop had been read in Paris and shown to another Jesuit. The Bishop replied to Father Gallwey telling him of what had occurred."

[69] Later evidence shows that Vaughan was not debilitated by a narrow understanding of his episcopal duties; with regard to his establishing a commercial college he wrote to its future Prefect of Studies, Louis Charles Casartelli, "I wish to provide for the children of my own flock in the first place, but at the same time I cannot fail to bear in mind that a bishop ought, as St Alphonso somewhere says, to be interested in and to work for objects

I should be quite safe in prophesying that if your Lordship grants us permission to do the work of our Institute by taking a part in education, the number of vocations to the priesthood, both for the Salford Diocese and for other parts of the globe, will be trebled and quadrupled.

I am writing all this not only on account of the kind tone of your Lordship's letter to me, but also in consequence of other letters that have been sent to me.[70]

It appears that it has been stated in very high quarters in Rome that we are unwilling to do anything for Middle-Class Education.[71] This is about as true as the reports concerning your Lordship to which you refer. This report and other representations on the subject have led to a correspondence between Fr General and the Propaganda. The Cardinal Prefect begs him to do all he can in England for Middle-Class Education, and names Manchester among places, and both he and some other eminent Cardinals have reminded us that this belongs to our Institute, and that wherever we are canonically instituted, it is part of our acknowledged work to open schools, that the permission to do so is already granted to us by the Holy See. Father General himself is most desirous to carry out the wishes of Propaganda, but I am sure that he would have the strongest objection to doing anything that would in any way prove an injury to your Lordship's Diocese, and very great reluctance to act against your Lordship's wishes. The happiest solution of the difficulty of the position will be if your Lordship going back in spirit to Mill Hill[72] – awakens old sympathies for souls outside the boundaries of Salford and makes an act of faith in the promise "date et dabitur vobis." This is the grace which I am hoping for during the octave of Our Lady.[73]

Very truly,
Your Lordship's servant in Christ,
P. Gallwey

---

which extend far beyond his own diocese. He who is of the Apostolic line ought to have the universal spirit of an Apostle." Salford Diocesan Archives (SDA), Box 179, Vaughan to Casartelli, 25 June [n.y.].

[70] See above, Beckx to Gallwey, 15 November 1874, in reference to Franchi's letter of 13 November 1874.

[71] See above, Weld to unknown, 11 May 1874.

[72] Mill Hill, an area approximately eleven miles from the centre of London; here Vaughan purchased a property as a foundation for a college for the training of missionary priests.

[73] Vaughan interpreted this letter, and the one Gallwey wrote to him on 19 December (see below), as having been written "in terms which seemed to have advanced from the nature of a petition to the assertion of a right and a threat." He understood from both that "The intimation is, that this will be done in spite of me, if I do not consent, upon the strength of the Card. Prefect of Propaganda's desire, and in virtue of their own privileges." *The Claim*, pp. 4 and 25.

P.S.
I shall be at Ackers Street on Monday.

["In answer to this the Bishop invited the Rev. Father to call and dine with him on Tuesday."][74]

Weld to Gallwey
San Gerolamo,[75]
Fiesole.
16 December 1874.

My dear Father Provincial,
I have been waiting to hear from Fr Armellini the final result of Cardinal Franchi's conversation with Archbishop Manning, but I hear this morning that he is sick with fever, so it is no use waiting. If I find that he is likely to be laid up long I will ask Fr Lambert[76] to call. He does not know the Cardinal so well as Fr Armellini. I trust all is right, as I think the Cardinal would have let us know if any difficulty arose, but I want to know if anything was settled about the limits. If not you can I think stand for the limits he formerly assigned me, i.e. east of Regent's Park which is over three miles from him, and at worst do what Cardinal Consolini suggested, say "give us a suitable place or we open a school at Mount Street." I was rather afraid of Manning's long interview with the Pope, but the Pope is not easily turned from a view he has once taken. I will let you know as soon as I hear anything further.

The question of the letter in Paris is very curious.[77] I cannot understand it. I feel sure I have not spoken of B[isho]p Vaughan's letter out of the Curia, and certainly only to say that he would not allow a college. Six months ago I told Monsignor Stonor that he and Manning refused colleges, meaning him to tell Howard and so get it to the Pope that it was not our fault. I certainly told some of the Cardinals that there was a great Protestant college close to us,[78] and the Bishop had nothing that could counteract it.

I think after B[isho]p Vaughan's civil letter about the chapel,[79] you will have to go with great tact when you announce your intention

---

[74] *The Claim*, p. 23. For the reply to this letter see below, Gallwey to Vaughan, 19 December [1874].
[75] ABSI, BN/6, Weld to Gallwey, 16 December 1875.
[76] George Lambert SJ, 1821–1882; Substitute (secretary) to the English Assistant in Rome 1870–1875.
[77] See above, Vaughan to Gallwey, 7 December [1874].
[78] Owens College, later to become the University of Manchester.
[79] Holy Family, Grosvenor Square: see above, 7 December [1874].

of opening [a] school. Of course the Cardinal's letter will be a great help.[80] Indeed, after that he cannot complain, but you must use it well. It occurred to me as a question whether it would not be worth while if there really is any respectable school near us which would be swamped, to give them something for a year or two as we did to Mr Fox,[81] not as a right, but only out of kindness to help them in their fall, and to keep the good will of the Bishop. He is a good fellow, though I always think he has learned too much from the Archbishop. It might be useful to remind him that Manchester people attributed the fate of the Rusholme Church to Mr Fox's own fault who had no idea of working a parish.

What you say of Fr Birch[82] has always struck me. He is too small for that place. I lost confidence even in his management of temporals at The Mount. Like many men of small ideas, he would sometimes burst into an extravagant speculation. I should like to see Fr Lawson in his place. He is a good preacher and could push on the College.

Ever yours sincerely in Jesus Christ,
A. Weld

Beckx to Gallwey
Fiesole,[83]
17 December 1874.

Rev. Father Gallwey, Provost Provincial,

I fully consent that Your Reverence's institution of Colleges in London and Manchester is a matter of the utmost importance, and that what His Eminence Cardinal Franchi has written to me in his own hand can help us in a marvellous way. But since it greatly matters to us that in our dealings we may have supporters or at least no manifest detractors, until we desire to exercise our right, let us be mindful of the words of the Apostle: "To me everything is permitted, but not everything is expedient," so I wish the matter to be somehow dealt with so that our Bishops may know our right and that they may agree we employ it for their good.

Peter Beckx S.J.

---

[80] See above, Franchi to Beckx, 13 November 1874, in which Franchi encouraged the Society do all it could for middle-class education in the great cities, especially Manchester.
[81] See above, 28 October 1874, Weld to Gallwey.
[82] Henry Birch SJ, 1828–1909; Rector of the Holy Name church; Wm Lawson SJ, 1834–1920.
[83] ABSI, RY/2/2, 12 December 1874, Beckx to Gallwey.

Gallwey to Vaughan
St Joseph's,[84]
Trenchard Street,
Bristol.
19, December [1874]

My dear Lord,

Owing to some unexplained blunder your note of the 14th *inst.* only reached me this morning in Worcester. I had to leave Manchester early on Tuesday, before the post came in – since then I have been on the move – and my letters were sent to the wrong place. I am very grateful for your Lordship's kind invitation, and must regret that I have lost the chance of a conversation on the subject of my last letter. It would be a very welcome Christmas consolation to give Father General if I could send him the news that all is happily arranged. In the natural order of things I shall not be going north again for some time, but if your Lordship thinks that difficulties could be better smoothed away in a conversation, I will gladly make the journey on purpose.

I forgot to mention when writing my last letter that Father Weld assured me that there was no compact whatsoever between him and your Lordship's predecessor, on the subject of a School or College, but merely an intimation from the Bishop that he did not want us to open a school.[85] I venture to hope then, my Lord, that as soon as your Advent Sermons are ended, you will have time to write a few Christmas lines of good tidings.[86]

---

[84] *The Claim*, p. 23; *The Case*, p. 85.

[85] See Appendix 10. The fragment of a letter written by Weld in 1878, in response to a request of Fr H. Coleridge SJ for information to enable him to draw up an account of the whole question from the Society's perspective – privately published as *The Case* – echoes Weld's earlier version of the conversation regarding the compact. In his account – *The Case* – Coleridge adds the following: "As it was important that these facts should not rest solely on Father Weld's word while there was another person living who could confirm them or deny them if they were inexact, Father Weld took the precaution of writing to Canon Benoit on the subject. 'On Nov. 18, 1878,' he writes, 'I wrote to Canon Benoit, reminding him of his presence on the occasion of my visit to the Bishop, and recalling to his mind the exact words I wrote, and asking him if he knew whether that document was still in existence.' In his answer, which was dated Jan. 7, 1879, he says: 'After the death of Dr Turner, I went carefully over all the papers which had reference to the administration of the diocese, and I did not meet with any manuscript such as you describe.'" *The Case*, p. 16.

[86] In response to this letter, and that of 11 December, Vaughan sent a summary of the case to Rome, dated 20 December 1874: see Appendix 3. In the 'Summary' Vaughan says that the correspondence he has received from Gallwey shows "how actively they have been endeavouring to obtain from Propaganda a permission – or even a command – while they admit I have many reasons, characterised by F. Gallwey as 'very valid,' not to grant permission." *The Claim*, p. 25.

Very truly, your Lordship's
P. Gallwey

Gallwey to Vaughan
14, Mount Street,[87]
New Year's Day [1875]

My dear Lord,

I heard from Father Parkinson last Sunday, that your Lordship is about to start for America with some Missionary Priests. I very heartily wish you God speed, and that the New Year may, among many other blessings, bring you plenty of vocations. As I have not heard from your Lordship, I venture to beg of you, before you start, to make an act of faith in the promise '*date et dabitur vobis,*' and to send me a line to say that you will not be angry if we use the rights given to us by the Holy See and carry our the wish of Propaganda by opening a school in Manchester. Both to F[ather] General and to all of us here it would be very disagreeable to use our privileges in opposition to your Lordship's wishes, but I hope that we shall have your consent and your blessing.

Very truly,
Your Lordship's
P. Gallwey

Vaughan to Gallwey
Bishop's House,[88]
Salford,
2 January, 1875.

My dear Fr Gallwey,

Many thanks for your good wishes for the New Year, which I heartily reciprocate.

As to your founding a College in Manchester, please not to take any steps until I have heard from Propaganda.[89] Vested interests are engaged which, you agreed with me in thinking, should be fully respected. There are several other considerations of a grave nature to be well weighed

---

[87] ABSI, RY/2/2, Gallwey to Vaughan, 1 January 1875. See *The Claim*, p. 24; *The Case*, p. 19.

[88] ABSI, RX/5, Vaughan to Gallwey, 2 January 1875. See *The Claim*, p. 24; *The Case*, p. 86.

[89] Vaughan was awaiting a response to the 'Summary' he had submitted on 20 December to his agent in Rome. The summary consists of reasons as to why it was impossible for him to grant permission to the Jesuits to found a college. For the text of the 'Summary' see Appendix 3.

before such a step as you propose to take can be decided upon. I must, therefore, beg of you to have a little patience. I shall be in England again by the end of February, and nothing need be done till then.

Wishing you every blessing,
I am,
You faithful and devoted servant,
+Herbert, Bishop of Salford.

From the Bishop's Agent at Propaganda[90]
   "In answer to the enquiry whether the Propaganda had given an order or expressed a wish in regard to the Jesuit scheme for a College, the following telegram was received January 4th: 'Neither order given nor wish expressed. This is official.'"

Weld to Gallwey
San Gerolamo,[91]
Fiesole.
11 January [1875].

My dear Fr,
   I can at length write to you, and have a good many things to say. First I have to thank you from Fr General for your kindness in sending us so many Masses which are a great boon, and for all your good work wishes and prayers, which are not less satisfactory. You are right about Eve. I shall try not to make such a mess of it as she did. I suppose we have no right to complain after all.
   Fr Armellini has at length seen Cardinal Franchi. He does not answer all my questions very categorically and I have written for something clearer. However the main thing is all right. He authorises us as he did before to me, to say to the English Bishops that he acknowledges our rights to open schools where we are established. He repeated what he had said before, that Manning urged that hitherto the Religious in England had been everything, and that now it was time for the hierarchy to have its right position. The Cardinal insisted that he must use us as auxiliaries and commanded it earnestly to him, and that Manning expressed his desire that we should help in his new College. This last point I do not understand as it is Fr Armellini's English version of what was said in Italian, it may mean anything. I have written for more light, and hope to have it before I send this off. Then comes a funny thing. Stonor went to Propaganda on the part of the Bishop of Salford to say

90 *The Claim*, p. 30.
91 ABSI, C/3, Weld to Gallwey, 11 January 1875.

they were in great alarm at the news that we had got leave to open a school in Manchester. The Cardinal answered that he had not spoken to the Fathers about Manchester. Either this was diplomacy or he had forgotten. It is true not much was said about Manchester, though it was spoken of, but it was included in the general principle on which I mainly insisted, and what is more, he himself asked Fr General in his letter to do something for Manchester. The Cardinal said nothing to the Archbishop about distance from the school, as he thought it better not to go into such details, but Fr Armellini asked him what he thought of three miles. He said he thought the Archbishop could not take objection to that.

On the whole I think there is a little weakness in his Eminence, and that he will be very glad if we can fight it out with the Bishop without loss, but did not want to fight himself; but I think he is committed too much – both by what he said and what he has written, to back out if it comes to a regular appeal to the principle and as we should certainly have four others of the most influential Cardinals of the Propaganda on our side I am for standing to our right.

After what you have done the Bishop of Salford can never complain of your way of doing things and I should not *ask* any more in case he holds out, but let him understand that the Propaganda has desired us to do it and that therefore we have no further leave to ask, and that in saying this you are not acting in opposition to him but simply carrying out the wishes of Propaganda. You may still put sugar on the pill without destroying the substance of it.

With regard to Manning, if I may suggest, I think I should not *ask* at all, but say that probably the Cardinal has told him as he has told Fr General that he wished us to open a school in London as we have the permission by virtue of our establishment in London and then ask him to let you take the old line east of Regent's Park.

In point of fact the new College at Notting Hill[92] does not make much difference. It is chiefly as a boarding College, but it is new, and that will not be affected by us, and after all as Cardinal Consolini said to me in a large place these things only affect one another very temporarily. In a short time new connexions are made and it is found that these are enough for all. I think you might say to B[isho]p Vaughan that you are in a difficulty, we wish not to oppose him but the Propaganda has not only declared our right but asked us to do it, and you might ask him to withhold his opposition to free you from a most unpleasant dilemma.

These are ongoing ideas. I think it better not to bring Fr General in now except in the general way that this has been done. He has suggested

---

92   St Charles's.

you to make use of what the Cardinal wrote to him, and it seems to me what I say is now the way to do it.

Fr General has had a letter from Fr Fitton which pleased him very much as he seems full of zeal and quite content, but he makes a strong appeal for men and also expresses the great want of money, and mentions that he had commended to you to give some of his money to the missions. Fr General was going to write to you about it, but as I told him I was writing he asked me to encourage you to do what you can saying, "it will have the same effect as if I write." He said "tell him to show compassion."

We had heard before that the Methodists are coming in and building schools and if something more is not done by us the next generation of these poor creatures who have hitherto kept the faith will be Methodist. A school costs so little there to build that a very moderate sum would go a long way. Somebody to teach the schools would be a great boon too. At Stann Creek Fr Parisi, one of the only four able Priests in the mission, is teaching the school. I do not think we have ever (at least for many years) given anything to Honduras. When I was Consultor they asked for a loan after the home at Belize had been burned down. It was refused.

One of the Assistants said to me the other day, "I know why the English Province is so sick: the reason is because it gives so much." So I think you will find God will give it back to you if you help the poor creatures who have no one else to look to for help.

I wish you could get up a series of afternoon (on Sunday) lectures in Manchester, I am afraid the intellect is running off to the Cathedral. If Frs Anderdon, Clere or other good ones could in turn give a month's lectures you would do the Society immense good in Manchester. They are sadly weak there now in learning. Fr Charnley is good, but there is some weakness about him, he used not to produce good effects.

Ever yours sincerely,
A. Weld

O'Callaghan to Vaughan
Rome,[93]
14 January 1875.

My Dear Lord,
    I send you a line, not to keep you "fizzling" as you call it. Simeoni[94]

---

[93] Archives of the Archbishop of Westminster (AAW), V1/63/1–259, Henry O'Callaghan to Vaughan, 14 January 1875.
[94] Giovanni Simeoni, 1816–1892; Secretary of Propaganda Fide, created Cardinal in March 1875; Prefect of Propaganda 1879–1892.

today told me that he had read the long document which I sent him[95] and spoke very strongly against Gallwey both in reference to his conduct and language. I fancy they will hold a preliminary *congresso* on the subject tomorrow or as soon as the Cardinal[96] has personally examined the paper. I have no fear of any thing being done contrary to your wishes as your case is so strong and so strongly put. The chief effect of this business will be to put S.J. in bad odour at Propaganda. Even at the best of times I fancy the atmosphere of that region is not most favourable to the Society as the whole Staff from top to bottom belong to a non-Jesuit if not anti-Jesuit section of the ecclesiastical world.

I hope to write again something more definite in two or three days in time to contact you before your departure for England. I had very hard work to translate your documents as I had my hands very full of work left by the other Bishops and was subjected to 10,000 interruptions owing to its being Xmas time.

I sincerely trust you will be able to put things on such a footing as to make it unnecessary for you to take such long and dangerous journeys. I shall be very pleased to hear of your safe return.

You need not be uneasy about the Gallwey business as it is a maxim at Propaganda to stand by a Bishop whenever it is possible.

Believe me with kind regards to your fellow travellers,

Yours affectionately,
H. O'Callaghan

Weld to Gallwey
San Gerolamo,[97]
Fiesole.
14 January [1875]

My dear Fr,

I received your letter yesterday (13th) and lose no time in answering it.

By all means get up facts about Manchester; the number of boys in the two schools you refer to, and what they are taught especially at the Xaverians, also some facts if you can to show how uneducated the Xaverians themselves are. I know that, for two young men presented themselves to me once for Brothers. I hesitated for some reason, and

[95] Vaughan's 'Summary' which he had forwarded to Propaganda *via* Mgr Henry O'Callaghan. O'Callaghan, 1827–1904, was Vaughan's Roman agent and Rector of the English College in Rome. See Leo Gooch, 'Henry O'Callaghan,' in Sheridan Gilley (ed.), *Victorian Churches and Churchmen* (Woodbridge, 2005), pp. 58–75.

[96] Alessandro Franchi, Prefect of Propaganda Fide.

[97] ABSI, C/3, Weld to Gallwey, 14 January 1875.

found afterwards that they had been snapped up by the Xaverians. They were quite uneducated, except as far as might do for a poor school. Another great point will be to find if there are Catholics attending Owens College and what numbers. If you could set on foot a petition for the Society it would be good. Be sure to send a good map that I may be able to explain the position of our church and Fr de Clerk's school.[98] I think that if we can carry on the contest in good humour, so that in Rome they may see that giving us our right will not make a rupture they will support us. They were all very much disposed in our favour i.e. the Cardinals I spoke to and I saw all the influential ones of the Propaganda who were in town. The only important one who was out of town was Cardinal Bilio, and he is a great friend of the Society and we may count on him, but every one dreads a rupture. Fr General wishes the school very much, but wishes it peacefully, and Cardinal de Luca begged me very much to try to keep peace. Cardinal Franchi will support us till it comes to a real fight, and then I begin to doubt him. I think the best thing of all will be this. If you can get your statement ready soon, whilst the Bishop is away, for me to take it to Cardinal Franchi and ask him to write to the B[isho]p to advise him not to oppose what really is our right, before he has time to bring it formally before the Congregation of Propaganda. I think he would do this if we can make a good case, but they are very averse to a formal decision against a Bishop. As the Cardinal Prefect now knows me, and told me to come again whenever I had anything to say, and called me *caro Padre* Weld etc. (though this does not mean much in the mouth of a diplomatist). I think I could get something from him if it has not already gone formally before the Congregation. In this view the Cardinal's answer to Stonor may be fortunate as it may serve as a blind and delay any formal appeal.

Ever yours sincerely in J[esus] C[hrist],

A. Weld

Weld to Gallwey
San Gerolamo,[99]
Fiesole.
15 January [1875]

My dear Fr,

It has occurred to me that in the Report of the Public School Commission[100] speaking of Lancashire there is a passage about the population

---

98 The Salford Catholic Grammar School. Augustus De Clerc, 1851–89, a Belgian.
99 ABSI, BN/6, Weld to Gallwey, 15 January [1875].
100 *Schools Inquiry Commission: The Bryce Report* (1868), pp. 712–732.

around Manchester in which it is said that there is no parallel to it in the world. I forget how many towns there are containing 90,000 each within a diameter or radius of 30 miles. It would be of great importance to get the passage copied and sent to me with your other facts, also a map of that part of Manchester, and to shew that there is not a single respectable school for all these souls. If you like to send me the vol. I will send all that is said in that part to the Cardinal. All that is said there about the need of education which is a great deal applies more to Catholics, for we have nothing.

They have the book at Stonyhurst, and that part was read in the refectory. Fr Purbrick[101] or others would find it in a minute for you. I think that an official statement like this would beat anything the Bishop could urge, especially if backed by proof of the want in Manchester itself.

Ever yours sincerely in J[esus]. C[hrist].
A. Weld

From the Bishop's Agent at Propaganda[102]
16 January 1875
"This morning I saw Cardinal Franchi, who said that the General S.J. having some time ago written to Propaganda to say that they would do nothing in opposition to the will of the Bishops, he would be requested to make that the rule of his conduct in reference to the Manchester College affair."

Weld to Gallwey
San Gerolamo,[103]
Fiesole.
2 February [1875]

My dear Fr,
This is in the first place to wish you prayers and all blessings after the retreat. You have not been forgotten: indeed I remember your intentions every day at Mass.

I have received a Blue Book which cost 3ˢ 10ᵈ in the post, but unfortunately it is not what I wanted. I wrote Your Reverence about a particular volume of the *Public* School Commission Report. It is the one containing the account of Stonyhurst and Manchester with neighbourhood, and was read in the refectory at Stonyhurst once, when I was Provincial five or six years ago.[104]

---

101   Edward Ignatius Purbrick, 1830–1914; Provincial 1880–1888; Rector of Stonyhurst.
102   *The Claim*, p. 30.
103   ABSI, C/3, Weld to Gallwey, 2 February 1875.
104   *Bryce Report.*

Br Foley has sent me the *Poor* School Report of 1874 printed since I came to Italy. It is of no use whatever for my purpose. Any one at Stonyhurst by referring to the volumes would tell you which is the right volume.

I also ought to know what is taught at the Xaverian Brothers' School and anything that will show their impossibility of giving a good education etc. as soon as you can. I cut out of *The Times*[105] this morning a letter in which it is shewn that there are great complaints against Owens College, to the effect that it is becoming very much of a technical school to prepare boys for calico printing, and though there is a class of scientific chemistry only 45 out of 200 scientific students attend it and that the professorship of Classics Literature [*sic*] are grouped together so as to shew that they are quite subordinate to practical science. This will strengthen us if we take a good position. My impression about your beginning in Manchester is that it would be best to do it simultaneous with my approach to Cardinal Franchi. I am afraid of him [Vaughan] making a formal appeal to Propaganda before Cardinal Franchi has time to write to him; whereas if I can put the case before the Cardinal, and tell him that you are on the point of doing it, and ask him to write to the Bishop asking him not to make difficulty as we have a clear right, I think we shall succeed. If I know the Cardinal, and I am beginning to know him by what I hear combined with what I experienced, I think he will do anything for us that does not bring him into real conflict but if it comes to a formal representation to Propaganda I do not trust him and this Fr General is very anxious to avoid. I might go so far as to say that you are doing it so that it may be too late to stop anything to prevent a formal representation from the B[isho]p to the S[acred] Congregation before I can get the Cardinal to write. I have not gone into this with Fr General yet. I would rather agree well with you first what is best, and he has been very busy during this last week.

I should like to know when you expect the Bishop back. If you will send me the Blue Book as soon as you can, and any other information, I will make out a case which will I think satisfy him.

I think I should time my visit to the Cardinal so as to coincide with your [illegible] close with the Bishop so as to precede your interview a little. If he would give me a letter open for the Bishop for you to give

---

[105]   *The Times*, 6 January 1875, letter from a J. G. Greenwood regarding Owens College. The letter, in defence of the academic standards of the college, is a reply to a Dr Appleton who, in a letter dated 31 December 1874, had claimed that the founders of Owens College had aimed at the setting up of "a great emporium of useful knowledge … where the manufacturer's son may learn enough chemistry and mechanics to be able to make more money than his father."

him, that would be best. Let me know what you think and the time as soon as you can.

A good map of Manchester will be better than one of the county as I have a list of the towns etc. around.

I have received Newman and Dr Ullathorne[106] and Vaughan for all of which I am much obliged. I shall be glad of Capel to complete the set. As far as I hear they do not like Newman in Italy, but I should not like to say much as I do not know who speak. I would rather it had been different in some points, but it requires reading very carefully. I mean to read it a second time.

The main things I want now is the right Blue Book and to know when the Bishop is expected.

Ever yours sincerely in J[esus] C[hrist]
A. Weld

Weld to Gallwey
3 February 1875[107]

My Dear Father,

I write you another line and take the opportunity of sending back Dr Vaughan's letter.

I have taken an opportunity to speak to Fr General about Manchester. His first answer was at the present juncture we must not fight as there is some unpleasantness about Madrasa[108] and he was afraid of annoying the Holy Father. I explained to him that we must not if possible let the present slip or else the matter will all have to be gone into over again when the Bishop will have had time to prepare, and thus we should lose all we have gained. He entered into that but fears very much a fight at the Propaganda. I told him I hoped to settle it with the Cardinal without going before the Congregation, and I think we must aim at that above everything. At present I like best what I said yesterday i.e. to shew the Cardinal the need of the College, tell him that we mean to act upon our right, that we are very good friends with the Bishop, and that all that is wanted is a letter from him to the Bishop or one which we can shew him. I think the worst would be if he were to refuse to write the letter. I hardly anticipate any prohibition from him because that could only, I

---

106   William Bernard Ullathorne OSB, 1806–1889; Bishop of Birmingham. No further information is given as to the nature of what Weld had received in connection with the names mentioned.
107   ABSI, C/3, Weld to Gallwey, 3 February 1875.
108   A Jesuit province in India.

think, come from the Congregation of Propaganda. Let me hear soon from you with whatever data you have to give me.

Ever yours sincerely in J[esus] C[hrist].

A. Weld

Weld to Gallwey
San Gerolamo,[109]
Fiesole.
17 February [1875]

My dear Fr,

I have been a little puzzled at not hearing again from you as I thought it important to have the memorial for Cardinal Franchi ready for Bishop Vaughan's return from America. I have made a memorial[110] however as far as I could and Fr General is pleased with it, and thinks it will do. I have represented again to him that we must not let our present position slip away; otherwise we shall never perhaps get it again. It seems to me that in England we talk so long about what we are going to do that other people have time to take the work out of our hands and do it themselves. Bishop Vaughan is now on the alert, and if we do not open a school in Manchester quickly he will.

I have some things quite to the point on the subject out of *The Times'* account of Mr Belaney's letter in the *Tablet*. These letters of Mr B[elaney][111] are shewing the necessity of just what we want to do; you should read them. I have explained all this to Fr General and I hope he will write to you very shortly; but you should be ready to begin if it is only half a dozen boys in the back room at No 46 Ackers Street.[112] Some thing that can be called a beginning. I have also explained to Fr General that if our memorial reaches the Cardinal in time he will probably never let a petition of B[isho]p Vaughan go before the Congregation, as it would be against himself as my memorial makes great account of his own letter and declaration on his own part and that of other Cardinals that we have a right.

If you send me what I ask for out of the Blue Book in time I will put it in, but in any case send me a map of Manchester and Salford, and one of the surrounding country would be useful too. Let me hear from you to know when the B[isho]p returns and when I must move.

[109] ABSI, C/3, Weld to Gallwey, 17 February [1875].
[110] See below, 27 February 1875.
[111] See the *Tablet*, 30 January 1875; 6 February; 20 February; 27 February; 6 March. These letters refer to the necessity of grammar schools.
[112] This was the address at which the Jesuit community lived in Manchester.

Bishop Vaughan is behaving quite *sui modo* with our Fathers in Baltimore,[113] and it makes me far less scrupulous about meeting him in Manchester. You spoke of having sent Fr General the Decrees of Westminster. He told me a day or two ago that they had not reached him.

Yours ever sincerely in J[esus] C[hrist],

A. Weld

Weld to Gallwey
San Gerolamo,[114]
Fiesole,
22 February [1875]

My Dear Fr Provincial,
    Enclosed with this is a letter from Fr General which I hope you will find according to your wishes. It is an order to go on with the Manchester College even independently of the Bishop's consent. For the meantime the memorial is finished and all of [it] copied. Fr General thought there was everything in it that could be of importance, and if you should send additional information it can be added by word of mouth. I found in *The Times* an extract from the Blue Book I spoke of which was very much to the point; pointing out the importance of Manchester for a scientific school as the centre of a great manufacturing district. This I have worked in; also the population of the district with the Catholic population, and have developed the importance of the Catholic middle class in England, as well as for forming missionaries etc. and have shewn the good S[aint] F[rancis] Xavier's is doing in Liverpool. The Cardinal is told that in consequence to his own declaration of our right and the wish he expressed in his letter to Fr General, Your Reverence is taking some action to execute this project etc. This will be sent to Fr Armellini to be presented to the Cardinal when everyone gives the word. You shall have a copy of it when we can get it copied.
    In the meantime you must have all ready to make a start as soon as the Bishop returns. You will very soon have to add a class of chemistry and physics. That is the great demand in Manchester, and it is

---

113 In 1871 the Josephites – the name given to the first missionaries who arrived in America with Vaughan – were assigned a church in Baltimore by the archbishop, Martin John Spalding, to serve the African-American community. The building was owned by the Jesuits and this led to conflict. The church was heavily in debt. The Society agreed to permit the Josephites to assume management of everything, including the debt. The Jesuits retained the right to reclaim and sell the property without conditions. This state of affairs was highly unsatisfactory to Vaughan. See below, 11 March 1875, Armellini to Franchi.
114 ABSI, C/3, Weld to Gallwey, 22 February [1875].

complained that at Owens College they are doing hardly anything else, and even in [*sic*] going too much into practical matters to prepare boys for trade instead of giving them sound scientific education.

The Bishop was to sail from New York last Saturday 20th so he will be in England soon after the first of March. Let me know when to have the memorial presented. We must take care to present it before the Bishop has time to write a protest, this way I think the matter will effectively be kept from going before the Congregation. Fr General says in the memorial that there may be difficulties, that there cannot be opposition because our right is acknowledged by his Eminence etc., but if there are complaints he hopes the Cardinal will calm them, as the Bishop himself will certainly be glad of it later.

The Bishop's people in Baltimore have got into great expense which will necessitate our depositing the deeds of the church to allow money to be raised, as the expenses were for substantial repairs. This is what he has been fighting for. In the circumstances it is necessary, but he says distinctly that if we do not he will fight us. Of course this must not be reported in England as it is our own affair, but it is right for you to know it, as to my mind, it takes away any cause of delicacy in the matter of standing on our rights.

I think the memorial should be presented about the beginning of next week, but there could be time for a letter if you write by return of post.

Yours ever sincerely in J[esus] C[hrist].

A. Weld

Beckx to Gallwey
Fiesole,[115]
22 February 1875.

Rev. Fr in Christ,

Having carefully considered the circumstances in which our Fathers live in the very large city of Manchester, it seems the opportunity should not be missed to do what for us is, according to our Institute, to the increase of God's glory. Therefore, I vehemently desire that Christian education be promoted among this most numerous populace. To say nothing about other things, I am now strongly urged by the wishes of His Eminence the Cardinal Prefect of the Sacred Congregation for the Propagation of the Faith, which he expressed in a letter to me on the 13 November; he earnestly recommended to me education for the young in the great Cities, in particular Manchester. I must add that the same

[115] ABSI, Litterae Annuae Provinciae Anglicanae Societatis Jesu 1865–1913, Letters 1875–1876, pp. 56–57, Beckx to Gallwey, 22 February 1875.

Eminent Cardinal Prefect and other Cardinals at the Sacred Congregation for the Propagation of the Faith have recognised that we have the right to open Schools where we are legitimately established, by force of the Apostolic Constitutions. Further, the teaching of children is certainly one of our Institute's particular duties, which we may perform in our houses. I therefore desire that Your Reverence employ means whereby we may satisfy the wishes of His Eminence, and may be able to open in that City schools with one or two classes as soon as can be conveniently achieved.

It will also be good if Your Reverence explains with all due respect to His Lordship the Bishop that we should kindly like his consent, but that, in beginning this work for the good of the faithful, we do nothing save that which the Eminent Cardinal Prefect has encouraged us to do, and that not only has this duty of teaching in our houses always been recognised by the Holy See as proper to our Society, but also it will become in time a consolation to His Lordship.

Moreover, it will not be futile to add that no one should be amazed that we abandoned a School shortly after its inception, for this happened only because His Lordship the Bishop, temporarily, did not wish a church of the Society; and because the Fathers at that time believed the Society could not exist in that City without a church.

Peter Beckx S.J.

Beckx to Franchi
Fiesole,[116]
27 February 1875.

Very Eminent Prince,

When some months ago there was talk of establishing colleges in the big cities of England and expressly Manchester, Your Most Reverend Eminence deigned to welcome such a project most warmly. You will therefore not find it unwelcome if I now acquaint you with particulars of this city which, as I believe, demonstrate even better the timeliness and necessity of such a College.

According to the last official government report the population of the two cities of Manchester, properly speaking, and of Salford (not including the suburbs) comes to 592,164 souls. This city is the centre of a highly populated area, which is becoming one of extraordinary activity. Suffice it to say that within a radius of 12 miles around Manchester, there are 26 towns, each of which numbers on average 25,000 inhabitants, besides a number of other villages of 2,000 to 3,000 souls. And

---

116   Archives of Propaganda Fide, Rome (APF), Anglia 20, pp. 195–99, Beckx to Franchi.

communication between all these towns and Manchester is now very easy, thanks to the railway and the mail coaches.

According to an official report from the Royal Commission for Schools in Great Britain, published in 1868, the district of which Manchester is the centre is perhaps that of the greatest industrial activity, and the most highly populated of any in the world, and therefore, in the judgement of this same Commission, has the greatest need of secondary schools, of which, outside the city of Manchester, there is a total want. In Manchester itself there is a big Protestant College,[117] or rather an atheist one, very rich and well established, which is currently making many approaches to the Government with the aim of creating a University for the north of England. We therefore, desirous of the Glory of God and the good of the souls included in the Government statistics, and of the aims of material prosperity of the very enemies of our religion, conclude that Manchester is a centre where it would be most opportune to found a Catholic secondary school.

In confirmation of the above, the extract of a document presented by Manchester gentlemen who are interested in the enlarging of this Protestant College, to the aforementioned Commissioners; a document that is printed in the official report of the Royal Commission and mentioned above.

"It is commonly felt that we should in England have, as in France and Germany, Colleges which give complete and sound instruction in all the principal branches of experimental and applied knowledge. There is no lack of workshops for teaching the various manufacturing processes, [but] there is a lack of schools of the technical knowledge, in which those who are to manage industry in the country, and those who are of an artistic bent who have shown special talent, can receive a complete education, in which teachers can be trained who will be truly able to teach the rudiments of knowledge (the sciences) soundly in primary and secondary schools.

"Manchester is now without doubt the best suited place for such a school of educational training. And if it be recognised to be of virtually national importance, that the district similar to that of which Manchester is the centre, should possess Colleges with such a goal, as demonstrated by the successful efforts being made to create Owens College almost anew, there should be no failure to compensate for such a lack in Manchester, where it is most keenly felt, and where everything makes it easier to rectify such a lack."

Up to this point the extract from the document, in which, even though there is mention by these men only of these sciences, there is a clear

---

[117] Owens College.

opinion about the importance of Manchester as a seat of instruction, and it notes its great influence on the whole area, of which it is so to speak the heart; and this is sufficient for my purpose of demonstrating the opportuness of setting up of a Catholic College in such a city.

It is even easier to demonstrate the utility, indeed the necessity, of such a college. According to the last diocesan report, the city of Manchester alone has 95,914 Catholics, but according to the same report the entire area of which we are speaking here should count between 130,000 and 140,000, that is more than two thirds of all the Catholics in this vast Diocese. Now, if the Protestant government, acting as it is, from material aims, shows itself so worried about the lack of higher education in this district, how much more justified should be our concern about the lack of Catholic higher education?

All the more because there is already in Manchester a grandiose Protestant College for the humanities, as we have said, whereas the Catholics, so great in number, have just two wretched little schools. Only one of the two is in Manchester, properly speaking, run by the Xaverian Brothers situated not far from the Protestant College; but it numbers only 75 young children and it does not inspire in Catholic parents any confidence that a rounded education is available. This is especially the case among the more respectable who do not send their children there, except perhaps when they are very young, because the teachers do not seem themselves to be educated men. There is another Catholic school,[118] run by a secular priest, which has about 90 children; but apart from the fact that this school is situated at the far end of the city, that is, Salford, two and a half miles away from the Protestant College, and distant from that part of the city in which many of the more respectable Catholics live, anyone can see, and even His Lordship the Bishop is also persuaded, that this school is utterly insufficient to serve so vast a population, with a complete education having a major concentration on the sciences, of which the middle class has great need, and in the procurement of which it sees great attractions. Since it is beyond doubt that in a manufacturing county *par excellence*, full of factories, like the county of Lancashire, it is very easy for the young, even those of the poor class, to improve their status, to obtain lucrative employment and, if they have the intelligence for it, to attain to very important posts in these factories. But for this it is necessary to be well trained in the Higher Sciences, as we have heard in the report issued by the Commission, and in the document of the Manchester gentlemen. From which there follows a great tendency and almost a necessity felt by the middle class parents of sending their children to accredited schools, where they

---

118   The Salford Catholic Grammar School.

can be qualified to pursue these advantages; and the Catholics, who for the most part have not the means to send their children to be educated in Catholic boarding schools outside Manchester, or rather for other reasons cannot harden themselves to sending them away from home, as in many cases happens, are tempted and perhaps allow themselves to yield to the temptation of sending them to the Protestant College, with such spiritual dangers and damage as can be feared when Catholic children mix with Protestant children, and are taught by teachers who are often also non-believers. This need could be met and this harm could be avoided with the establishment, of which we have been speaking, of the Catholic College in our house in Manchester, situated in the most suitable place, because near the Protestant College, and in an area inhabited by many Catholics, who would be delighted to entrust their children to it, to receive a sound and complete education, together with a Catholic upbringing.

But in addition to this more immediate advantage, which is of the highest degree of importance and one which everyone can see, there are others, which cannot perhaps at first sight be discerned, which are no less real and of the highest significance. It is undeniable that the chief weakness of Catholics in England is felt in the middle classes. There is a lack of an intelligent middle class, and it is perhaps the case that nothing could be of such advantage to those with an interest in the Church in this country, as the establishment of good schools in the big centres of population and industrial activity, where children of the middle class or even of a lower class could receive a good literary, scientific and religious education. It is scarcely necessary to say how great an advantage to society and to religion would result from the strengthening of this class, which is the most numerous, the most skilled, and the most influential. This is already beginning to be experienced at first hand in Liverpool; the only city in England where to date the Society has been able to open a College for *external* diplomas. It has already between 260 and 270 young people who come to the school every day from the city and from the outskirts and devoutly attend Mass and follow all the pious practices of our College. Those who have known this city for many years assure me that the good effects of this College are already being felt, and that the children who attend it are having a salutary influence on the youth of this same city: and it is well-known that having been a pupil of the College of St Francis Xavier is a good recommendation for a young person, even with the Protestants, in attaining the best posts. Since, as has been said, in these parts knowledge applied to practice, with a foundation of solid, classical literary studies (which are lacking), opens the way to good jobs and high ranking positions when the young person is intelligent and well trained.

There could be added another advantage of most appreciable value to the Church. When young people of high intelligence and with the best disposition cannot dedicate themselves to the sanctuary because they lack an education in letters, who is to prepare them? Let a solid classical grounding be available and many could answer the divine call and enrol in the secular or regular clergy, and also bring the faith among the unbelievers in so many Missions in the greatest need of workers, mostly English-speaking.

To facilitate the attainment of these advantages would be the Society's aim in setting up the College in Manchester, a most suitable, needful and on the part of good Catholics the most desirable district for such an institution. It would seem impossible that there should be opposition or even difficulty on the part of the diocesan authority. I say difficulty since by the Pontifical Constitutions, which give the right to open Colleges in places where there are already some established, the Bishop cannot put forward opposition, as recently Your Eminence in conversation with the English Assistant Father has recognised. That notwithstanding, *perhaps* this good Bishop might make some complaint, in the illusion that he himself could later open a College. But it is foreseeable that this good desire will not be allowed to come to fruition, lacking the means and particularly the appropriate personnel to sustain the teaching in such a College. Furthermore, were he to succeed, it seems to me that two Colleges would not be too many for so numerous a population. On the other hand, I am sure that, when His Lordship the Bishop sees the good effects of our College, which with the help of God we hope to see, he will be the first to rejoice and to bless the Lord. Therefore, if perhaps in the beginning some illegal action has been taken, I dare to beg Your Eminence not to be dismayed and to succeed, as your prudence dictates, in calming things down. It would be very painful for me, if this great opportunity to provide a significant benefit for this country were lost; all the more so, because at another time, about 20 years ago, we had already started a College here; but then we had no church of our own, and the then Bishop dug his heels in against allowing a church to be built, and for that reason the Fathers, believing they could not succeed without one, judged it necessary to abandon the College. What we were at that time prevented from having will, I hope, be more fully achieved, the more so because we have for some years now had our own Church, and the Fr Provincial of England, having been notified of the letter of 13 November 1874 sent to me by Your Eminence, in which you deign to encourage me to open a College in Manchester, the execution of the project is being prepared.

Pray forgive, Your Eminence, the prolixity of this letter and believe the most profound respect and veneration with which I kiss the Sacred Purple.

Rev. Eminence.
Your humble and devoted Servant in Christ,
Pietro Beckx S.J.

Weld to Gallwey
San Gerolamo,[119]
Fiesole.
4 March 1875

My Dear Father,

I have read your letter into Italian to Fr General, and hasten to give you the result. He approves the substance but suggested some changes which I will give you here following your numbers.

1) Is all right as far as it goes, but before coming to Nº 2 he proposed some ideas which I have put into form [*sic*] and read to him, and which he approved. He thought that the part about the complaints etc. had better come last – you will see the word petition scratched out in your letter, this was Fr General's wish, but what I have written makes it unnecessary.

At the end of Nº 1 Fr General would add something to this effect: "In speaking of a school here, I mean one in a new position to be determined with your Grace, because there is no doubt, and the point is fully recognised in Rome, that we have the right of opening schools where we are canonically established; this has been declared to us by several of the Cardinals, and possibly the Cardinal Prefect of Propaganda has spoken on the subject to your Grace but we wish to be more amongst the middle class than we are at Farm Street, where the want of education is more manifest, and Fr General desires us not to use the right granted us by the Holy See till we have done all in our power to obtain the good will of your Grace.

"I wish with great frankness and respect to explain our sentiments on this matter. We are instituted to assist the Bishops in the labour of the salvation of souls, and especially in the education of youth. His Holiness Pius VII declared that he restored the Society specifically for this object, and we feel it hard and strange that so many difficulties are put in our way to prevent us from exercising this our first duty. We are certain that we seek only the salvation of souls, and if your Grace had any complaints to make against us or against any of us, as if we sought ourselves instead of God, I should be very glad to know it that I might correct it, as I know well, that we cannot expect all to be perfection in a body consisting of so many men. Your Grace has assured me that you

---

[119]   ABSI, C/3, Weld to Gallwey, 4 March 1875.

have no reproaches to make against us. I know that it may seem to some Bishops that we are too independent of them, but I may submit that this independence is approved by the Holy See and by the Council of Trent and is really nothing more than a right which the Holy See reserves to itself. I have then but one request to make and it is that your Grace will give us liberty to work according to our Institute for the salvation of souls, and I am bold enough to prophesy that your Grace will thank God for the result.

"The movement now being made for Grammar Schools in the large towns, and especially London, and made as we understand with the sanction of your Grace gives me confidence in the success of my petition, for it shows that [*sic*] my idea in general, that London is not sufficiently provided with schools of this class, and that a good College in a fit situation would do an immense good to religion by educating the lower middle class, rendering children of even poorer parents capable of raising themselves in life, and then thus supplying the general want of the Catholics of this country, to say nothing of preparing for the sanctuary so many boys who could not obtain reception into our boarding Colleges, and even who would not travel three or four miles to a day school. This removes also the chief difficulty which could be opposed to our project, the fear of injuring existing establishments.

"Here I would wish to touch a point of another kind; I feel a great delicacy in doing it, but I know your Grace would like me to speak with full frankness. It seems to me that this concession on the part of your Grace will do much, even more than can be said, to promote union of minds, and a refusal in this matter, that is the exclusion of the Society from the chief function for which it was instituted by the Holy See, in these particular circumstances, when the necessity of such schools is acknowledged by all, would increase, I very much fear, an impression which I and all of us would deplore no less than your Grace."

You would here introduce the point about charity and the impression existing that he is unfavourable.

Fr General thinks you should not extend it as much as you have done, introduce it rather more delicately with more compliments etc. (if the English way will allow of it), and soften expressions down as much as you can so as not to spoil it.

He would omit the passages about appealing to the Holy See, which looks like a threat, and the latter part of Nº 3 where you speak of exceptional severity etc., he thinks that part is rather too strong.

These are all the remarks he has to make, and with these he approves the letter. Though we read together very carefully the part I have introduced at the end of No1 and literally the expressions are his translated from Italian and he approved it all, he did not mean to dictate it to you but leaves it to your judgement.

If he refuses we shall be free to open schools at Mount Street, and it will be for you to consider whether it is better to do that or to make a formal request to the Holy See for a distinct College.

Perhaps you might add that it is hard to withdraw *without notice* the written permission given to me in 1869 and which you wished to act on in 1873. The only reason it was not acted on being that with his encouragement we were occupied with ideas of higher studies.

Let me know immediately you have taken any steps in Manchester.

Yours ever sincerely in J[esus] C[hist].
A. Weld

Armellini to Franchi
Rome,[120]
11 March 1875.

Most Reverend Eminence

Allow me to return to the issues of Manchester, to further clarify the matter. A conversation took place last Thursday with Monsignor Rinaldini; I found out that someone had issued a formal complaint to Propaganda concerning the behaviour of Father Gallwey, the English Provincial, towards the Bishop of Salford. From a letter of this very same Father, which I am enclosing here, translated into Italian, you will see, Most Reverend Eminence, with what kindness and simplicity of manners Father Gallwey treated Monsignor Vaughan.

To better understand our relations with that Prelate it may be helpful to refer to an event that occurred not long ago in the United States. A few years ago Monsignor Vaughan obtained from us, on a three year loan, a church in Baltimore for his Missionaries, on condition that in the meantime they would procure for themselves other accommodation.

Now it would seem that they, without a word to the Superiors of the Society in America, incurred a debt of 26,000 dollars on the said church for repairs. To get out of this embarrassment, Monsignor Vaughan requested that we yield to him the title deeds of ownership of the church, threatening otherwise to let the matter go before the secular tribunals.

It is clear that he has no right at all to that church of ours, and that he could well have avoided this embarrassment prior to it happening by advancing to the Missionaries money he had in New York.

Given all this, Father General authorized the Provincial of Maryland to hand over the title deed of that property, were it asked for.

---

[120] APF, Anglia 20, Armellini to Franchi, 1875–1877.

That is the situation in America. Now please kindly observe the situation in England. The necessity of schools for Catholics in Manchester is unquestionable. The Society a very long time ago obtained a residence in that city with the intention of eventually opening a school. Most of the property (in Manchester), if not all of it, was purchased by the Society in advance of Monsignor Vaughan becoming Bishop of that diocese. It is clear that he cannot prevent us from receiving students in our house, but despite our rights and the necessity to provide for the education of Catholics, he wants us to desist from executing our intentions. Does this not seem like using two different weights and measures; one for America – to his advantage against us, – and the other for England, – to the detriment of young Catholics? The *memorial* of Father General aims to demonstrate that the Bishop's refusal does not favour those poor souls. And I humbly pray Your Eminence to let me know when I may see you, so that I may show you, with a map of Manchester at hand, the distances between the locations mentioned in the said *memorial*.

Meanwhile, please consider me most respectfully yours.
Your most devoted servant,
Torquato Armellini

Weld to Gallwey
San Gerolamo,[121]
Fiesole.
12 March [1875]

My dear Fr,
I have written to Rome to urge that the Cardinal will write a letter at once to B[isho]p Vaughan. I am afraid of a crisis if he holds out. We must take care not to give any scandal, though I do not know what he can do when he sees the General's letter.[122] The Cardinal cannot deny it now, for Fr General has reminded him of it. Did you see a letter from a Manufacturer in [the] last *Tablet* about Owens College? We shall have hard work to compete against that. You must try. It will be well to study the complaints against Owens College and avoid them in yours.

Ever yours truly in J[esus] C[hrist]
A. Weld

---

[121]   ABSI, C/3, Weld to Gallwey, 12 March [1875].
[122]   This refers to the above letter of Beckx to Weld dated 22 February 1875; it was read to Vaughan on 15 March.

Gallwey to Vaughan
8, Salisbury Street,[123]
13 March [1875]

My dear Lord,

Out of respect for the wish expressed by your Lordship before your departure for America, I have abstained, notwithstanding some very urgent pressure, from taking any action during your Lordship's absence with regard to the Grammar School which we desire to open in Manchester. Now however, I have received from Father-General a letter[124] which makes it my duty not to remain inactive any longer. This letter I have forwarded to the Superior of the district, Fr Ullathorne,[125] who will, if you permit, read it to you Lordship, and I have good hopes that helped by the prayers of your Patron S. Joseph, it will make clear to Y[ou]r Lordship that we are not acting disloyally towards you or in a factious or intriguing spirit, as has been said, but following a course that is reasonable, right and dutiful; and that Father General has good grounds to prophesy, as he does, that before long Your Lordship will look upon our project not as an unwelcome intrusion but a source of much consolation. For as your Lordship will observe, Father General lays down the principle that we are fully authorised and encouraged by the Holy See to establish such a school as we propose; and that the right to do so is one of the essential features of our Institute. He then further states that the Cardinals of Propaganda whom for greater security he consulted on these points, fully acknowledge that we hold this privilege from the Holy See.[126] Now S[aint] Alphonsus teaches that a Religious Superior sins grievously if he fails to maintain the status granted to his Order by the Holy See; moreover, as Father General goes on to observe, the Cardinal-Prefect of the Propaganda not only declared emphatically that we are within our rights, but with his own hand wrote to beg of him to further education in the great towns of England, and more especially in Manchester. As I am told this last statement which I have already once before made to your Lordship has been called into question, it may be well for me to extract from the copy of the Cardinal's letter, sent me by Fr General, the following words: "pregandola ad un tempo a favorire sempre più l'insegnamento nelle grande cità e particolar-

---

[123]   ABSI, RY/2/2, Gallwey to Vaughan, 13 March [1875]. See *The Claim*, pp. 30–31; *The Case*, pp. 118–119. By this letter, which Ullathorne delivered by hand to Vaughan on 15 March 1875, the Society announced the actual establishment of their College in Manchester.
[124]   See above, 22 February 1875, Beckx to Weld.
[125]   Thomas Ullathorne SJ, 1817–1900.
[126]   See above, 16 November, Weld to Gallwey.

mente a Manchester."[127] On the copy sent to me Father-General writes these words: "desumptum ex litteris manu propria scriptis ab Em. Card Franchi S. C. Prop."[128] If to all this we add the solemn declaration of our Fourth Council,[129] in which your Lordship sat: that such schools as we design are greatly needed; and the earnest recommendation addressed in Decree XVII[130] to Priests in charge of missions to establish them wherever it can be done,[131] I think your Lordship will agree with me in thinking that I am not unreasonable in asking in the name of your Patron that we may have the great consolation of beginning this work with Y[ou]r Lordship's cordial blessing and good will.

Very truly,
Your Lordship's servant,
P. Gallwey

Manning to Vaughan
Rome,[132]
14 March 1875.

My Dear Herbert,
    Thank you for your letter, which is a real comfort to me. I have had a great anxiety lest this change should in any way hinder my work for the good of the Church in England. Yet I ought not to fear when the Vicar

---

[127]   "Requesting it [i.e. the Society] at the same time to give more and more support to teaching in the large towns and especially in Manchester."

[128]   "Taken from a letter written in his own hand by His Excellency Cardinal Franchi of the Sacred Congregation of Propaganda."

[129]   Fourth Provincial Synod of Westminster, 1873.

[130]   "In view of the daily increase of the class of family which can be regarded neither as rich nor poor, we make a ... decree for rectors of the larger missions to that most wisely passed at our First Provincial Council: that is, we recommend that as soon as possible schools should be set on foot, even small colleges, in which children of the better class may be carefully taught subjects bearing upon the pursuits and business of life, in addition to the ordinary elements of education." Robert E. Guy, *The Synods in English* (1886), p. 246.

[131]   Vaughan later disputed this point *vis-à-vis* the Holy Name: "It is argued by the Provincial S.J., that the decree XVII of the Fourth Provincial Synod justifies the Society in founding a College of the Order attached to the Mission of the Holy Name. But putting aside other considerations, the text of the Decree is directed to the Rectors "*majorum missionum*." The Mission of the Holy Name is not among them. In Manchester and Salford there are fourteen Missions, and, according to the official return of the Catholic population of each, they rank in the following order ..." The Holy Name appears in the penultimate position with a population of 1,580, above that of St Edward's with 220. *The Claim*, p. 34. For Jesuit refutation of this claim see below, 20 April 1875, Charnley to Gallwey, n. 216.

[132]   Snead-Cox, *The Life of Cardinal Vaughan*, vol. 1, p. 292; Manning to Vaughan, 14 March 1875. The letter refers to Manning's becoming a cardinal.

of Our Lord acts. It was He that willed it, as I know. I am glad, too, that the English are in this, as they are in themselves, just and kindly. I hope what you say – that they will not count me less one of themselves in all lawful things. Here, apart from the … I have had real friendship shown. I am very sorry to hear that you are unwell. You must take what from habit your system requires. I have no doubt that you need stimulants as medicines. Have no hesitation about it. *Media ad finem*. Last night I had a full conversation with Cardinal Franchi, and to-day with Rinaldini, about the Jesuit College in Manchester.

I hope the whole business is at an end.

Believe me always, my dear Herbert,
Yours very affectionately,
Henry Edward, Archbishop of Westminster.

Fr Henry Clarkson to Birch
16 March 1875[133]

My dear Fr Birch,

I do not myself care for artificial flowers but I accept them with grati-tude and shall use them as a token of good will from the FF. S.J. I return your very heartfelt and sincere thanks for your kindness, for the gift tendered in good will. I hope that you will never hear my name joined in any disrespectful mention of SJ. It becomes us all who labour for souls and not for an earthly reward to emulate one another in good works and not to let jealousy show itself in our intervention with our flock in words that are unfortunate and dis-edifying. We priests have to build up this work of His and not to pull down. I know in times past I may have said harsh things of SJ but if I have I sincerely repent, I hope you will succeed in all that you propose for the good of religion in Manchester. Indeed, there are wants that you can supply which are very inadequately supplied. I do not see with the many irons the Bishop has in the fire how he is to succeed in what he has promised to the Catholics of this city.[134]

---

[133] ABSI, RX/5, Fr Henry Clarkson to Birch, 16 March 1875. See Anon., *Facts and Documents*, p. 43.

[134] In his memorial to the Cardinal Prefect of Propaganda, *Facts and Documents*, Gallwey enlarges on the difficulties which this letter alludes to and also gives an insight as to why some of the secular clergy were not entirely supportive of Vaughan. Gallwey pointed out the following: "His Lordship has certainly worked since his consecration with untiring energy to provide for the wants of his diocese, but I think it becomes more evident that without the assistance of Religious Orders this will be impossible. For although by his remarkable energy and his talents, and through the goodwill and favour with which the people regarded their new Bishop, he has been able to collect considerable sums of money for his pastoral Seminary and other works, yet it is certain that to carry out his purpose he has been obliged to use methods new and unusual, at least in this country, that

I recommend my infant mission to your prayers.

Your humble servant,
Henry Clarkson[135]

Vaughan to Birch
Bishop's House,[136]
Salford.
16 March 1875.

To the Rev Henry Birch, S.J.
     Superior of the Church of the Holy Name, Manchester.
     Notice having been given to me by one of your Superiors that you have actually opened a College in Manchester against the expressed and known prohibition of the Ordinary; determined as this prohibition was by many good reasons, which were admitted by your Provincial to be "very valid",[137] and learning from the same Superior that he declines to have the College closed at my desire, or to recognise my authority in the matter, it becomes my painful duty to inform you as follows:
     That the opening of this College is a grave act of disobedience and insubordination: that it is a direct violation of the agreement made by one of the Provincials S.J. with my predecessor, upon which alone the Society was again admitted into Manchester;[138] that it is based upon a

---

notwithstanding these industries, financial difficulties are great, and that it is not probable that after the novelty is worn off the same methods can continue to work. When I speak of new and unusual methods, I mean, for instance, moving the bodies of the dead, to the number of five thousand, from their graves in order to secure a site for his Seminary; claiming by Episcopal prerogative a right to preach in all the churches of his diocese, Regular as well as Secular, in order to make a strong appeal in person for an increase in funds; convoking his clergy, and obtaining large donations from them; laying an annual tax, or quasi tax, on the clergy in addition to the cathedraticum; requiring heavy fees for dispensations; enjoining that by all who do not fast an alms should be paid into the Episcopal treasury; ordering his Pastorals, and certain other publications, to be sold at the door of all the churches." pp. 7–8. Gallwey also quotes evidence from the bishop's circulars that the diocesan debt stood at £18,000, and that £5,000 was still required to complete the Pastoral Seminary. Gallwey concludes, "therefore it seems quite necessary to adopt the spirit and views of the Apostolic See, and to allow the Religious Orders to provide in part for the wants of the diocese, rather than burden too much the faithful, and injure many charitable institutions by excessive collections, in order to maintain the theory that the souls of men must not be saved except in their own parish churches." p. 9. The injured "charitable institutions" were the "Convents and Hospices which depend on the alms of the faithful [and] suffer much loss" because of the constant appeal for funds.

[135]   Henry Clarkson 1831–1880; Rector of Cuthbert's, Withington.

[136]   ABSI, RX/5, Vaughan to Birch, 16 March 1875. See *The Claim*, p. 31; Anon., *Facts and Documents*, pp. 24–25; *The Case*, pp. 119–120.

[137]   See above, 20 August 1874, Gallwey to Vaughan.

[138]   See above, Vaughan to Gallwey, 7 August 1874.

claim put before me by the actual Provincial to a right in the Society to found Colleges attached to any church they may serve in the Diocese, independently of the carefully formed judgement of the Bishop as to what is due to existing vested interests and for the greater good of religion, and even in spite of the Bishop's prohibition. I do not accept this claim, or admit it to be proved; nor do I allow, even if it were legal, that it would entitle the Society to override and cancel an agreement made with my late predecessor. I may add that I have received official communication from Rome that Propaganda has "neither given an order nor expressed a wish" that the Society should establish a College in Manchester. Moreover, the right set up by the Provincial having been denied by me, and the matter referred to the Holy See, you are not competent to act upon your contention *pendente lite in curia.*

Wherefore, for these and other grave reasons, I hereby give a second admonition, that if the School or College be not entirely closed and the pupils dismissed by Thursday, 18th instant, you as local Superior of the School, and the clergy employed in it will, *ipso facto,* cease to hold faculties in the Diocese and be suspended absolutely *a divinis.* Should you contumaciously persist, and God forbid that you should, in disobedience to this command, I shall proceed upon Sunday next to such further measures as may become unhappily needful.

Given at the Bishop's House, Salford, this 16th day of March, 1875.
+Herbert, Bishop of Salford

Gallwey to Vaughan
46, Ackers Street,[139]
17 March [1875]

My dear Lord,

Since I received from Father Ullathorne the report of his conversation with your Lordship on Monday last,[140] I have naturally suffered a good deal of anxiety, lest by any fault of mine I should give occasion to the scandal which must ensue in case your Lordship carries out the threat of suspension and other more severe measures, which has now been officially communicated to us. It would be wickedness and great folly on my part if I did not do all in my power to avert the

---

[139]   ABSI, RY/2/2, Gallwey to Vaughan, 17 March [1875]. See *The Claim*, pp. 32–34; *The Case*, pp. 121–124 (where a full text of this letter is reproduced).
[140]   Gallwey noted in *Facts and Documents* that he received no written answer to his letter of 13 March, "but the Rev. Father Ullathorne came back from his visit to the Bishop on March 15th, bringing this verbal answer: That unless the school was closed by March 18, His Lordship would withdraw faculties from all the Fathers of the Society in Manchester." *Facts and Documents*, p. 23.

great misery which seems impending. I have every wish to do so; but I venture to beg of your Lordship to consider my position. The time allowed me for consideration in a case of the greatest importance is so short that I cannot properly discharge my duty. I must go to London and call together the Counsellers [*sic*] of the Province, whom I am bound to hear on such grave matters as this. One of them is to-day starting for his mother's funeral, and the feast of St Joseph, just at hand, will make it very difficult for me to have them together before the end of this week; but I will certainly use all my diligence. Then, moreover, as Father General has been long and carefully considering the question, and has been in communication with Rome, and has now sent me his deliberate judgement and definite orders, it is my clear duty to lay the case before him, and let him know your Lordship's wishes, that he may instruct me how to act.

Your Lordship's right will not in any way be prejudiced, if you kindly grant the extension of time for which I beg, before proceeding to extreme measures.

I ask this favour the more confidently, as your Lordship knows, that at your request, I have waited for nearly three months and taken no action, though much blamed for delay, during your Lordship's absence in America. I should probably have waited much longer had not Father General's order arrived.[141]

And now, with regard to the heavy censure which your Lordship proposes to inflict. I lost no time in seeking counsel from the best theologians within my reach, and I venture, in all respect, to invite your Lordship's attention to certain Pontifical Bulls and Decrees of the Sacred Congregation of Bishops and Regulars, which they have pointed out to me. It will be sufficient to cite the Decree of the Sacred Congregation of Bishops and regulars, November 20, 1615, the Bull *Superna* of Clement X, 21 July 1670, the Decree of the Sacred Congregation of Bishops and Regulars, November 28, 1732. *Vide* Bizzarri and also Ferraris, Decree, March 24, 1645.

From these Decrees and Bulls it seems:

1. That Bishops are strictly forbidden to inflict suspension on religious communities *inconsulta Sede Apostolica.*[142] Bull, Clement X, July 21, 1670.

---

[141] "The Bishop's version of this letter, in the copy printed 'for official use, and circulated in his pamphlet' [*The Claim*], breaks off here, with the remark, 'Here follows a long disquisition on the censure of regulars, which for its length and irrelevancy to the College question is omitted.' As many persons will not think it at all irrelevant to see what high authorities think of the Bishop's claim to suspend the Manchester Fathers, the original is here quoted, rather than his Lordship's mutilation of it." *The Case*, pp. 121–122.

[142] "Without consulting the Apostolic See."

2. In the Decree of 1732, the sacred Congregation, after reciting and renewing former Bulls and Dcrees and Orders sent to particular Bishops, concludes thus: *Quorum quidem Decretorum tenorem et aliorum plurium in subjecta materia saepissime emanatorum ab omnibus quibuscumque Archiepiscopis, Episcopis, locorumque Ordinariis eadem S. C. praecipit atque mandat adamusssim servari.* Bizzarri, *loc. cit.*[143]

From these same Decrees it appears further that Bishops are not only forbidden to suspend regular communities, but even to withdraw faculties from so many that only two remain with faculties to hear confessions in their Church.

3. Moreover, it is enacted in these Decrees of the sacred Congregation above cited that a Bishop must not suspend a religious whom he has once approved *ad audiendas*,[144] unless for some cause connected with the confessional, or for violating an interdict imposed by the Bishop himself. '*Emi. Ejusdem S. C. PP. statuunt ac decernunt Archiepiscopis Episcopis, aliisque locorum Ordinariis, ad quos confessarios approbandi jus spectat, confessarios regulares alios ab ipsis libere approbatos ab audiendis confessionibus suspendere posthac minime licere, nisi ex nova causa ad confessiones ipsas pertinente, aut ob non servatum interdictum ab ipsis Ordinariis impositum.*'[145] Bizzarri *loc. cit.*

The Decree ends with these words. *Quod quidem Decretum Emi. PP. inviolabiliter jubent observari.*[146]

It is needless to add that none of the Fathers are in the present instance charged with any crime connected with the confessional, or with violation of interdict.

In addition to these Bulls and Decrees, the Theologians whom I have consulted have called my attention to these principles laid down by Moralists and Canonists.

1. That if a Community is punished by censure, those who are innocent do not incur the censure.

2. That no one can be censured *pro delicto alieno* [for another's wrongdoing].

---

[143] "This same Sacred Congregation commands that the measures prescribed in those decrees, and in others covering the same or closely related area, which have been sent out times without number, are to be scrupulously observed by each and every Archbishop, Bishop, and local Ordinary."

[144] "For the purpose of hearing confessions."

[145] "The most Eminent Fathers of this Sacred Congregation declare and command that Archbishops, Bishops and other local Ordinaries, to whom the task falls of approving confessors, should not afterwards suspend confessors belonging to religious orders whom they have already approved unless it is on account of some new case related to the hearing of confessions, or if an interdict imposed by the Ordinaries themselves is not kept to."

[146] "Which decree the Eminent Fathers command to be inviolably observed."

3. That a grave censure cannot be inflicted on any one who has not
been guilty of a grievous sin.

I think it must be clear that whatever sin is committed, must be
committed either by me or Father General. F[ather] Birch and the FF.
in Manchester have no power to close the school, therefore cannot be
guilty of contumacy.

Father General, acting on the authority given to him by the Holy
See, after advising with the Cardinal Prefect of Propaganda and several
other Cardinals of the same Congregation, has directed us to do what
the English Bishops have in Council decreed. Father General sends us a
copy of the letter which the Cardinal Prefect wrote with his own hand,
to request him to help in Manchester. I have cited it to your Lordship.
If our FF. obey Father General's order, no theologian would hold them
guilty of grievous sin and deserving of suspension.

This being the case, am I not right, my dear Lord, in begging you to
pause for a little while before taking a step which must have grievous
consequences; and which seems to be a violation of solemn decrees? If
I have done wrong in opening the school, I will make full reparation.
As I have already said, all your Episcopal rights will be secured in a
peaceable manner by a delay of a few days. I will only add that we all
most sincerely regret the trouble and disturbance of which we are in
some sense the occasion.

Your Lordship's servant in Christ,
P. Gallwey
P.S.

To prevent a mistake, I add with reference to the official document sent
to F. Birch: 1st. That I have not in any of my letters to your Lordship,
if I mistake not, stated that Propaganda had either "given an order or
expressed a wish". I stated that the Cardinal Prefect had written with
his own hand to Father General, to beg of him to help on education in
Manchester, and that several of the leading Cardinals had given their
judgement that our right in this matter was quite certain. 2nd That the
words, in the document, "many good reasons which were admitted by
your Provincial to be 'very valid'" seem to me to go much beyond what
I stated in my letter to your Lordship. 3rd That I am assured by my predecessor in office *that no agreement* existed between the Society and the
late Bishop on the subject of a school or college. 4th With regard to the
words "the right set up by the Provincial", it is clear from what I have
already said and from Father General's letter, that the claim does not
originate with me, it is a right founded on the Apostolic Bull, on which
our Institute is based, a right of ancient date and fully acknowledged by
men much wiser than I am. 5th I submit respectfully that in the present
instance there is no case of *pendente lite in Curia*. At the same time, I

think if your Lordship will kindly allow time for a reference to Rome before having recourse to measures which seem to go against law, and which are likely to cause great scandal, the cause of Christianity and religion will gain.[147]

Manning to Vaughan
Rome,[148]
18 March 1875.

My Dear Herbert,

I have had two full conversations about Salford, and Father O'C[allaghan] had been with your letter to Cardinal Franchi. I will see to your case as if it were my own, and in Low Week I mean to bring the whole relation of the Jesuits to the Church in England before the Bishops, and to lay it before the Holy See. I am very sorry you have this pain, but you are called to do a great service to the Church in England and to bear the odium of which I have not a little. Be of good heart. These things are more keenly trying than worse things. Let me know anything and everything I can do for you.

Yours very affectionately,
Henry Edward, Archbishop of Westminster.

---

[147] In *Facts and Documents*, Gallwey comments: "To this letter no written answer was sent. The Bishop expressed his determination to enforce his sentence of suspension on the following day. As, however, His Lordship expressed a wish to see me, I waited on him in the evening of March 17. In our conversation, he reproached me with considerable severity for what we had done, and complained of the manner in which it was done, and urged me strongly to close the school on the following day, according to his order." p. 31. Gallwey explained that he could not close the school without consulting Peter Beckx the Jesuit General. He therefore requested a few days' grace in order to secure a reply from the Father General; in return he agreed to take no new pupils and to close the school for the Easter holidays on the following Monday [22 March]. Vaughan consented to these terms. In his account of the conversation between Gallwey and himself, Vaughan adds, "The next morning the Provincial returned with overtures for an adjustment of differences. His proposals were: that he should give the Bishop money for his Seminary; that he should educate some boys for the Diocese; that he should make some compensation to the Xaverian Brothers if they were to suffer injury, – and that in return for this, the Bishop should consent to the Society carrying on a College in Manchester. The Bishop felt unable to accept these overtures." *The Claim*, pp. 8–9.

[148] Snead-Cox, *Life of Cardinal Vaughan*, vol. 1, p. 292, Manning to Vaughan, 18 March 1875.

Weld to Gallwey
Observatory,[149]
Roman College.
19 March [1875]

My dear Fr,

I have waited till today to have something to tell you. I received [a] telegram on Tuesday morning and on same evening started for Rome, and went immediately to see the Cardinal even before saying Mass as I hoped to catch him in his house before he went to the Vatican. I found the horses at the door and the servant would not let me in on any account. I then went and said Mass at the altar of St Ignatius in the Gesu[150] for your intention. Then went to Mgr Simeoni, who was mighty surprised at the idea of suspending a community. I found from him that the Cardinal would dine at the Irish College, it being St Patrick's Day. There I went and came in for dinner too! After dinner I had a short conversation with him. I asked him to let me send a telegram to Vaughan in his name, however he preferred to do it himself and sent this: "Write at once about the school and mean time suspend action."[151] He wanted me to telegraph to stop you too. I told him that as you had begun (if you had already done so) on authority of his Eminence's letter to Fr General it would be a little compromising to him to tell you to stop, that probably you had only begun quietly with half a dozen little boys, and it would be better simply to tell you to take no new measures till further orders. He was satisfied with this, so I sent my telegram that afternoon.

The Consistory and other things have made him very busy so I only got a conversation with him this morning. He is certainly desirous of the school and will help us through it if he can. I feel convinced of this. He was astonished at the size of Manchester. The maps made great effect. He said I think we shall find some way of combining it, and repeated this more than once. Vaughan has written to the Rector of the English College saying that he was on the point of coming to an agreement with you but you have taken the matter into your hands and proceeded by way of fact. I told him how gentle you had been about that and Vaughan had positively refused, and it was a matter within our house; that Vaughan is a man who expects to gain everything by firmness, it was unnecessary to ask. He knows that you are not stopping but that I told you to take *no new measures* and is quite satisfied with that. He expects Vaughan's letter tomorrow and I have an appointment with him

---

149 ABSI, C/3, Weld to Gallwey, 19 March 1875.
150 The Jesuit church in Rome.
151 APF, Weld to Franchi, 17 March 1875. On the reverse of this letter, in which Weld requests that Franchi telegraph Vaughan, are written the words: "I ask you to write to me and suspend all action, 18 March 1875."

tomorrow at 4 p.m., but I do not think the letter can reach by that time. At any rate I stay here till we can settle something. The Cardinal told me he had spoken to the Pope (I think he said yesterday) lately and told him that those English Bishops now that they have got the hierarchy think they are to develop it and have everything in their hand whereas they ought to make use of Religious too. He said the Pope quite agreed with him, and told him to speak to Manning in that sense. The conversation was interrupted by one of the new Cardinals coming in, but whilst I stood there they talked for some minutes together in great praise of the Society, and Cardinal Franchi said the most cruel blow in all their time is the suppression of the religious orders. He has the character of being a diplomatist but I should say I think him friendly. Much will depend on the statement which Vaughan makes. He has promised to talk it over with me, and I am in fair hopes.

He asked me if Manning could help us in the matter, I said no it was better not to consult him who would not let us have a school himself! Still there will be a strong fight made. I said Mass yesterday at [the] altar of B[lessed] Berchmans for your intention, and today for the same.

If there is anything important after my interview with the Cardinal I will telegraph. I hope to finish all and return to Fiesole early next week.

Ever yours sincerely in J[esus] C[hrist]
A. Weld

Ullathorne to Gallwey
Lowe House,[152]
St. Helens,
Lancashire.
21 March 1875.

Dear Fr Provincial,
When I told his Lordship that I commenced a school in Manchester and hoped for his blessing and good will to the undertaking he asked on what authority I had done so, I said that I thought I was right as we had a special duty in our Society of having schools etc. but perhaps the letter I had come to present would explain better than I could. His Lordship then appeared to read the letter and then said – well I cannot allow such a thing – you must at once send away the scholars and close (or break up) the school. I said I could not do so. His Lordship said if you do not I shall "*withdraw the faculties from the Society in Manchester*" – I am perfectly certain of these words underlined – after talking and arguing his Lordship said – "*if you do not close the school by Thursday next I*

---

[152] ABSI, RX/5, Ullathorne to Gallwey, 21 March 1875.

shall withdraw the faculties." I don't think he used the word suspend or interdict but what word he used implies withdrawal of faculties from *all* the Fathers.

In my second interview he spoke of the note in which he had sent to Fr Birch as including only Fr Birch and the Priests in the school and I reminded his Lordship that he had threatened to withdraw faculties from all the Fathers. I said your Lordship told me these very words that you would withdraw faculties from the *Society* in Manchester.

Your Reverence's obedient servant,
Thomas Ullathorne
P.S.
In my second interview I do not exactly remember how it came on but I think his Lordship brought it on himself. I say that he does not mean to deprive the people of Confession, and only withdraw the faculties from Fr Birch and those employed in the school. I reminded him of his words to me. *'Luckily'* I have got a copy of the document sent to Fr Birch. He did not deny it.

Birch to Gallwey
46, Ackers Street,[153]
Manchester.
22 March 1875.

Dear Fr Provincial,

Rev Mr Gadd[154] called this afternoon, from the Bishop (luckily just after the pupils had been sent home) to ask if we had carried out the Bishop's instruction about closing the school. I answered that we had carried out Your Reverence's instructions, agreeable to arrangement with the Bishop. I suppose there will be mis-understanding. Rev Mr Gadd was hearty, but a little awkward. I said as little about the matter as possible, and we passed on to other matters in no way connected with us.

Obediently yours in Christ,
Henry Birch

---

153   ABSI, RX/5, Birch to Gallwey, 22 March 1875. See *Facts and Documents*, p. 32; *The Case*, p. 124.
154   Charles Gadd, 1838–1907; secretary to Vaughan.

Weld to Franchi
Collegio Romano,[155]
22 March 1875.

Most Reverend Eminence,

I would ask with deepest respect that your Eminence explain to His Lordship the Bishop of Salford that the Fathers of the Society are urgently desirous of co-operating with the Bishops in the salvation of souls, and that the Father General and also the English Fathers, as I can assure you, 1) are most desirous of doing nothing which could be contrary to the right of the Bishops or which could harm their enterprises; on the contrary they wish to aid them with humble homage according to their Institute.

2) That this Manchester school was not begun until after it had received from Your Eminence and parish priests and other Eminent Cardinals the assurance of the right of the Society to open a school where the Fathers are legitimately established, and Your Eminence prompted the Fr General also by letter to favour the work of teaching, especially in Manchester. Since therefore the house has been built on this basis, and since the Holy Father Pius VII announced the restoration of the Society especially for the education of the young, it is hoped that it will not be displeasing to His Lordship that the Society has taken this step, which could not have been taken without authority.

3) One can add that the population of Manchester and its surroundings reaches to nearly two million within a radius of 12 miles, and that within the same limits there are more than two thirds of the Catholics in the entire diocese of Salford. It is true that many of these Catholics are poor, but there is general agreement that it is mainly in the middle class that Catholics are lacking in England, and that the only way of expanding this class is by providing education. In a county full of factories, a little knowledge is sufficient to render a young man capable for a good job, and if he has also received an introduction to letters, there is no post which a young man with ability cannot hope to attain. It seems certain that in this way and this way alone a good Catholic middle class will be created. For that reason the IV Westminster Synod in the XVII decree reads thus: It is greatly recommended to all heads of larger missions (or as it were, parishes) to set up such schools, and in the Catholic magazine the *Tablet*, every week there appears letters written with the express aim of promoting the foundation of these schools.[156]

4) It is likewise certain that many vocations to the priesthood and to the religious life are lost because the parents cannot send their children

---

[155] APF, Anglia 20, ff. 206–207, Weld to Franchi, 22 March 1875.
[156] See above, Weld to Gallwey, 2 February 1875.

to boarding schools in the country, and there are not enough scholar-
ships available for the children to go free, although if these schools
of which we speak existed in abundance they could at least receive a
basis of education. Your Most Rev. Eminence knows how frequent these
days is the request for missionaries speaking English throughout the
whole world. Various places ask for English Jesuits, and they cannot
be sent, because they are not here. I know that the Bishop of Salford is
proposing to enlarge the school he already has, but it is two and a half
miles away from our Church. There are, in fact, two centres of respectable Catholics, one around the Cathedral and the other in the vicinity
of our Church, and it is not very likely that children of the one group
would go to the more distant school of the other group, in such a way
that one school would much damage the other. In fact, some of those
who live in our area, instead of crossing the city to go to the Bishop's
school, already go to the Protestant College which is in their area. In
fact, someone calling himself Catholic, writing recently in the *Tablet*,
spoke with praise of this school (in fact atheist) as if Catholics should
have nothing to desire apart from knowledge. It is obvious how useful
a good Catholic school would be in this part of the city. I have heard
that the Bishop is proposing a boarding school, which our day school is
even less likely to harm.

5) If I may add that such is the development of religion in England
that there is a comparable multiplication of churches and schools and
also colleges, so there is no lack of Catholics for all of them. In fact
the number of Catholics is increasing in proportion to these institutions.
What is more, within so vast a population no-one can really know the
true number of Catholics. The Father Provincial has explained to Your
Reverend Eminence the feelings of the Protestants within Manchester
about the city as a centre of education. It seems to me therefore that
Religion will receive a great benefit from the establishment of this
school without harming the Bishop's school.

6) If our schools are now being created in the house in which our
members live, this position is simply provisional until the new house is
more or less built; and since this state cannot last many months, it does
not seem that there should be delay in the matter under discussion. I
would hope that on this point His Lordship will be able to agree with
the Fr Provincial.

7) About the idea that I might have promised the predecessor of the
present Bishop not to open a school, I have explained to Your Eminence
what happened, and I can say that I did this with all openness, without
hiding anything, so as not to be lacking in the most scrupulous veracity,
and Your Very Rev. Eminence assured me that there would be no difficulty on that score, but if the Bishop wished also to have details from
me on this point, I would be very pleased to give them.

Your Most Rev. Eminence will be kind enough to convey these details in writing to the Bishop in the sense in which I have expressed them, and to say to him that considering the basis upon which we will have begun the work, and the hope of benefit to the region, Your Eminence hopes that he will be satisfied and not displeased to see this new aid to the education of people in his diocese; I am persuaded that his Lordship will be not only pleased but gradually will rejoice in the Lord.

A. Weld S.J.

Gallwey to Vaughan
111, Mount Street, W.[157]
23 March 1875.

My dear Lord,

Father Birch writes that Canon Gadd[158] called yesterday to know whether we had closed our school *according to Your Lordship's instructions*. To prevent mistakes or prejudice to rights, I will tell Your Lordship in a few words what I have done. When I called on Thursday morning I mentioned that I had received a telegram from Rome, and I was told in that telegram that Your Lordship had also received one. The telegram which I received exonerated me from carrying out the agreement we had come to the evening before, and empowered me to carry on the school till Rome should adjudicate. As, however, we had come to an agreement amicably on the previous evening,[159] I said to Your Lordship on Thursday that I would adhere to our arrangement. I have since received a letter from Rome giving the sense of the telegram in detail, but the situation remains as it was last Thursday. The school has broken up, as Your Lordship suggested, for the holidays a day or so sooner than otherwise it would have done, simply because I had agreed to the arrangement with Your Lordship, and did not wish without necessity to oppose Your Lordship's wishes.

Since my return I have looked at the new Poor School Code, and it seems to me quite clear that your College and our College and another will not be too much to save our children from the havoc which the Board Schools with their improved education will work in England – as they have already done, I am informed, in New York.

---

[157] ABSI, RX/5, Gallwey to Vaughan, 23 March 1875. See *Facts and Documents*, pp. 33–34.
[158] Charles Gadd was not in fact made a Canon of the diocese until 1880.
[159] See above, n. 147.

Notwithstanding our lawsuit, I wish Your Lordship many graces from this Holy Week, and a large share of Easter Blessings upon all your works both at home and abroad.

Your Lordship's servant in Christ,
P. Gallwey

Vaughan to Gallwey
Bishop's House,[160]
Salford.
24 March 1875

My dear Fr Gallwey,
    Fr Gadd denies having used the words attributed to him. It is of no use to carry on a paper discussion as the matter has past to a higher tribunal.
Wishing you every grace and blessing,

I am Your faithful and obedient servant,
+ Herbert, Bishop of Salford.

Manning to Vaughan
Rome,[161]
23 March 1875.

My Dear Herbert,
    I wrote to Cardinal Franchi last night and asked him to write to the General and say that the College Jesuits must go back to their house. I said also that the question I intended to bring before the Bishops is not whether the intended College shall go on – which I consider to be settled already in the negative – but what are the relations of the Society to the Bishops. I am sorry that you have had to bear this cross, but I rejoice that it has come. I have long felt that the English Province is altogether abnormal, dangerous to themselves, mischievous to the Church in England. I have seemed to see it and feel it with more than natural intellect and natural discernment. I am now convinced that I am right, and I propose to go through the whole work or warfare which has now been begun – for their sakes as well as for ours.

Yours very affectionately
Henry Edward, Archbishop of Westminster.

---

160   ABSI, RY/2/2, Vaughan to Gallwey, 24 March 1875. See *Facts and Documents*, p. 34; *The Case*, p. 125.
161   Snead-Cox, *Life of Cardinal Vaughan*, vol. 1, p. 293, Manning to Vaughan, 25 March 1875.

Vaughan to Birch
Bishop's House,[162]
Salford.
4 April 1875.

My dear Fr Birch,

I have been told that the Acker's [*sic*] Street School has been re-opened. Is this true? And if not, have you received orders to open it this week?

In case you have reopened, I should be obliged if you would inform me what number of pupils have been admitted.

The bearer will wait for an answer. I am sorry to have to trouble you on this subject again.

Wishing you every blessing I am,
Your faithful and devoted servant,
+ Herbert, Bishop of Salford.

Birch to Vaughan
46, Ackers Street,[163]
4 April 1875.

My Lord,

Forgive me if I say that I feel bound to communicate with my Superior before I give any further answer, than that the school was reopened last Wednesday.

With profound respect, believe me to be,

Your Lordship's obedient servant in Christ,
Henry Birch

Vaughan to Gallwey
Bishop's House,[164]
Salford.
4 April 1875.

My dear Fr Gallwey,

I hear that you have re-opened your school in Manchester. Pray excuse me if I say that I consider this to be contrary to your promise of

---

[162]   ABSI, RX/5, Vaughan to Birch, 4 April 1875. See *Facts and Documents*, pp. 34–35; *The Bishop of Salford's Reply: Uncanonical Reopening of the Jesuit College and Summary of the Whole Case* (1875) (hereafter *The Bishop's Reply*), p. 11; *The Case*, p. 126.
[163]   ABSI, RX/5, Birch to Vaughan, 4, April 1875. *Facts and Documents*, p. 35; *The Bishop's Reply*, p. 12; *The Case*, p. 126.
[164]   ABSI, RX/5, Vaughan to Gallwey, 4 April 1875. Cf. *Facts and Documents*, pp. 35–36; *The Bishop's Reply*, p. 12; *The Case*, pp. 126–127.

March 17th; and that I must request you to send me the evidence upon which you justify this act, so that I may examine it officially. Meanwhile the school should be closed until I have proof of the right which you claim to re-open it.

My address for this week will be: Archbishop's House, Westminster, London.

Believe me to be,

Your faithful and obedient servant,

+Herbert, Bishop of Salford.

Telegram from Weld to Gallwey[165]

Firenze

5 April 1875

Suspend re-opening of school question of house all going well. I have written.

W. A. Johnson to Gallwey

Archbishop's House,[166]

Westminster, S.W.

6 April 1875.

My dear Father Gallwey,

The Cardinal desires me to say that the Bishops ask you to let them have by tomorrow evening the statement that you wish to send to them; and that their Lordships will afterwards be glad to receive on the following morning[167] any verbal statement that you may wish to make in person.[168]

---

165 ABSI, RX/5.

166 *Facts and Documents*, pp. 37–38.

167 Thursday 8 April 1875.

168 Gallwey's decision not to address the bishops in person led to some misunderstanding as his decision not to do so was misconstrued, as can be seen from the following letter. "My dear Lord, Fr Jones has written me the substance of what your Lordship said to him at your recent visit to St Beuno's. I very much wish that I had met your Lordship at [the] ordinations as it is pleasanter and more easy to clear up misunderstandings by conversation than by letter. I think it will be a very suitable work for the year of the silver wedding [*sic*] if your Lordship can help to clear up any misapprehensions that disturb peace and concord between the Bishops and the Religious Orders. I will say a few words on each of the points in Fr Jones' letter. 1. With regard to my not appearing before the bishops in Low Week, if your Lordship had been in London you would have received a note from me which would have prevented all [illegible] on this point. I wrote to your Lordship, to Dr Ullathorne and to Dr Clifford. For as I took for granted that the Manchester question would be discussed in the Bishops' meeting, I wrote to your Lordship and to Dr

I remain, dear Rev. Father,
Yours sincerely in Christ,
W.A. Johnson.[169]

The Provincial's Memorial to the Bishops[170]
111, Mount Street,
London.
7th April 1875.

I shall be able to spare their Lordships' time, and to make my memorial much shorter than I originally intended, as the Bishop of Birmingham has kindly told me that the correspondence that has recently passed between the Bishop of Salford and myself is already before their Lordships.

I think it highly desirable that the Bishops should see the whole of that correspondence, as in one or other of the letters which I wrote will be found, I think, almost everything of importance that I would desire to lay before them, both as regards the act of Father General, and the suspension threatened by his Lordship.

It would suit my own inclinations very well to pour out all my thoughts to their Lordships – but in the first place the task would be a very long one; secondly, in order to clear up matters in a satisfactory way, I should require to have before me the statements made by the Bishop of Salford; and thirdly, to introduce occasionally matter of a personal character.

Add to this that the legal question must necessarily be now settled in Rome, and therefore I need not enter into that portion of the subject.

The points on which I wish to make a brief comment are these: 1) The Bishop states in his monition of suspension that I had admitted his reasons in refusing us a College to be very valid, etc. 2) In a recent

Ullathorne, and to Dr Clifford before the meeting pressing for an interview. Hearing afterwards that your Lordship was unwell I did not post my letter to your Lordship but B[isho]p Clifford and B[isho]p Ullathorne both kindly saw me and I begged of them to [illegible] to their Lordships to permit me send in a memorial before they came to any decision. This originated with me – on the following Tuesday in Low Week I received a note saying that their Lordships would receive my memorial – and also hear anything I wanted to add on the following morning. This was clearly not an invitation or summons to meet their Lordships but an answer to my petition. I wrote in reply that I thought my written memorial would be sufficient if the correspondence between the B[isho]p of Salford and myself was laid before their Lordships." ABSI, RY/2/2, no date, the handwriting is that of Peter Gallwey. The recipient of the letter was James Brown, the Bishop of Shrewsbury, who was absent from the Low Week meeting due to ill health.
[169]   Secretary to the Cardinal-Archbishop of Westminster. This letter refers to the bishops' Low Week meeting, 5–9 April 1875.
[170]   APF, Anglia 20, 1875–1877, ff. 220–223; *The Case*, pp. 128–131.

letter he expresses his opinion that I violated a promise made to him on the 17th March.

1) It is true then that in my reply to the Bishop's letter of August 17th, 1874, I made use of the expression that some[171] of his reasons for refusing us permission to establish a College were "very valid." I will explain these words:

Of the reasons alleged by his Lordship two seemed to me at the time to carry weight.

a) The compact which the Bishop asserted to exist.

b) The respect due to vested interests.

In both cases I assumed the facts alleged to be correct, when I called the reasons valid, and I should still consider them valid if the facts could be established.

1) With regard to the compact said to exist between the late Bishop and the Society, I had never heard of it till I found this mention of it in the Bishop's letter, and when I saw the statement, it seemed to me that our case was at an end, and I certainly would not subsequently have taken any part in the establishment of a school, had not Father Weld, who was Provincial at the time, assured me that he knew of no contract or engagement binding the Society not to open a College. He fully admitted that Bishop Turner had forbidden him to establish a College, but this prohibition Father Weld never considered to be a compact by which he had bound himself. Furthermore, he assured me that for the security of his own conscience he laid fully before the Cardinal Prefect of Propaganda all that passed between Bishop Turner and himself, and that the Cardinal declared that on this score there was no difficulty.[172] It

---

171   Vaughan reacted to Gallwey's memorial to the bishops by publishing another pamphlet – *The Bishop's Reply* – in which he takes Gallwey to task for being inexact. In his letter to Vaughan of 20 August, Gallwey wrote "I cannot but admit that *many of your* Lordship's *reasons are very valid*" while in his memorial he used the phrase "that *some* of his [Vaughan's] reasons ... were valid." From this Vaughan concludes that Gallwey "seems to have forgotten the extent of the admission he had readily made in the earlier stage" of the proceedings, p. 3.

172   Here, too, Vaughan finds reason to criticise: "The Bishop of Salford begs to point out that the slightest consideration of the case clearly demonstrates that the Cardinal, in the opinion attributed to him, gave no official judgement. Father Weld carried to him his own case of conscience, and upon his own statement of it, the Cardinal, with the clarity and condescension of a Bishop and pastor of souls, gave him his opinion. But it is too obvious to need insisting on that the Cardinal never intended as Prefect of Propaganda to decide a question on litigation by the expression of an opinion on a case brought to him as a private and personal matter of conscience. The Bishop of Salford begs further to express a doubt as to whether the Cardinal has been made aware, at the time he expressed his opinion, of the nature of the contention between the Bishop of Salford and the Society as to the agreement. The Bishop feels that it would be highly disrespectful to his Eminence to suppose for a moment that the opinion quoted by the Provincial is the official judgement of the Cardinal-Prefect. And he cannot refrain from adding that it is sad to experi-

is true that the Bishop of Salford told me recently that a memorandum exists, and that some of the Canons can bear witness to a compact. Whether the memorandum and the evidence of these Canons can establish more than the fact that the Bishop laid no injunction on Father Weld, I have no means of ascertaining. I can only say that if sufficient evidence can be produced that the Society is bound by a real compact, that compact must of course be respected, and I am quite sure that Father General would at once direct me to repair any wrong done by closing our school without delay.

2) As to the vested interests of the Xaverian Brothers, if the good Brothers had by perseverance brought their school to a great state of efficiency, and that the people of Manchester were well contented with the education which they offer, I should consider this is a valid reason why we should not be allowed to do grievous damage to this existing Institution. But to say nothing of the statistics of the school, of the testimony of the Brothers themselves, or the voice of the public – when I find that his Lordship himself, because he considers this school quite inadequate to existing wants, publicly declares his intention of absorbing it into his proposed College, and that in his letter of August 17th he asks me to pledge myself that the Society shall help him to form staff of the said College, it seems to me clear that his Lordship agrees with the common view that the vested interests of the Brothers is but a very small one, and must not stand in the way of the souls that are in danger, though it might be quite reasonable to compensate them for any loss which they might sustain.

I am still more confirmed in my present opinion that the vested interests of the Xaverian Brothers is not a valid reason for excluding us from a work especially allotted to us by the Holy See, by the fact that his Lordship has more than once quite recently stated to me and to others that he fully intended to allow us to have a College a little later, when his own College had been established, and that he was on the point of coming to an agreement with me when I suddenly took action. These assurances took me quite by surprise, as I had before my mind the words he wrote to me in August, "I must beg of you entirely to dismiss the idea that it is permitted for the Society to establish another house of education in Manchester," which seemed to me quite final.

Still more did our exclusion seem final when he made known to me last Passion Week that the site which he had purchased on the borders of

ence another instance of the way in which a private and unofficial opinion is forged into a weapon by the Provincial to destroy the position of the Ordinary of the Diocese, and is then brandished before the eyes of the entire Hierarchy as a verdict given in his favour by the Prefect of Propaganda." *The Bishop's Reply*, pp. 6–7. See *The Claim*, pp. 14–16.

our district, and very near to our church,[173] was not, as I then supposed, for a new church, but for his future College, and when he went on to say that he considered our system of teaching was one not at all suited to the needs of his people, and, in fact, that we were not wanted in Manchester. Probably had not our conversation been a hurried one, all these statements would have been modified so as to harmonise better. Meanwhile I think some of them go to show that the vested interests of the Brothers is no serious obstacle to the establishment of another College in Manchester.

I will only add a few words respecting the promise made by me on the 17th of March, and which the Bishop considers me to have broken. On that day I went to his Lordship at his request, to see if some means could not be devised of preventing the scandal that would ensue if the suspension were to be enforced on the following morning. I begged for time to consult Father General, as I had been acting under an order given by him, after long deliberation and communication with Rome. I did not think it right to close the school without instruction from him. The Bishop feared that if we continued to keep the school open the number of scholars might increase, whereby the difficulty of closing would be made greater. He however at last consented to my request, and allowed me four days. I on my part promised three things-

I. To write without delay to Father General, and I did so that night.

II. Not to allow the number of scholars to be increased during the short interval allowed me, and this was faithfully observed.

III. To close the school for the holidays on the following Monday. This was also done.

I made no other promise than these.

On the following morning I received Father General's telegram from Rome, which informed me that one had been sent to the Bishop, staying his proceedings against the Society. I hereupon went back to his Lordship to tell him of the arrival of this telegram. To me it seemed to meet all agreements of the previous evening. I however told the Bishop that as we had come to an amicable arrangement I would stand by the terms of it, and close the school on Monday for the holidays. This I accordingly did.

In conclusion, I hope that I have not, either in this paper, or in any part of my correspondence with his Lordship, used any word that is either disrespectful or unkind, and as I do not in any way complain of his Lordship for upholding what he thinks to be his Episcopal rights, or protecting what he conceives to be the interests of his flock, so on

---

[173] Grosvenor Square, All Saints, within ten minutes' walking distance of the church of the Holy Name.

the other hand I hope that neither his Lordship of Salford, nor any of their Lordships, will take it amiss that we strive by all lawful means to preserve our rights to take part in education, which is as essential to our Institute as the choir duties are to cloistered Orders.

P. Gallwey

Gallwey to Vaughan
111, Mount Street. W.[174]
7 April 1875.

My dear Lord,

A great press of work has hindered me from replying to your Lordship's note of the 4th inst. as soon as I could have wished. I am sorry that your Lordship thinks I have acted contrary to my promise of March 17. I cannot see that I have done so. I promised three things and no more to the best of my knowledge.

1. To write to Fr General without delay. I did so that night.

2. Not to let the number of our scholars increase during the interval of four days which you allowed to me; that is to say till we have broken up for [the] Easter holidays. This we kept to faithfully.

3. To break up school on Monday for the Easter holidays. This we also did.

These are the only requirements that I am aware of, if I had known of any more I certainly would have kept them. The telegram which arrived on the following morning suspended, as I have already mentioned to your Lordship, the arrangements of the day before – but still I called on your Lordship to say that as we had come to a friendly agreement I would adhere to it and close the school on Monday for the Easter holidays. Your Lordship further asks for the evidence upon which I justify the act of reopening the school after Easter. In your Lordship's note of March 24 you write, 'the matter has past to a higher Tribunal.' This being so, my Lord, I respectfully submit that it is to this Higher Tribunal that I must furnish evidence to justify my act.

Very sincerely,
Your Lordship's servant,
P. Gallwey

---

[174] ABSI, RX/5, Gallwey to Vaughan, 7 April 1875. See *Facts and Documents*, pp. 36–37; *The Bishop's Reply*, pp. 12–13; *The Case*, p. 127.

Weld to Gallwey
San Gerolamo,[175]
Fiesole.
7 April [1875]

My dear Fr

I have just received a line from Rome written on Monday 5th to the effect that the Cardinal will write to B[isho]p Vaughan to say that according to the information received we are according to Canon Law, but that if he has been put to loss through the misunderstandings about the promise you will do something to the benefit of the diocese on which point you will agree with him. Still I am told not to tell you to go ahead, as the Secretary asked whether things were kept in suspense, to which Fr Armellini answered yes. This was written on the day I telegraphed. I have since written to tell them your answer, and the instructions I sent after. I fancy they wish to give Vaughan the opportunity of making a reply. He cannot say much as we have his reasons, and they have all been answered over and over again. I am told that if the question of the *house*[176] had been understood from the beginning, the letter would have been written long ago. It is a great loss of time, my being here. It takes two days to get a letter from Rome, so that I should have gone again this week, but the matter seems to be going so well, that it seemed no longer necessary.

The most important news however is this: we know for certain that the Holy Father has spoken to Cardinal Manning in our favour. This you must keep very quiet. I expect it will prevent the memorial against us which I considered to be a certain consequence of the meeting of the Bishops at this juncture, and a memorial from an entire hierarchy could not help making an unfavourable impression.

The question of making compensation to the Bishop could I think only come in case he has really bought land near us, in which case we might have to take it off his hands, as we had to the house in Burlington Street.[177] The school of Xaverian Brothers and his one in Salford existed before our time.

[175]   ABSI, BN/6, Weld to Gallwey, 7 April [1875].

[176]   In a letter of 11 May 1912 Fr Walmesley SJ, who had been researching the correspondence between the then English Provincial, Fr Peter Gallwey, and the Jesuit Superior General, Peter Beckx, commented "The Bishop of Salford (Bp Herbert Vaughan) seems to have made a point out of the fact that the school which Fr Birch set up was *locally* separated from our church, or chapel such as it was then." ABSI, RY/2/2.

[177]   This refers to the property belonging to Canon Toole which Turner stipulated as being a *sine qua non* for the Society to purchase before he could allow them to make their second entry into Manchester. See below, 23 April 1878, Harper to Coleridge.

The letter of Gregory XVI to the English Bishops[178] has not reached us. I should be glad to see it. I should be very glad if you would send Fr Armellini a copy of the new decrees of the Westminster Synod. We owe to him more than anyone else all that we gained in that business. He worked for us very hard, and would be much pleased with such a recognition. If it is posted to the Collegio Germanico, Rome, addressed to him it will be all right.

I wrote yesterday to ask whether we are not in *regula* in either of the two houses in Ackers Street, I can only say that I have no doubt of it, but have had no answer, and will give you all information as soon as I receive it.

Cardinal Franchi has spoken once or twice of sending me to England to help smooth things with Vaughan so as to bring him amicably to accept his position, but I said I thought you could do it much better than I could, and that there was not the least utility in my going.

Stonor whom I drew out a little upon Vaughan's plan, told me he intended to spend £40,000 on his college, and saw his way to it! I pressed him as to whether he had actually bought land, he could not say that he had actually done so. About a year ago I spoke to Stonor and told him Vaughan was against our having a college, he said "What a shame, I'll scold him for that." I reminded him of this with the view of keeping him from saying anything to the Pope against us as I knew Vaughan had written to him. He did not remember it, and said it must have been some one else. Poor fellow, he has had such a blow on the head, it is a wonder if he remembers anything. He looked very languid

---

[178] 20 June 1835. This letter is referred to in *Facts and Documents*, pp. 14–15. "To an earnest recommendation from the Sacred Congregation of Propaganda, given he says, *Nobis annuentibus*, the Fathers of the Society of Jesus should be permitted to have a church in his district, one of the Vicars Apostolic had answered, '*Se non posse nisi vulnus infensissimum infligendo conscientiae suae, adeoque nullo modo posse approbationem atque consensum praebere illi negotio*' ['He could not do so except by hurting his conscience very severely and so in no way coud he give approval and consent in that matter']. And he added by his representative, '*Ab universo ejus Clero haberi ut Religioni summopere injuriosum templum illud Jesuitis deferre.*' ['All his Clergy held it to be extremely injurious to Religion to hand over that church to the Jesuits.'] To this answer Pope Gregory XVI, replied with his own hand, '*Quid minus gratum hac responsione? Quomodo poterant injuriosius rejici Congregationis Vota quam denuntiando injuriosum Religioni quod ipsa valde utile edixerat insuper et profitendo nonnisi inflicto propriae conscientiae infensissimo vulnere iisdem obsecundari posse.*' ['What could be less acceptable than this response? How could they reject the decisions of the Congregation more damagingly than by denouncing as injurious what it itself had decreed to be very useful, as well as claiming that he could only comply with the decisions by inflicting serious damage to his own conscience?'] And then he adds, '*Quid praeterea Jesuitis magis opprobrio esse potest quam sic probrose repelli a missionibus adeundis!*' ['Furthermore, what could be a greater insult to the Jesuits than to drive them away in such an ignominious manner from starting up missions!']"

and is still suffering from a broken rib [?]. The wonder is he was not killed on the spot.

Monsignor Nardi[179] has sent me a card to say that he will be here in a day or two. I think he is going to England. He is very near the Pope, and I think it is good to be attentive to him.

Ever yours sincerely in J[esus] C[hrist],
A. Weld

Armellini to Gallwey
Collegio Americano,[180]
Rome,
7 April 1875.

Dear Fr,
    I write directly to Your Reverence not to lose time. The Bishop of Salford wrote some time ago a thundering letter to the Rector of the English College saying that the Jesuits were following the theory of accomplished facts and that he would take very strong measures, if they reopened their schools, and that scandal would arise from it etc. This I heard from the Cardinal Prefect of the Propaganda, from whom I come. The Bishop added that he would notify to the Rector (of course always for the Cardinal) by telegraph, whether the FFrs would re-open the schools. This in fact he did last night. After all this I had to tell the Cardinal that Fr General's letter and Fr Weld's telegrams did not reach Your Reverence in time, and that consequently the schools were reopened according to our Rule on Wednesday after Easter. I told the Cardinal that Your Reverence asked through a telegram: what should be done? and that Fr Weld had answered you, to keep the schools in the older part of the house. Then I asked the Cardinal, what was to be done? He was afraid of scandal and rather inclined to the suspension of the schools, saying that he did not wish to have the responsibility on himself. I then remarked that I thought the Bishop could and would do nothing in fact: especially if His Eminence would be so good as to tell him at once by a telegram to wait for his answer. This he will do this evening through the Rector of the English College. But at the same time he wished us *at least* not to receive new scholars for the present, till the question is arranged. As to the letter of the Cardinal to Bishop Vaughan, it was read to me by the Secretary of the Propaganda this morning. It tells the Bishop: "not to do any thing which could not be supported according to Canon Law." For, according to the

---

179 Mgr Francesco Nardi, Consultor at the Congregation for Sacred Rites.
180 ABSI, RX/5, Armellini to Gallwey, 7 April 1875.

exposition of the FFrs we are in good order with regard to the religious house where the schools have been opened. And besides, it invites the Bishop to write to the Cardinal. As yet the Bishop has never written to His Eminence, and that seems to be very inconvenient to the Cardinal Prefect. In consequence of this communication Your Reverence will see what is to be done in order to prevent any scandal, according to the wish of the Cardinal. For my part I consider this question as settled according to the Propaganda. However euphemistic be the letter of His Eminence to the Bishop, it is substantially in favour of our schools.

Yours very sincerely in Xt.,
T. Armellini, SJ.

Bishop Ullathorne to Gallwey
Archbishop's House,[181]
9 April 1875.

Dear Father Provincial,

In compliance with your request contained in your letter of today, I put your two questions to the assembled Bishops. In reply to the first, we were distinctly assured by the Bishop of Salford that every letter and note that had passed between him and you or Fr Birch had been produced and read with the exception of one letter of His Lordship's of which he had kept no copy, but of which he gave the substance.

In reply to the second question, I am authorised to say to you, that no personal statement affecting the case respecting the Fathers and Manchester have [*sic*] been put before the Bishops, except that they had canvassed the parents of children for their College[182] who were already placed in the school or College of the Xaverian Brothers.

The brief reply to two particular points in your letter I likewise placed before the Bishops.

Praying Our Lord keep you,
I remain, dear Father Provincial, your faithful servant in Xt.
B. Ullathorne.

---

[181] ABSI, RX/5, Bishop Bernard Ullathorne to Gallwey, 8 April 1875. See pp. 59–63 above, 'Provincial's Memorial to the Bishops', 7 April 1875.
[182] See *The Claim*, p. 10.

Weld to Gallwey
San Gerolamo,[183]
Fiesole.
9 April 1875.

My dear Fr,
     I have received your letter and that of Gregory XVI, also the cheque. Fr General does not think it desirable for me to go again to Rome now, and I feel so much confidence in the spirit of obedience that I am quite content. Though I put the matter before him as clearly as I could. As things are just now I am not sure it would be of much use, but I have written very strongly to Fr Armellini [and] sent him your letter and developed the argument and told him if possible to get a telegram sent to Vaughan not to oppose us as we have a right, and to telegraph to you at the same time. I have shown how much scandal will come if this agitation goes on and how much the Catholics will be alienated from the Bishop if we are not allowed to educate their children etc. I have told him to urge [in] every possible way the importance of doing this immediately. I have also told him to communicate with me by telegraph when he wants information or has news to give.
     I still hope that after what the H[oly] Father said to Manning which is quite certain, the latter will not send anything against us in Rome. Fr General wishes you if possible to get and send a copy of the pamphlet.[184] Fr Armellini is well on the alert now and is not afraid of speaking out, so that I think that by keeping him well informed he will do all that is wanted at present.
Ever yours sincerely in J[esus] C[hrist],
A. Weld.

Weld to Gallwey
San Gerolamo,[185]
Fiesole.
10 April [1875].

My dear Fr,
     As Fr General is sending you today his gatherings out of the Consultors' letters I send you another line to tell you more clearly a thing which will console you, but Fr General wishes you to keep it to yourself. It is certain that the Holy Father *told Manning not to oppose our*

---

183   ABSI, RX/5, Weld to Gallwey, 9 April 1875.
184   Vaughan's pamphlet, *The Claim*.
185   ABSI, RX/5, Weld to Gallwey, 10 April 1875.

schools; also Manning told Cardinal Franchi that in his latest interview the H[oly] Father had given him a gentle admonition about his treatment of the Society. In these circumstances, I doubt very much whether the Bishop will think it prudent to send anything to Rome against us. Fr General is very sanguine and thinks the present affair cannot be decided against us. Vaughan is under a disadvantage. I fancy he cannot write Italian, and is not fresh in Latin so he does not write direct to the Cardinal but when Manning was in Rome to him and now to the Rector of the English College who carries the message to the Cardinal. I hear a thundering letter came the other day to him threatening all sorts of things if you re-open the school. This brought out another telegram to him to do nothing till the letter arrived and the one I hear of to you to take no more boys.

I wrote yesterday very strongly to Fr Armellini on the dangers to religion and Religious in general if we are stopped, and told him [*illegible*] to urge every way he could to get this state of suspense stopped as it is only increasing agitation and producing scandal.

If anything turns up to make my presence in Rome important, Fr General will let me go in a moment. Meantime I shall keep Fr Armellini up to the point. I should like to know if Vaughan ever made complaints to you or Fr Whitty of our Fathers in Manchester. If not his printing his pamphlet is unpardonable. I am telling Fr Armellini to resist the *dispersion* of the school by all possible means. I should like to know what Vaughan does when he receives the Cardinal's letter. Telegraph if anything important.

Ever yours sincerely in J[esus] C[hrist],
A. Weld.

Vaughan to Franchi
Bishop's House,[186]
Salford.
10 April 1875

Your Eminence,

I have the honour of receiving today a letter from Your Rev. Eminence dated 3 April. I have not to date sent to Your Rev. Eminence a full account of the Manchester affair with the Jesuit Rev. Fathers, 1) because I thought that the clarifications sent both to my Procurator[187] and to Cardinal Manning would be all that Your Eminence wanted for the moment; 2) because having understood that given I had to submit an

186 APF, Anglia 20, Vaughan to Franchi, 10 April 1875.
187 Henry O'Callaghan, Rector of the English College, Rome.

account to the Bishops assembled in London and that the Bishops had to give a report on the matter to Your Eminence, I thought that everything would be sent together to Your Eminence with the opinion of the Bishops.

Moreover there was in my mind the possibility of some indication on the part of the Bishops that it would be better for reasons of keeping the peace to accede to the wish of the Jesuit Fathers. And in this case it would not have been perhaps necessary to do anything more than write a letter indicating the submission of my judgement to the impartial judgement of those who add to the intimate knowledge of the critical state of the Church in England an experience and a wisdom superior to mine. Now everything is in the hands of His Eminence the Metropolitan Cardinal – my report along with that of the Fr Provincial and the opinion of the Bishops. When they have been translated into Italian they will be sent to Your Most Rev. Eminence.

But concerning the site of the Father's school in Manchester it is true, *as I indicated most particularly* in my letter to Fr O'Callaghan two weeks ago, that it is attached to the house of the Fathers, and I regret that Your Eminence had understood that it would be distant from it. The question, however, in my opinion is not whether it should be physically attached to the Fathers' house or not, nor even whether there exists in the abstract the right which they claim. But the question is 1) if the bishop should have to sacrifice an educational task canonically undertaken with the agreement of the Chapter in order to satisfy the wishes of the Fathers of the Society. 2) If the Fathers can freely dissolve an *agreement* supported by the Chapter and the secretary of the late Bishop, that is, a *"prohibition"* as it is called by the Fr Provincial, not to erect a college in the district given to the Fathers by the late Bishop, when he gave them permission to erect a church of the Society? 3) If the rights and educational interests invested in an existing establishment near the Fathers (including the property of great value already purchased by me for the development of the said establishment) should be destroyed to make room for a work of the Society, not required in the present circumstances of Manchester? 4) Whether the Fr Provincial has not publicly injured the Bishop among the dioceses with the declaration of his Fathers that they would decide to give public proof of the aforementioned authority – as he has in truth done by establishing the said college in spite of his prohibition? 5) Whether ecclesiastical subordination, canon law, and above all the honour of the Sacred Congregation of Propaganda is not injured when, the Bishop having given notice of his appeal to the said S. Congregation, the Provincial, without further communication with the Bishop, sends after some time to announce that *the matter is settled*; and this without any rescript of Propaganda?

I limit myself for the moment to these lines, begging Your Eminence to suspend any judgement for as long as you have not received all the *ponenza*.[188] I have already requested permission through my Procurator to come in person to Rome, when I hope to satisfy in full as much my good disposition with regard to the Society as concerning my conduct in this sorry matter.

I am, your Eminent Reverence,
Herbert Vaughan

Weld to Gallwey
San Gerolamo,[189]
Fiesole,
12 April 1875.

Dear Fr,

I have just found out that Bishop Vaughan's pamphlet has arrived in Rome and is in the hands, as I understand of several; Archbishop Howard and Mgr Stonor have it. The latter is said to be furious against us. I have had some of the heads of complaints sent to me, but we can do nothing till we see it. The points given me are: 1. the original exclusion of schools; 2. that B[isho]p invited us to open a school and we refused; 3. B[isho]p is going to do it himself; 4. impossibility of two Colleges in Manchester; 5. our lacking influence especially with the sick. 6. B[isho]p's College would be useless. 7. B[isho]p would have no Priests as all would go to Jesuits etc. etc. We claim privileges which [we] do not have in England. We are also accused of injustice, insubordination etc. It is making [a] great impression on those who have read it, and will I fear do us great harm. I have told Fr Armellini, and am also writing to Fr Lambert[190] to do all that is possible to guard the Cardinal not to be led astray by it till we have time to answer it, and to get some one to do the same with the H[oly] Father, and to insist on our having a copy.

It will be necessary now to print a regular defence and it may possibly turn out for the best after all, but the letter which I have received from Rome makes Fr General very anxious.

What would you think of writing to the Bishop yourself and asking for a copy? Every man has a right to know the accusation brought against him; and if he refuses it is a point to be noted. In the mean time we must get up matters for a defence. Could you find out how many

---

[188] A formal written proposal submitted to higher authority, in this case Propaganda Fide, for decision.
[189] ABSI, RX/5, Weld to Gallwey, 12 April 1875.
[190] George Lambert SJ, 1821–1882, secretary to the Society's English Assistant in Rome.

secular priests there are who have been boys in our Liverpool College, and how many in the Society? It could be useful to know. It would be easy to show how one-sided the money question has been, but it is hardly any use speculating about an answer till we see the pamphlet. I fear the impression in Rome very much. We must get many prayers that it may be for the best.

Ever yours sincerely in J[esus] C[hrist],
A. Weld.

Vaughan to Gallwey
Bishop's House,[191]
Salford.
13 April 1875.

My Dear Fr Gallwey,

There is one point in the statement you laid before the Bishops, which I think it desirable to set right, as it might lead to misunderstanding in the future. You said, I think, that I had, on more than one occasion stated that I intended to allow the Society to have a College in Manchester, and that I was at one time on the point of coming to an agreement with you on the subject. My meaning seems to have been entirely misapprehended. The argument several times used by me has been that it was indecent to frustrate the plan of the Bishop by anticipating it in establishing a Jesuit College – that later on the Jesuits might have one, *if there were need* of another College in that part of the town. But I cannot foresee that such a need will arise for long years to come. It is true that I emphatically denied having said you should "*never*" have a College in Manchester – first because to have used that word might have seemed indicative of an animus which does not possess me, and next because I never laid claims to so lengthened a jurisdiction.

As to our having been on the point of coming to an agreement on this subject, I am at a loss to know what occasion this can refer to. I write these lines, not for the purpose of carrying on a controversy but simply as a word which may be useful.

Wishing you every blessing,
I am, your faithful and devoted servant,
+ Herbert, Bishop of Salford.

---

[191]   ABSI, Vaughan to Gallwey, 13 April 1875.

Weld to Gallwey
San Gerolamo,[192]
Fiesole.
13 April [1875]

My dear Fr,

I have just received news from Rome that Bishop Vaughan asked leave to come to Rome and is to start on the 19th. I shall no doubt be there to meet him, so you must hold up your hands whilst I fight. In a letter written yesterday morning before this news Fr Armellini says, from what he can gather from conversations with Cardinal Franchi, the Secretary, and others at the Propaganda, the cause cannot go against us.

He added in his second letter that B[isho]p Vaughan now relies most on the *condition* of admission into Manchester. It certainly was never put distinctly as a condition. I am quite sure of that.

If you can send me any facts relating to secular Priests from our College in Liverpool and Jesuits, also comparison between Priests in the two dioceses born in the country etc., it will help to answer one of his points.

Fr Armellini tells me he had read *legally* in your letter instead of *loyally* but did not make great case of it. I noticed his translation and wrote to tell him of it. He is quite alive to our work and I feel sure omits nothing that can be done. The question will now be brought to issue at once I think, the great danger I feared of it becoming the occasion of a general question against religious, will I trust be arrested. If we gain the point the importance to the Society cannot be over estimated.

Ever yours sincerely in J[esus] C[hrist],
A. Weld.
P.S.
Cardinal Franchi has not seen Vaughan's pamphlet yet. He wrote to tell him to write to him not to other people. I suspect this is what brings him to Rome. When I go to Rome I shall go to the Observatory, Roman College.

---

192   ABSI, RX/5, Weld to Gallwey, 13 April [1875].

Weld to Gallwey
San Gerolamo,[193]
Fiesole.
14 April 1875.

I sent you a hasty line yesterday and told you the latest news is that B[isho]p Vaughan has asked leave to come to Rome. I shall be there to meet him. There are one or two more little things I had not time to say.

Cardinal Franchi has not secured a copy of Vaughan's pamphlet; if *he can get one* he will let us have it. This sounds rather strange in a controversy before the Propaganda! I told Fr Armellini to take care that he and the Pope are warned against impressions against us on account of it. Cardinal Franchi has undertaken to do this with the Pope himself. As I believe he stands very well with the H[oly] Father, this will counteract anything Stonor can say. I am told Howard will say nothing against us.

The more hints and bits of information you can give me the better in the mean time. I have a copy of Vaughan's documents sent to Fr Birch. I should like to know the points I asked the other day, i.e. if any complaints had before been made against the Manchester Fathers and Superior, and any facts to prove that Secular Priests are not diminished in numbers but rather increased where we have Colleges, as at Liverpool. I should like to know if the B[isho]p has entered into any details about the agreement and promise alleged to have been made with me. What has he to shew? Has he any account of the conversation? Does he bring any evidence or what? I am quite certain there was nothing beyond what I told you, which I also told substantially to the Cardinal. I wonder if you could find the Bishop's letter to me inviting us. It must be in the box left with Fr Johnson, either in a bundle of Bishops' letters, or a bundle of miscellaneous things which came out of my travelling desk. It was a half sheet of note paper doubled up I think. If you could find it, it would be very useful but I can swear to the words as it was only a line or two, and not a word about a school. I look on that letter as the invitation, and after that it was too late to put conditions; and those I have asked here say there can be no doubt of it, besides he never put it as a condition at all, but the letter would convince if I could shew it.[194] A copy of your memorial to the Bishops might be useful to me, especially if they send up anything against us.

Also did Vaughan say anything when you took on the second house? He seems to me to hang first on one reason and then another, which is a sign that they are none of them the real one. His holding fast to the idea of a second house is absurd. I think he is conscious that his arguments

[193]   ABSI, RX/5, Weld to Gallwey, 14 April 1875.
[194]   No evidence as to any condition or agreement is provided by Turner's letters.

will not stand when put on paper and that is the reason he is coming to Rome.

Everyone here seems so impressed with the idea that Regulars have little chance in a contest against Bishops that you must pray hard. I think the persecution of Religious here produced a favourable change in feelings towards us and on the whole am very hopeful that God means to bring it through.

Pray for yours ever sincerely in J[esus] C[hrist],
A. Weld.

Vaughan to Gallwey
Bishop's House,[195]
Salford.
17 April 1875.

My dear Fr Gallwey,
   In reply to your note of yesterday you must allow me to say I still adhere to my version of the remarks I made to you and Fr Ullathorne, and that I cannot accept your account as representing my words, and still less my meaning. With regard to the other point I beg to say that the mode of procedure is that each should send in to Propaganda his own statement and the justification of his own conduct. If the Card[inal] Prefect thinks it necessary to verify the evidence by further reference or cross examination, of course he will act according to the approved system of the S[acred] Cong[regation] of Propaganda.

With every blessing,
I am your faithful and devoted servant,
+ Herbert, Bishop of Salford.

Armellini to Franchi
Rome,[196]
19 April 1875

Most Reverend Eminence
   Please allow me to express to you *in a confidential manner* a thought of Father Weld's regarding the Manchester question.
   If the Holy Father knew that it is a matter concerning the eternal salvation of numerous Catholic children and youths, and that if Religious (who do not demand a salary, as neither do the seculars) were

---

[195]   ABSI, RX/5, 17 April, Vaughan to Gallwey. The note referred to is missing.
[196]   APF, Anglia 20, ff. 257–58.

excluded from providing education, it would not be possible for the Bishops to compete with the Protestant Schools maintained by the Government, because they do not have the means to pay for adequate teachers, Father Weld is of the opinion that His Holiness would say to Monsignor Vaughan what he said, as Your Eminence suggests, to Cardinal Manning.

It is to be noted that Monsignor Vaughan is one of the *Oblates* of the Cardinal, and follows entirely his suggestions; new to episcopacy, and rather precipitous in operating, precisely for that reason he is in need of a fatherly warning from His Holiness. Unfortunately, he has in the Chapter a priest who is very adverse to the Society, and for about twenty years has done everything possible to keep it away from Manchester; speaking of this priest, Monsignor Vaughan's predecessor said one day to Father Weld: "You now have only one enemy in Manchester".

Your Eminence knows of the great need, of which there is for many missions to have Fathers whose mother-tongue is English. If the English Bishops manage to prevent us from having schools in England, we would have to wait for miraculous vocations to have missionaries from that nation. It also seems to me that a word from His Holiness, well informed of the real reason of this dispute, would do a lot more than any conference held between Monsignor Vaughan and Father Weld in the presence of Your Eminence.

Please act, Your Eminence, as you deem most prudently appropriate and consider me always most respectfully yours.

Your most devoted servant,
Torquato Armellini

Report of the Archbishops and Bishops on the College in Manchester[197]

The undersigned Bishops of England, having received commission from His Eminence the Cardinal Prefect of Propaganda to examine and to report upon the question which has arisen between the Bishop of Salford and the Society of Jesus in respect to a College founded by them in the above named diocese, have carefully read over the correspondence between his Lordship and the Rev. Father Gallwey Provincial of the English Province of the Society.

The Rev. Fr. Provincial of the Society was requested by the Bishops to lay before them in writing a statement of his case and to attend in person, if he desired, to add any information in conversation. The

---

[197]   APF, Anglia 20, 1875–1877, ff. 234ff. The report is dated 19 April 1875.

latter course he declined,[198] but forwarded to the Bishops the statement accompanying this Report.

Before the undersigned proceed to state the conclusions to which they have come they desire to extract the following passage from a letter of the Rev. Fr Provincial addressed to the Bishop of Salford on the 17th March last.

"Fr General, acting on the authority given him by the Holy See, after advising with the Cardinal Prefect of Propaganda and several of the Cardinals of the same Congregation, has directed us to do what the English Bishops have in council decreed. F[ather] General sends us a copy of the letter, in which the Cardinal Prefect wrote with his own hand to request him to help on education in Manchester."

The Bishops feel, that if the Cardinal Prefect of the Sacred Congregation and other Cardinals of the same should have given authority to the Fr General of the Society to found a college in Manchester, the undersigned would not venture to express themselves as they do in the following Report, which has been drawn up upon the supposition that the question referred to them for their opinion cannot have been as yet decided by a judgement, which would make all reference to them superfluous. From the correspondence above mentioned it would appear:

1) That the college in question was founded without the knowledge of the Ordinary.

2) That it was founded with a full knowledge on the part of the Provincial, that the consent of the Ordinary had been more than once on previous occasions refused.

3) That for this cause, as the Provincial alleged to the Bishop in conversation, he proceeded to its foundation without further endeavours to obtain the Bishop's consent, once he knew such consent would be refused, and that he therefore proceeded in obedience to the order of the Fr General to found the college with the intention of contesting the authority of the Bishop afterwards.

4) That no evidence has yet been afforded to the Bishop of the existence of the privilege so claimed, the Provincial in his last reply declining to exhibit proof of the privilege claimed by him on the ground that 'the question of law' would be decided in Rome; the Bishops confine themselves to remarking that the Bishop of Salford has been carefully guarding against opposition to any Pontifical privilege or concession, that he has asked only as the Ordinary is bound to do in Canon Law for proof of the privilege claimed, which has not, as yet, been laid before him.

---

[198] See above, n. 168, for Gallwey's explanation as to why he chose not to appear personally.

5) That on receiving from the Bishop an inhibition to proceed the Provincial refused to comply alleging his obedience to the Fr General.

6) That in the judgement of the Bishops the foundation of the said college is in violation of Episcopal jurisdiction, unless the Society of Jesus possess such a privilege in virtue of Pontifical concessions, of which no proof has yet been exhibited to the Bishop.

7) That the foundation of the said college cannot fail to destroy a college already existing within a very short distance, which has been meritoriously conducted for some years by the Xaverian Brothers: and that this disregard for fraternal charity is rendered more grave by the fact that the SJ Fathers gave up the same school or college some years ago on the ground that it did not succeed; the late Bishop and the Xaverian Brothers then taking up the work, raised the number of pupils to eighty or ninety. The founding of another such college could not fail to frustrate the intention of the Bishop to improve the college and would perhaps even destroy it, and would also seriously affect the school attached by the late Bishop to the Cathedral Church.

8) That it is alleged by the Bishop and confirmed by a written declaration[199] of the V. Rev. Canon Benoit, secretary to the late Bishop of Salford, that the then Bishop, in consenting to admit the Jesuit Fathers into his diocese, made it a condition that no school should be founded by them except for the poor of their district. The late Provincial denies that this was a *contract*, but admits that the Bishop gave this *prohibition* or *injunction*. The fact therefore is so far admitted. Three of the Canons of the Chapter of the diocese are willing to declare on oath, that the *contract* was by the late Bishop intended and believed to be made, and to this engagement the Bishop subsequently appealed, when he anticipated some such scheme as has now been attempted.

9) That at this time the Bishop of Salford possesses neither a sevior nor a junior seminary in the diocese.

10) That he is responsible for the care of more than 200,000 souls, and is scarcely able to find vocations for the maintenance of the clergy of his diocese, and is unable to find vocations except among the poorer and even the poorest classes of his flock. The hope of elevating the clergy would be for ever taken away, if a college of the Society was founded in Manchester.

11) That the Bishop had already made publicly known in a Pastoral Letter dated November 30, 1872, that he was about to open a college of a higher kind in Manchester and also a diocesan seminary for Pastoral Theology in Salford.

The Bishops are therefore of the opinion, so far as the evidence laid

---

[199]   See Appendix 2.

before them appears to show, that the college in question ought not to be founded and that on the following grounds:

First – because a grave example of opposition to Episcopal authority, unsustained by any proof of privilege or authority to justify it, has been set, which may affect injuriously the spirit of obedience in his own clergy, and endangers the peaceful relations of the Bishops with the Society: and because much dissension among the faithful has unhappily been caused by the founding of the college in question, and the opposition of the Society to this injunction of the Bishop has become notorious, so as to cause partisanship, from which scandal and ill-will can hardly fail to arise.

Secondly – because the duties of fraternal charity appear to be gravely disregarded in respect of the laborious and meritorious Xaverian Brothers, who at this time are teaching more than a thousand children in Manchester, and are greatly respected by the clergy of that city.

Thirdly – because such action on the part of any Religious Order in the present state of the Church in England would render impossible the organization of the newly-erected dioceses, the foundation of diocesan seminaries, and the supplying of such seminaries with students, and would be therefore *non in auxilium sed in obstaculum – non in aedificationem sed in destructionem.*[200] The Bishops insist all the more on this point, because it is from grammar schools and colleges of this class, that the diocesan clergy must in the present state of England be recruited and maintained. To this common and general good of the whole Church any partial good accruing to the Society ought in their judgement be subordinate.

The force of the last reason is greatly increased by the three following facts:

1) The Society of Jesus at this moment possesses four large and flourishing colleges. The whole Hierarchy of England possesses only five of an equal magnitude.

2) The Society, in a *memorandum* forwarded to *Propaganda Fide* last year, claims to educate at this moment a number of youths equal to the number in all the colleges of the Hierarchy, that is to say almost seven hundred. The numerical statement is excessive, but it is true that the Society has a disproportionate number of the sons of the rich and the higher families, a fact which bears with serious disadvantage upon the secular clergy of England.

3) The Society has already in the diocese of Salford the college of Stonyhurst, which is equal to the largest of the colleges of the Hierarchy, and twofold or threefold larger than any others in England. By

---

200 'Not to help, but to hinder – not for building up, but for destruction.'

the founding of a college in Manchester the whole higher education of the diocese of Salford would thereby be transferred from the Bishop of that See to the Society.

Thus far the Bishops have treated the question of the diocese of Salford alone, as referred to them by the Cardinal Prefect of Propaganda, but they cannot conclude this report without laying before the Holy See a much graver aspect of the question, which affects not one diocese but the whole of the Church in England.

The hierarchy in England has existed no more than five and twenty years.[201] So complete was the wreck made by the so-called reformation, that not a vestige of the external order of the Church remained. Everything was to be created anew, clergy, churches, colleges, schools, the whole external and material organisation of thirteen dioceses. The Bishops at the time of the restoration of the Hierarchy found themselves responsible for the cure of more than a million souls. The number of the clergy was insufficient. Three mixed colleges founded in the last century by the Vicars Apostolic served as seminaries for the thirteen Bishops. The education of the poor was very scantily provided: the education of the middle class was altogether without provision. For all these works the Bishops had scanty means: the richest had little, many had none. Nevertheless in the last 25 years the Bishops aided generously by the faithful have multiplied their clergy and their churches, but neither is as yet sufficient. The poor-schools have been more than doubled. However at this time only two dioceses possess a seminary. In Westminster and Birmingham seminaries have been founded within the last six years. Clifton, Southwark, Beverley and Salford are preparing to found their seminaries. On the foundation of seminaries in all the greater dioceses will depend the multiplication and education of the clergy of England, and upon the adequate supply of clergy in number and culture equal to that of the English people will depend the future of the Church in England. Anything which can seriously thwart or retard this paramount and vital work will hinder and obstruct the development and maturing of the restored Church in England.

The Bishops therefore desire to lay before the Holy See their united judgement, that valuable as the action of Religious Orders has always been *in auxilium saecularium*, the action of Orders and Societies asserting such privileges, as are here in question, without limitations of charity and subordination, would be abnormal and not helpful under the exceptional circumstances in England, in as much as it would anticipate and obstruct the diocesan organisation of the Church itself. The auxiliary would thus supplant the principal. The order wisely contem-

---

[201]   The English Hierarchy was restored in 1850.

plated by the Supreme Pontiff would thus be inverted and the relations of the Hierarchy and the Religious Orders would become abnormal, and their higher interests would be in conflict with each other. In no case could this follow – the Bishops are constrained to say, in no case has this followed so visibly as in the relations of the Society of Jesus to the Dioceses in which their chief houses exist. The Bishops desire to express their veneration and love for all Orders of religion. In them they see the special provisions of the Holy See, and in their privileges they respect the authority of the Sovereign Pontiff. All this they feel with an especial force in reference to the Society of Jesus. The Fathers of the Society stood and suffered side by side with the Secular clergy in the terrible persecutions of the Tudors and the Stuarts. They have deserved well for their constancy and perseverance in keeping alive the faith of multitudes in England. Their example, their learning, their piety, their missionary zeal command the love and gratitude of the English Hierarchy. The Bishops earnestly wish them Godspeed in the perfecting of their own Society, subject only to the supreme and vital condition that it be for the furtherance and not for the hindrance of the Divine Order, authority and mission of the Church. They cannot fail to see that by reason of the exceptional circumstances of the Church in England it may obstruct its development, for the Hierarchy is as yet only developing the organisation of its dioceses, which though rapidly advancing is yet far from complete.

The Bishops are fully aware that the action of the Religious Orders is most beneficial, where the Bishops and secular clergy are inert or worldly. This cannot, they trust, be said of the clergy in England. Indeed it may be affirmed, that in the dioceses where the action of the Society has been felt by the Bishop and clergy to be at times adverse, the clergy at least are zealous, self-denying and laborious in a high degree. True as this is of London and Liverpool, it is especially true of the diocese of Salford.

The undersigned desire to close this statement of their reasons with one remark of universal application.

They can conceive no good to result either to the Church or the Society, so long as the Society shall fail to gain the confidence and act in harmony with the Episcopate. They can conceive no more fatal source of evil to the Church or to the Society than any breach in the relations of charity, or any conflict with the jurisdiction of the Ordinary. The privileges of the Religious Orders were granted by the Pontiffs for the aid of the Episcopate. The Bishops of England will never by the slightest act hinder or restrict them, but under the exceptional circumstances and conditions of the rising Church in England they must regard any such exercise of privileges, especially when not proved, which shall conflict with the welfare of the diocese, as a defeat of the benign intentions of the Supreme Pontiff. The Bishops, however, do not venture to ask that their judgement should be final in a matter where the authority of the Holy See is present before them.

They conclude, therefore, this Report to the Sacred Congregation with a unanimous petition to the effect that, in consideration of the exceptional and abnormal state of the Church so recently restored In England, whensoever it shall appear to the Ordinary that the exercise of any privilege by a Religious Order is at variance with the general good of the diocese, the Religious Superior shall not proceed to use such privilege, until the case shall have been heard and decided by the Holy See.

The Bishops also ask:

1) Whether the Society since its restoration has the privilege of establishing colleges independent of the permission of the Ordinary?

2) Whether, in the case of the Society possessing such privilege, the Holy See deems this privilege applicable to the peculiar circumstances of England?

3) In the case of these questions being answered in the affirmative, the Bishops most earnestly entreat the Holy See to provide, that in the case the Society should be disposed to establish a college without the approval or concurrence of the Ordinary, the Religious Superior shall be bound to suspend all proceedings on the part of the Order or Society in question, until the Holy See has been informed of any difficulties presented by the case, and its instructions received.

Henry Edward, Cardinal Archbishop of Westminster.
(Signed in behalf of all the Bishops except the Bishop of Shrewsbury who was absent by reason of ill health.)
19 April 1875.

Armellini to Gallwey
Rome[202]
19 April 1875

Rev Fr Prov[incial],

I have to thank Your Rev[erence] for two letters, one of the 11th and the other of 15th of this month. The first of them seemed to be so much to the purpose that I went to the Propaganda and read it to Mgr Rinaldini.[203] He advised me to read it to the Cardinal[204] and I did so in the afternoon. It made a good impression on both and will produce a good effect in due time. I say in due time, for as Your Rev[erence] may

---

202   ABSI, RX/5, Armellini to Gallwey, 19 April 1875.
203   Mgr Achille Rinaldini, an official at Propaganda Fide.
204   Cardinal Franchi.

know, B[isho]p Vaughan has asked and obtained from the Card[inal] permission to come to Rome. He intends to leave today, but he shall find Fr Weld who is ready to answer his objections before the Cardinal. At the suggestion of Fr Weld, I have today written to the Cardinal asking him to do with regard to B[isho]p Vaughan what he did with Cardinal M[anning]. He suggested to the Holy Father to say something to that latter in respect of his relations with Religious and the H[oly] F[ather] did so, as Cardinal Franchi assured me. One word said by the Holy Father to that Bishop who is a follower of the Cardinal and one of his Oblates, may do more good than any conference before the Cardinal Prefect.

I heard that Mgr Clifford[205] also is coming. Could Your Rev[erence] speak to him in our favour? If he were to speak to the Holy Father of the necessity of Catholic schools and of the impossibility of starting them, if the Religious were excluded, because the Bishops cannot give large salaries to the teachers, as the Government does, I think it would make a very good impression on the Holy Father. As regards the pamphlet, we are trying to get it but it is not easy.

Mr Palmer[206] also is going to impress on the Cardinal the opinion of Catholic laity on the subject and will prove to him the necessity of entrusting education to the Religious. He is *convinced* of it and will use with the Cardinal the most convincing language.

I remain in union with your holy intentions and prayers,
Yours faithfully,
T. Armellini

Weld to Gallwey
San Gerolamo,[207]
Fiesole.
19 April 1875.

My dear Fr,

I have received both your letters, that of the 14th on Saturday and the other written I presume on the 18th yesterday. The letter, in which Vaughan said he was on the point of coming to an arrangement with you, was not written to Fr Callaghan [*sic*] but to Cardinal Manning. My authority for it is Cardinal Franchi to whom Manning had given the

---

[205] William Clifford, 1823–1893; Bishop of Clifton.
[206] William Palmer, 1811–1879; a convert to Catholicism, lived in Rome from 1852 until his death. He specialised in the theology of the Eastern Church; this no doubt brought him into contact with Propaganda Fide.
[207] ABSI, RX/5, Weld to Gallwey, 19 April 1875.

substance of the letter. According to Card[inal] F[ranchi] he was on the point of coming to terms, but that you had tried to settle it *per modum facti*. It would be difficult to verify this exactly, as no doubt Cardinal Manning kept the letter.

I start for Rome tomorrow morning so as to have another conversation at the Propaganda before Vaughan comes.

He has written to say that if the majority of the Bishops had been against him, he would have yielded, but that the majority were in his favour. I think this rather a favourable report for us, as it shows they were not unanimous and therefore a unanimous memorial from them against us is not likely.[208]

At any rate the letter of Gregory XVI which is in Cardinal Franchi's hands is most opportune as it will give good precedent for opposing even the united bishops.

I feel in very good spirits about the business. If reason avails I think we are sure to win. He has done wisely in coming to Rome as his presence and character will have more weight than his reasons, and this is where I fear him. I mean to shew on the map besides all the other reasons that the old bishop put us as far as he possibly could from the Cathedral that our influence might not clash with that of the Bishop! so as to leave us form a centre of work and influence in the south of Manchester.[209] It is too bad now coming down close to us and then complaining that we interfere with him. I see the school in Salford is entered as the Diocesan Grammar School, I shall ask the Cardinal to persuade him to stick to that, and develop it as much as he likes. I believe there is quite room for both, as there is a large Circle of Connexion of the Cathedral and boys will not cross the commercial part of Manchester in large numbers. I shall also point out what I believe to be the element of opposition all through: Canon Toole[210] and one or two others who are I believe pushing the Bishop on. It was he who chiefly kept us out of Manchester for nearly 20 years and shortly after we had got in, he bought land for a chapel on the very skirts of our district, close to All Saints; it may be

---

208   One dissenting voice could have been that of Bishop Ullathorne, see below, 6 May 1875, Waterworth to Gallwey.

209   See the map (p. xvi above) showing the relative positions of the Salford Catholic Grammar School and the church of the Holy Name, Ackers Street.

210   Lawrence Toole, 1808–1892; original member of the Diocesan Chapter, Rector of St Wilfrid's, Hulme. Toole was very hostile to the Jesuits opening a college in Liverpool, see ABSI, College of St Aloysius, District Accounts 1700–1849, Toole to Lennon, July 1840. See also Maurice Whitehead, 'The Contribution of the Society of Jesus to Secondary Education in Liverpool: The History of the Development of St Francis Xavier's College, c. 1840–1902' (unpublished Ph.D. thesis, University of Hull, 1984).

the very piece of land, but I don't know; W[ilding][211] pointed out to Dr Turner, that it would never do to have a chapel there and he stopped it. Dr Turner said to me once, referring to him, 'you have only one enemy in Manchester'[212] and now he wants to have a great school in his own district so as to exclude ours. It could hardly have been a very large zeal for souls that made the Bishop forbid our church to be called the Gesu as he did in a letter to me,[213] or in the Eccl. Statistics of Liverpool to omit notice in the list of Orders, Congregations etc. of there being a single Jesuit establishment in the Diocese, as it does, or of there being such a thing as a Jesuit College in Liverpool. I shall point these things out to shew the point … I have some important bits from Benedict XIV to shew that in schools we are entirely exempt, and that the Bishop had no power to suspend any body.

Ever yours sincerely in J[esus] C[hrist],
A. Weld.

Charnley to Weld
46, Ackers Street,[214]
20 April 1875.

Dear Fr Provincial,

I have read carefully with great interest the "Facts and Documents"[215] this morning. It occurred to me that more might have been made of the application of the words "larger missions" to our own, in this ground: that our congregation (of the people living in our neighbourhood) is much more largely made up of the middle class than any congregation in Manchester.[216] Even absolutely I think it contains a larger number of

---

[211] James Wilding, 1820–1883; Canon of the diocese and Rector of St Augustine's, Granby Row.

[212] Turner had wanted the Jesuits to return to Manchester much sooner than they did, but the opposition of the Diocesan Chapter made this impossible. Only one member of the Chapter – Canon Wilding – was in favour of the Society coming back to Manchester. See below, 23 April 1878, Thomas Harper to Coleridge.

[213] See ABSI, Letters to Bishops and Cardinals, Turner to Weld, 21 October 1871. Turner writes: "To call it the Gesu, which is an Italian word, would scarcely be right, and I wish it to be named by the proper title."

[214] ABSI, RX/5, Charnley to Weld, 20 April 1875.

[215] The document drawn up by Gallwey and sent to Rome to present the Society's side of the argument. The Italian version of the memorial is addressed to the Cardinal Prefect of Propaganda Fide.

[216] See above, n. 131. Gallwey states in his *Facts and Documents*, "I do not forget that His Lordship, when this Decree of the Fourth Council [Decree XVII of the Fourth Westminster Synod with regard to establishing middle schools in larger missions] was pointed out to him, had a double answer ready. For he said in the first place that the Decrees of the Synod had not as yet been published in his diocese. But surely a laudable zeal which

the class for whom such schools are designed than any other parishes. It is also true that our quarter of Manchester is that in which this class is most likely to develop.

It struck me also as a pity that detailed explanation of the supposed "contract" does not appear in an earlier part of the pamphlet. There is a reference to this explanation in a foot-note, but an impression is left on the mind until one arrives at the memorial to the Bishops that there is no fully sufficient answer to this difficulty.

I had a long conversation a few days ago with Fr Ramsey who succeeded Fr Clarkson as Head Priest of the Cathedral church, and who consequently lived in the house where the Bishop's school is held and with the men who teach it. He told me that that school was quite incompetent for the purposes of a good middle-class school, that such was the opinion of the laity (or many of the laity) from whom he himself had heard it, and that they in consequence would not send their children to it. As for the school of the Xaverian Brothers, he added, five minutes conversation with any of them would be sufficient to convince any one of their incompetence to carry out such work.

He further expressed his conviction that the Bishop was absolutely without the means (at least within his own diocese) of establishing a school or College which would satisfy the public needs.

A Catholic family in our district informed me the other evening that they had been told by a secular priest (and the information produced some dismay among them) that the Bishop had gone to Rome to effect our removal from Manchester. The quarrel and the *disobedience* of the

---

forestalls the publication by a week or two to do a good work which all the Bishops enjoin as urgent does not deserve a heavy censure. In the second place, he said that whereas the Council addresses this injunction to the Rectors of large Missions, the Mission of which the Fathers S.J. have charge is not a large one ... First, the Council, while laying an injunction on larger missions, nowhere forbids smaller missions to have their Grammar School. Secondly, a mission may be called a large mission in more senses than one. If the Priests in charge have committed to them a large district, then, in one sense, the mission is a large mission. Again, if the number of Catholics in the district is great, the mission will be justly considered a large mission. Or again, though the number of Catholics in the neighbourhood be comparatively small, if there is a large Protestant population that can be influenced, the mission might be reckoned among large missions. Lastly, if the church be a large one, and for one cause or another an important one and well frequented, the Head Priest of that church may fairly be classed among those addressed by the Synod. Consequently, though at present there may not be more than two thousand Catholics in the district assigned to the Church of the Holy Name, while the neighbouring district may have ten or twelve thousand, yet I think that no one that was not in search of objections would think of denying that the Fathers in charge of that church would deserve blame if they neglected the commendation of the Synod in the plea of not having a large mission." *Facts and Documents*, pp. 10–11.

Society are now well known in Manchester and matters of daily talk, I think without fault on our side.

I hope S[aint] Joseph befriends us.
Yours very sincerely in Xt,
Alex Charnley.[217]

Weld to Gallwey
Osservatorio,[218]
Collegio Romano.
23 April [1875]

My dear Fr,

I have received all the papers and have talked over the petition to the Pope with Fr Armellini; we both think it better not to present it, 1) because a petition to the Pope should be in the name of Fr General only, and 2) because the matter being in the hands of Propaganda, it would not do for us to go over their head to petition the Pope, but Fr Armellini thinks it might do great good if a short petition signed by three or four of the principal laity were sent to the Pope begging him not to allow the Society to be prevented from executing its chief function of teaching and pointing out the urgent necessity especially at the present time, and the impossibility of the Bishop to meet the want on account of pressure of other work, naming Manchester, but not entering into details of the case. This should be done so as to prevent any agitation or scandal and as quickly as possible for that object. The Pope has promised to speak to Vaughan in our favour, but from what I know of him and from what has taken place I fear nothing will bind him, and if there is no possibility of coming to an agreement the question will go before the Congregation of Propaganda. Fr Armellini thinks this will be good for us, I am not very sanguine about it.

I have seen the Cardinal this morning and given him your pamphlet. He tells me the Bishops are all excited about it and unanimous against us for having acted in the teeth of the Bishop, and Vaughan is bringing a memorial from them on the subject. No one questions our abstract right here, but those I have spoken to, I mean the Cardinal Prefect and Howard, think us imprudent in asserting it. The Cardinal will do what he can to get Vaughan to come round, and has told me to see him as soon as ever he arrives, to try to calm him, so as to prepare him for seeing

---

[217]   Alexander Charnley SJ, 1834–1922; taught at the Jesuit College in Manchester. "He would say afterwards: 'had they allowed us to work that school, for every one priest provided by the others we would have given them forty.'" *Letters and Notices* 28, p. 88.
[218]   ABSI, RX/5, Weld to Gallwey, 23 April [1875].

the Cardinal. You may rely on our doing all that can be done. It is not so much now a question of arguments, except to answer his objection, for all see the reasons in favour, but finding some way out of the clash without sacrificing the Bishop. We expect Vaughan tonight. Clifford has arrived. I think I could not circulate the correspondence even among Ours: I fear the passage at the end will produce irritation.

Ever yours in J[esus] C[hrist],

A. Weld.

P.S.

Since writing the above I have seen Mr Ricard, also Mgr Agnozzi,[219] this morning. The latter is secretary of the Propaganda and has been Nuncio in [illegible] and seems well up to these questions and has great influence – he told Mr Ricard that the matter must end favourably though it may take time. I hope he is not too sanguine.

Armellini to Franchi
Rome,[220]
23 April 1875

Most Reverend Eminence,

I saw Father Weld after his conversation with Your Eminence and he seemed rather deflated and afflicted by the displeasure caused to Your Eminence by his commentary on the schools of Manchester.

The proven kind-heartedness of Your Eminence encourages me to talk to you with the utmost sincerity and confidence. It seems to me that no one can justly complain about that letter, and least of all the English Bishops. What else did Your Eminence do if not comply with the decrees of the Synod of Westminster, that recommend that all the Superiors of larger missions create such schools to satisfy the very serious needs of young Catholics?

It seems to me that nothing was done against the decorum of Your Most Reverend Eminence.

The English Provincial maintained, with all the respect that he was capable of, a right that in the end goes back to a right of the Holy See, and he maintained it for very serious and fine reasons, and that is for the eternal salvation of the young Catholics of England. There is a great necessity, by establishing Catholic schools, to prevent Catholics being lost (as they already are) to Protestant schools. It is not possible for the Bishop to provide for this – with the debt on the Cathedral, declared by himself publicly to be £18,000; onto which must be added another

---

219   Mgr Giovanni Battista Agnozzi, pro-secretary to Propaganda Fide.
220   APF, Anglia 20, 1875–1877, Armellini to Franchi, 23 April 1875.

£5,000, that he has requested to complete the Seminary. But even if the Bishop could, for more or less a long period of time, manage to run such schools, the compatibility of two Catholic schools in a city so vast and populated as Manchester, is manifest. The Provincial knew he had the right to start a Catholic school in our house in Manchester, and he declared so respectfully to the Bishop. Should he have allowed the Bishop to violate such a right? He believed with St. Alphonsus Liguori that he could not do so, and he acted following this judgement. If some English Bishops, incited by Monsignor Vaughan, manifest their irritation because the Provincial of a Religious Order acted according to his right – that is in fact a right of the Holy See – it seems to me that a pure and simple declaration by Your Most Reverend Eminence should be sufficient to appease them; just like the firm and dignified response of Gregory XVI was sufficient for the Vicars Apostolic, whereupon they were forced to allow us to have a Church in London and in Liverpool. Without going into the conditions of London, which are known to everyone, the effect of such a permission on Liverpool has been that there are now seventy-two priests, whilst in 1843 there were only ten.

But I dare to hope that the cause of young Catholics of England does not diminish in strength due to despicable jealousies, and I entrust it to the heart of Your Eminence.

I beg you to forgive the liberties I take with this letter,
and to consider me always yours most respectful and
most devoted servant.
Torquato Armellini
Secretary of the Society of Jesus

Weld to Gallwey
Osservatorio,[221]
Collegio Romano,
Rome.
24 April 1875

My dear Fr,

I came away rather discouraged from Cardinal Franchi yesterday, and feel I may have made you feel the same. Today I think I can restore the balance at least to some degree. The Cardinal was put out that we had used his letter to Fr General[222] as we have, and is desperately afraid of having committed himself, and he let out his feelings a little to me, very

---

[221] ABSI, RX/5, Weld to Gallwey, 24 April 1875.
[222] See above, 13 November 1874, Franchi to Beckx; in this letter Franchi asks the Jesuits to do all they could for middle-class education, especially in Manchester.

kindly, but so as to shew me that we were not safe not to be sacrificed at the last moment.

Last night Fr Armellini wrote him a capital letter, encouraging him to stand firm and to tell Vaughan openly what he always acknowledges that we have right with us. He will do all he can to keep the matter from going before the Congregation because then he will be fully committed and this is in every way desirable if it be possible to get B[ishop] Vaughan to come to terms.

This morning I have had a long conversation with Cardinal de Luca who is a sincere friend of the Society. I explained to him and satisfied him entirely with the map before him of the unreasonableness of the Bishop. He has promised to speak to the Bishop and to try to get him to an arrangement and to persuade him to develop his school in Salford and leave South Manchester to us.

I have thought of a compromise that might be made if you approve. We to agree not to receive boys from Salford for a certain time or till such time as the Propaganda released us from the agreement. It would be an answer to one of his objections and would not be a very great sacrifice, as I think families attached to the Cathedral will generally not send them across the City to us. Cardinal de Luca advised me by all means to keep the question from going before the Congregation.

I also hear from Fr Armellini that Mgr Rinaldi asked Dr Clifford to act as peace-maker, and that he accepted the proposal, I think this will do good. He is good at that, and will be less suspected as he is a Bishop. I explained the chief points to him, and he seemed to agree to the justice of our views, but was certainly staggered at the idea of our going in the teeth of the Bishop. On the other hand all the men here condemn Vaughan utterly for his threat of suspension as being quite out of his powers and for his secret pamphlet. The Cardinal has not received it yet and so I think it will do us no harm here. I am inclined to think that as your memorial is inscribed to the Cardinal Prefect of Propaganda[223] it would not do to send it to the Pope through a layman. The Pope will certainly shew it to Franchi, and as it compromises him a little or rather commits him he may be annoyed especially as he begged me not to distribute it till I heard from him, and I promised not to do so. I had already given one to Clifford, and told him so. If the matter does not go before the Congregation there is no need of its being distributed, if it does it must of course. I think Cardinal de Luca would give one to the Pope for me. You can let me know if you have done it. The Duke of

---

[223] This is the Italian version of *Facts and Documents*: *Fatti e Documenti relativi al Collegio della Compagnia di Gesù in Manchester presentati a Sua Eminenza Rma, il Cardinale Prefetto di Propaganda*.

Salviati has hitherto been our immediate lay agent, and is thoroughly staunch. Cardinal de Luca would be very grateful for a copy of the Blue Book containing the returns on the laws concerning religious orders in foreign countries. Would you kindly send me a copy here by post, as he is a sincere friend, and of great authority, and particularly kind to me. I think you have not yet sent Fr Ballerini[224] a copy of the *Decrees of the Synod*. *Will you please do so* and send it to me. He deserves it for he worked hard for us. If you saw how he laughed at the idea of Vaughan's suspending the Fathers you would have enjoyed it richly.

You must get our Fathers in Manchester to do all possible to allay scandal and to pooh pooh the quarrel etc. for that will do mischief whatever else happens. By [illegible] to be very loyal and to get the people to do the same, as religion demands that. I am praying very hard that God will not allow any blunderings and imprudence to be an injury to the Society, for I feel that if harm comes out of this I have most of it on my shoulders, and if good comes I do not think I shall deserve praise.

Pray for yours ever sincerely in J[esus] C[hrist],
A. Weld

Weld to Gallwey
Osservatorio,[225]
Collegio Romano.
25 April [1875]
My dear Fr,

I have nothing of importance to say today except that if anything is sent to the Pope it is better to say nothing about the Cardinal's letter to Fr General. He is put out about it, and it will not do to make the matter worse. He has no reason to be put out as the letter was surely meant to be used, but it has done its work and it would rather do harm to push it now. I hope all will be settled this week, as great efforts will be made to come to a conclusion without sending it to the Congregation.

Fr Rossi, who is confessor to Cardinal de Luca, has promised me this morning to get him to speak to Cardinal Franchi to make him firm and get him to tell Vaughan boldly that we have the law, and besides that no compact would be an obstacle except a clear expression in writing. If we finish this way it will be probably all over before anything could reach the Pope. As far as he has heard the story I believe he is favourably disposed to us; but of course Vaughan will tell his own story, and then we shall have a conference in [the] presence of the Cardinal.

---

[224] Antonio Ballerini SJ, 1830–1907; consultor at Propaganda Fide.
[225] ABSI, RX/5, Weld to Gallwey, 25 April [1875].

I have not heard of Vaughan's arrival in Rome. I hear he was expected on Friday night with Mgr Gadd. I shall telegraph as soon as there is any news.

In haste, ever yours sincerely in J[esus] C[hrist],

A. Weld.

P.S.

I have received everything. The pamphlet will not be distributed unless the case goes to the Congregation – but I shall put in a formal request for a copy of Vaughan's pamphlet to be able to defend ourselves. I shall do this through the Cardinal.

Weld to Gallwey
Collegio Romano,[226]
Rome.
26 April 1875

My dear Fr,

I write a few lines though there is not much news. I went to see Vaughan in a friendly way this morning,[227] as the Cardinal was very anxious I should. He seemed a little surprised but got friendly though I did not think very hearty. He said "you have had your say and now I shall have mine and then the Cardinals will decide, and I suppose you will obey". Certainly said I be quite sure of that; "but you have not done so hitherto" was the answer. Of course I asked him in what we had failed, he said in not shutting the school when you were told. I said we never were told (meaning of course from Rome); this surprised him. He then said, "then you are going on receiving more boys after being told not to," I said are you sure? "Yes. There were 15 when I left" – but when were they received? "Oh I don't know," – I said that's it exactly. The order to take no more boys was sent very lately and I feel quite sure it has not been disobeyed, but will ascertain exactly. Clifford was in the room while this was going on and was giggling as hard as he could.

Please let me know about this point. It is important I should be able to say positively that the Cardinal has been obeyed. Fact is, it is well I saw him, as he would have told the Cardinal what he told me.

I doubt whether we shall get much help from Clifford. I see he is very sore about our taking action in spite of the B[isho]p but if we beat Vaughan well on the point of right I think he will help to make him bend without driving it on to the Congregation of Cardinals which must be avoided if possible as it might bring on a decree annulling our privi-

226   ABSI, RX/5, Weld to Gallwey, 26 April 1875. Punctuation as in original.
227   See below, Vaughan's Diary, 25 April 1875.

lege in practice. A great deal now depends on the personal firmness of Cardinal Franchi and I am sorry to say his antecedents in this point are not good, but he is compromised if it goes before the Cardinals, and that is strongly in our favour. I hope to have our conference in two or three days and then we shall soon see which turn things are likely to take.

Ever yours sincerely in J[esus] C[hrist]
A. Weld
P.S.
Can you find out whether Vaughan's pamphlet has been given to others besides the Bishops and if to any of the laity – it is important to know this.[228] I shall ask the Cardinal to let us have a copy in Vaughan's presence for common justice. Everyone here as far as I know condemns him for it.

Thomas Greenan to Gallwey
Holy Name,[229]
27 April 1875.

Very Rev. and dear Fr,

I have just had a conversation with Dr Noble about our school. He is most indignant, and proposes to head a petition or expression of opinion in favour of the school and in deprecation of any opposition to it. He thinks that it should be signed only by representative men – say half-a-dozen of the leading men in Manchester – if only we could get them. He seems to think we could easily. Your Reverence would know the best terms in which such a demand should be conceived.

I write this in haste to catch the post.

Your obedient servant in Xt,
A. Greenan[230]

E. J. Purbrick to Gallwey
Stonyhurst,[231]
29 April 1875.

Very Rev. and dear Fr Provincial,

I was at the Pendleton opening yesterday.[232] At luncheon an address was read from the Chapter to the Cardinal in which the Chapter regretted

---

[228] Vaughan later denied that he had done this, see below, 27 May 1879, Vaughan to Bishop of Clifton.
[229] ABSI, RX/5, Thomas Greenan to Gallwey, 27 April 1875.
[230] Thomas Greenan SJ, 1834–1905.
[231] ABSI, RX/5, E. J. Purbrick to Gallwey, 29 April 1875.
[232] St James's church, Pendleton, Salford.

"the absence of the Bishop who had gone to Rome on urgent and unfortunate business, now that he had completed his first great work, to lay before the Holy Father his designs for the future, with a vision to saving souls and promoting intellectual culture both of the clergy and laity. However he had gone with the full knowledge and concurrence of the Chapter."

His Eminence, of course, had the good taste to steer clear of unpleasant topics and in his reply simply regretted the Bishop's absence on local grounds, such as the pleasure he would have had in seeing his accomplishment of a good work by one of his zealous priests. The address from the clergy, secular and regular, omitted anything offensive.

E. J. Purbrick.[233]

Fragment of Fr Birch's letter regarding the clergy address mentioned in the previous letter.[234]

As to the meeting of clergy about the address, I may mention: 1) that the address previously prepared and submitted for our revision and approval, contained the statement that the Bishop had gone to Rome on business of very great importance to the Diocese. One of the priests from St Chad's (Rev Mr Darley) got up like a brick, and objected to this on the ground that nothing ought to go before the people hinting at the object of the Bishop's journey to Rome – he stuck to his point and carried it, I feel grateful to him. 2) The address also said that the Bishop had so identified himself in every way with his clergy that they felt they might speak also in his name, or words to that effect. This was objected to by several, on the ground that as it was an address from the clergy themselves alone, they had no right to assume in his absence to speak in the name of the Bishop – and so this was expunged. The address when brought into final shape as to the wording by three of the clergy appointed (the *substance* being already settled) was to be signed by the Chairman (the Provost) and the secretary, in the name of the clergy, secular and regular of the Diocese.

As I am writing, I may mention that various rumours are afloat – e.g. that our business of the school is the town's talk amongst Catholics – that some person has offered the Bishop £80,000 to put us out altogether from the place – that the Bishop has said he will yet bring the Fathers on their knees – that some of the secular clergy are saying scandalous things about us etc. But what is more definite – I was told yesterday by one of our congregation, more in the confidence of the clergy than

---

233   Edward Ignatius Purbrick SJ, 1830–1914; English Provincial 1880–1888; Rector of Stonyhurst.
234   ABSI, RX/5, no name other than the signature 'Henry Birch', no place and no date.

any layman I know, and who assured me he had his information from a reliable source as having come from the Bishop – 1) that he had said, that one reason why we wanted to have a college was to help us to meet the burden on our church, and that the Bishop had insinuated that he was ready to take the burden and had a Religious Order ready to take our place. 2) That the Bishop had threatened to suspend us unless we closed the school last Thursday. 3) That when a telegram had come from Rome staying the Bishop's action, the Bishop had said that this was only another trick of the Jesuits. My informant was not very clear on this latter matter, or else I picked his brains badly. He of course does not want *in any way to be committed.*

Henry Birch

Charnley to Gallwey
46, Ackers Street,[235]
30 April 1875.

Dear Fr Provincial,

We have only 13 scholars and none have been received since your Reverence gave orders to the contrary – 4 or 5 days *before* your Reverence's order came I had received a boy whose actual coming was from accidental circumstances delayed till after the receipt of the order – I could not well refuse him admission after having accepted him, three applications have been refused since.[236]

Fr Jackson tells me that one who frequents our church though in Fr Vermeulen's parish informed him that Fr Vermeulen[237] told her he had the Bishop's pamphlet, Fr Greenan also says he has been told that each of the Canons had one, of course that is only likely and natural. Rev R[ichard] Brindle,[238] whom I met the other day, told me that Canon Cantwell[239] is a staunch defender of ours in the Chapter; unfortunately

---

[235]   ABSI, RX/5, Charnley to Gallwey, 30 April 1875.

[236]   The names of these scholars and the schools they came from are preserved in the Archives of Propaganda Fide, Rome, they are: Ward, Alton, Alton (brother of latter), Turner, Murphy (these five came from the Xaverian Brothers' school); O'Neil (Douai); Finnigan (Mount St Mary's); Scott, Annacker (from the Jesuit elementary school in the Holy Name parish); Powel, Heilmann, Heiltzman (all three were taught at home by a governess). APF, Anglia 20, 1875–1877.

[237]   Peter Vermeulen, d. 1898; taught at the Catholic Collegiate Institute; Rector of St Edward's, Rusholme, 1873–1874.

[238]   Fr Richard Brindle, 1832–1894; Rector of St Patrick's, Oldham; three brothers of his were Jesuits.

[239]   Edmond Cantwell, 1820–1881; Rector of St Patrick's, Livesey Street, Manchester; an original member of the Diocesan Chapter.

he has less weight as he has the reputation of frequently forming the opposition.

We all hope and pray that Card[inal] Franchi may have the gift of fortitude.

Very sincerely in Xt,
Alex Charnley

Weld to Gallwey
Collegio Romano,[240]
30 April [1875]

My dear Fr,

I have just returned from Cardinal Franchi and almost at the same time received your letter and the Blue Book for Cardinal de Luca, for which many thanks. I went to the Cardinal to urge on the conference he had promised. I found him sadly perplexed about our business. He told me the Bishop would not yield an inch. That he had proposed various modes of compromise but that he would hear nothing etc., that he wanted to reform his clergy and so on. I told him that the way to bring him to terms was to tell him clearly that we were according to Canon Law and that once that is understood it follows that he acted quite beyond his jurisdiction and therefore it is he that is in the wrong. As to forming his clergy we should help him immensely and I told him what went on in Glasgow, Liverpool, Belgium, France etc. and shewed him how low was the state of the clergy of Manchester as compared with other dioceses precisely because Religious have been excluded. I said I would undertake to answer any argument of Vaughan. He had not a word to say against my argument and did not name the compact so I think it did not make much impression on him. I had in fact explained it well to him before.

He asked me if we could not take part in the B[isho]p's school, and I said after all we are not mere school masters. Our influence over youth is in the management and government as well as the teaching. He said the H[oly] Father was going to speak to him about it and finally said he would try to find some accommodation. He said Vaughan disdained money, I said that money on the plea of compensating the Xaverians would be the most honourable way out for him, and reminded him of what I told him in the beginning that Vaughan's policy is to stand firm and not hear reasons. The Cardinal told me the Bishop wanted the Congregation to go into the whole question of right, but he did not wish to do that, it was a large affair, I quite agreed, and added that there was no need of it, it was perfectly clear. I would demonstrate it to anyone.

On the whole my interview has rather encouraged me, as I think the right is felt, as well as the reasonableness, and weak as he is, he will probably find some means to avoid deciding directly against right. Tomorrow I shall go again to Cardinal de Luca and shall give him the memorial and leave with him a note on the question of the right which I shall help Fr Armellini to draw up.

Since writing the above I have been to see Fr Rossi who is Confessor of Cardinal Antonelli[241] to ask him to beg the Cardinal to read to the Pope the little memorial which Fr Armellini left with him. As the Pope is going to speak with Franchi and wants the thing to be finished, this may do good.

Whilst I was out Vaughan called on me. Perhaps it was only to return my call and I do not think it likely to be for anything else; but I shall see him and try to talk him into reason, but shall see what Cardinal de Luca thinks first. It seems to me that the case is so strong that it is better to put it before the Congregation than yield and when we should have to make an elaborate memoir and insist on having a copy of Vaughan's to answer it. The conference is deferred but is still promised. Stonor is organising us but I told the Cardinal he is excited by Vaughan's pamphlets and his opinion is worth nothing.

I am in fair hopes because I think to close the school will be such an evil in the present circumstances that the Holy Father will not allow it. It is weary work, and I wish myself back at Fiesole. Pray for me I shall do all that is possible.

Ever yours sincerely in J[esus] C[hrist]
A. Weld

Weld to Gallwey
Osservatorio,[242]
Coll[egio] Romano,
Rome.
2 May 1875

My dear Fr

I think I have a little progress to report today. As I found from my conversation with the Cardinal Prefect on Friday, that the real difficulty now is how to save the honour of the Bishop without sacrificing us,

---

[241] Giacomo Antonelli, 1806–1876; Prefect of the Public Ecclesiastical Affairs (Secretary of State).
[242] ABSI, RX/5, Weld to Gallwey, 2 May 1875.

he having so pledged to make us close the school. I consulted with Fr Armellini as to a mode of meeting him and we agreed on the following – that we should close the school for a short time, say till the new scholastic year, or till we can open our own College on the two conditions: 1) that the Bishop be bound not to open [a] school in the mean time within a mile of us, and 2) that the Cardinal tell the Bishop that we have not gone beyond the Canon Law. This would save the honour of the Bishop in the main point of our having opened in spite of him, and will secure all we care about. Fr Armellini went this morning to propose it to the Cardinal Prefect. He liked the proposal, and undertakes to make it from himself to Vaughan. I in the mean time spoke of it to Cardinals de Luca and Bilio who carry great weight, and they both approved of it very much and promised to support it if the Cardinal Prefect speaks to them.

The latter all along says there is no question about our right and when Fr Armellini urged that the B[isho]p had gone far beyond his jurisdiction he said, "yes I saved him from that", referring to his telegram not to suspend the Fathers. In the meantime the Pope has spoken to Vaughan, so he will probably be more disposed to knuckle under.

Cardinal Sacconi[243] whom I saw this morning and who is a great friend of the Soc[iety] told me we must make some compromises as it is almost impossible to expect a decision against the whole hierarchy if it goes formally before the Congregation. He wanted me to go off to Vaughan to make terms but it would not do to shew any sign of yielding to him. He had seen Vaughan who had told him that if we would close our school he would let us have one later! He appears also to have said something about resigning if he cannot carry his point, but I think this will not last. He must be disappointed with the reception he has met from the Cardinal Prefect as he finds it not so easy to bring us on our knees. The Cardinal propose [*sic*] a conference on the basis of the compromise I spoke of above and am very confident that in a conference we can shut him up. Wherever I come across his story as coming from him or Stonor it is this: that having failed before, now that the B[isho]p has got a school we want to come in again, that he wants to reform his clergy, that the Catholics are chiefly poor and that we cannot claim privilege in England as in other places etc. All this I can demonstrate abundantly to be all nonsense. I do not hear a word of the compact so I think he has found that that does not hold water.

With a bit more prayer and patience, and yielding something to save the honour of the Bishop I expect word that all will come right. The declaration that we have not gone beyond Canon Law will save our principle.

---

243   Carlo Sacconi, 1808–1889; Prefect of the Economy at Propaganda Fide.

We are giving out your pamphlet[244] where we think it will be of use; always *confidentially* to save the Cardinal Prefect who is caught by his letter to Fr General, but of course the letter was asked for this very purpose. He complained to me on Friday that Fr General had in his answer promised not to go against the Bishop. I was surprised at this, and he then read me the letter which was merely to the effect that he wished and should always endeavour to act according to the wishes of the Ordinary. I answered that all that had been carried out most carefully but that the Bishop had gone out of his jurisdiction so it was necessary to resist. I think your letter sent to the Pope, and our representation through Cardinal Antonelli will do the work and the compromise will open the way to do it. Fr Maxwell will have his audience with the Pope tomorrow. I told him to say a word if he could get an opportunity, but not to let Stonor hear him. No one here thinks anything of Stonor's influence. Howard is more serious but he will not go out of his way against us ... Stacpols has been in retreat for sub-diaconate. I mean to see him tomorrow and set him to work, he has great influence.

Bishops [*sic*] have asked three questions. 1) Whether we have the right to open schools. 2) Whether we can do so in spite of prohibition of Bp. 3) I forget the 3rd; it is contained in the first. The Cardinal Prefect does not wish to go into the question.

Ever yours sincerely in J[esus] C[hrist]
A. Weld

Weld to Gallwey
Collegio Romano,[245]
Rome.
4 May 1875

My dear Fr,

Yesterday I had a great alarm and went to bed with a heavy heart and did not sleep very well. Today however I am up again. I heard in the course of yesterday morning that the three Bishops with Howard and Stonor had gone that day in a body to the Vatican "on important business". Of course I knew what that meant, and as they are all well up in Vaughan's pamphlet, I feared the influence that might have on the Holy Father. What increased my fears was that Mgr. Nardi[246] called on me in the evening and left word that he had an important communication to

---

[244] *Facts and Documents.*
[245] ABSI, RX/5, Weld to Gallwey, 4 May 1875.
[246] Mgr Francesco Nardi, consultor at Propaganda Fide. He may have been one of the 'three Bishops'. See below, 5 May 1875.

make to me. Of course I went the first thing this morning. There was no news of what took place at the Vatican, but both he and Cardinal de Luca this morning told me it was very unlikely for the Holy Father to take action without fully hearing both sides. Nardi is strongly in our favour, and has promised me to do what he can for us with the Pope and also with Cardinal Franchi.

We are also asking Cardinal Antonelli so that the Pope will I trust be on his guard. I do not know how long the Bishops think of remaining here, but they are going about dining here and there together with Howard and Stonor, Lady Herbert[247] too is there. The feeling for Manning here is not too great. I am told the Pope did not like the great shew he made in Rome when he was made Cardinal, also the letter he lately published in the newspaper contradicting the report of his conversation with the Pope is said not to have pleased. His views about the union of Italy are becoming well known and I hear do not give satisfaction. All this is not of much consequence to us, but as Vaughan is looked on as a child of his it may tell in our favour.

What you tell me about his resigning may have more in it that you think.[248] I told you I had heard of it here. I have since heard a rumour going about in high places, that Manning is trying to make him Coadjutor with right of succession in Westminster and to have a new Bishop in Salford.[249] This has been put to Vaughan, but though he said he had no such ambition and denies any knowledge of it, he was said to look confused. Another report here is that the Bishops are trying to get young men above a certain age forbidden to go to Stonyhurst so as to force them to go to the college in Kensington.[250] I asked Cardinal de Luca if there was any fear of the Holy Father granting such a request himself, he said not the slightest without hearing all that has to be said on both sides and taking a long time about it. We have two or three real friends in the Propaganda and should be certainly told if such a question were brought before them. Our present business may drag on for all I know, there was a general meeting of the Cardinals of Propaganda yesterday, but it was not spoken of, Cardinal de Luca thinks there is nothing to be done except to insist on a meeting with Vaughan before the Cardinal,

247   Lady Herbert of Lea, 1822–1911; see Shane Leslie, *Letters of Herbert Cardinal Vaughan to Lady Herbert of Lea 1867 to 1903* (London, 1942).

248   Vaughan had in fact threatened to resign if he did not carry his point, see Vaughan's Diary, 7 May.

249   When Manning submitted the *terna* to Rome, headed by Vaughan and strongly recommended by Manning, the latter added a further request: that he be given an auxiliary bishop in Westminster without right of succession. Manning further asked that Vaughan, if not named Bishop of Salford, be appointed as auxiliary in Westminster: APF, Anglia 20, 1875–1877, ff. 762–771.

250   The Catholic University College.

this I have asked for and it has been promised, but still it does not come. I suppose Vaughan does not wish for it, but it is the only fair thing, then we shall see who has better reasons. I think I can hold out in Rome longer than he can, though I am sadly tired of the life for anxieties come in fits that wear me out.

When I told Mgr Nardi that the school was still going on (don't let this out) he threw his arms round me and embraced me! He would not have us yield an inch. I have this morning received an excellent letter from Dr Noble[251] of Manchester in which he tells me that the regret among Catholics at the effort to stop our school is considerable. He complains too that the laity are not consulted as to the education they wish for. He also tells me that he heard of the question first from a layman in London. I have sent the letter to Mgr Nardi and asked him to read it to the Pope. Fr General will be here tomorrow, the Pope having expressed a wish to see him, not principally I think about our affair but that of Makisa [?], but we shall have him well got up on our business in case the Pope speaks about it. Mgr Nardi also proposed to get an audience by the Pope [sic], I did not decline, but left it to depend on the state of mind in which he finds the Holy Father on the subject. It is not everyone who can speak well with the Pope. Fr General has great influence with him and might spoil it.

Of course I am still somewhat anxious as to the effect of the audience of yesterday, but they tell me the Pope would decide nothing and I think he would at least wait till he saw Fr General. Any rate it shews that the Pope spoke to Vaughan to some purpose. Cardinal de Luca is very grateful for the Blue Book. He says there is an appendix come out later, which he would like. Please send it to me. He is very kind.

Ever yours sincerely in J[esus] C[hrist]
A. Weld

Weld to Gallwey
Collegio Romano,[252]
Rome.
5 May 1875

My dear Fr,

I am able today to give you some report of the audience at the Vatican on Monday. Three of the party, and a fourth, i.e. Vaughan, Howard, Stonor and *Lady Herbert*! lunched with Stackpols immediately after.

---

[251] Daniel Noble, 1810–1885; surgeon, author of authoritative works on famine epidemics.
[252] ABSI, RX/5, Weld to Gallwey, 5 May 1875.

Stonor came in rubbing his hands, saying I think this affair is well finished now. I think we shall hear no more of it etc. Vaughan said I don't think it's finished at all. There will be a fine row before that comes etc. He was very preoccupied all lunch and so was Howard.

After lunch, they adjourned to another room and had one hour's consultation or confab. It came out during lunch that the Pope told them he would leave all to the Congregation. In the mean time Nardi went to Franchi who entertained him with remarks not particularly favourable to M[annin]g and great praise of the Society in England, told him that the Bishops were willing to let us have college [*sic*] in *small* towns but not in the large cities, that they said if we had them there, all would come to us. That all the good respectable lads would be Jesuits instead of secular Priests. Though he said he knew this was false, as he knew excellent seculars who had been scholars of the Jesuits. Nardi shewed him the real meaning of the argument and seems to have pleaded hard and well for us. Several times he rose to leave but the Cardinal kept him to encourage him to come to him again and he assured him no *coup d'etat* would be taken but all would be most carefully examined before any decision was come to.

All this is satisfactory. I think Vaughan will have to leave town, and it will be a case of who can make out the best case in a memorial. I am not afraid if it comes to that. We shall have some of the most influential Cardinals certainly in our favour. I think a few more good letters of laymen signed in their name written to Mr Palmer or other seculars would tell very well when worked into a memoir. We shall proceed to prepare it at once, and as a matter of course Vaughan's will be communicated to us. I hear all your letters, your documentation and our memorial will be presented to each Cardinal if it goes before the Congregation, but it may be kept to a small committee as the Cardinal Prefect is averse to it going before the Congregation. I conceal no names from you, but please don't let them out. I mean Stackpols, Nardi etc.

Ever yours sincerely in J[esus] C[hrist]

A. Weld

P.S.

Just got your telegram, all right. Now I think we shall fight it out, but if compromise is accepted we'll stand for August 1. They understand more and more that it is an affair of Manning exalting the hierarchy which does not find much favour here.

Weld to Gallwey
Collegio Romano,[253]
6 May 1875.

My dear Fr,

I have received yours of the 3rd. You must not be afraid of speaking freely to me. You are not more sensible than I am of my unfitness for fight. However I do nothing without Fr Armellini who though very quiet in his way, is very bold and ready in speech and with his pen. However I think finally all will have to be done in writing. We shall make a full memoir – shall not hurry it, and for this the more material you send the better. You might work the pressing wants of England. Also some good facts illustrating repression of the Society: such as refusal of faculties to you when at Roehampton. I am getting some statistics from France relating to boys who come out of the Collèges Apostoliques. The more we can bring out the system of jealousy and repression the better. It will tell well with some of the principal Cardinals. The admission that they don't want us in the large towns is of great importance to us. The Cardinal Prefect has promised to do nothing in a hurry, so I expect Vaughan will have to return home very much as he came. I have no doubt he would like to be home for Pentecost. Cardinal Chigi[254] is quite in our favour, though Manning tried to win him round, also Bilio, Consolini, de Luca and Sacconi, but the latter thinks we should try to make terms.

Fr General arrived last night, and we have explained the case well to him, in case the Holy Father speaks to him about it. We shall insist on having a copy of Vaughan's pamphlet but it will not do him much good at the Propaganda unless he has got it put into Italian, in that case I dare say he will modify it but we shall insist on the original as a matter of justice.[255] The Cardinal has promised it to us.

---

[253] ABSI, RX/5, Weld to Gallwey, 6 May 1875.

[254] Flavio Chigi, 1810–1885; member of the Congregation of Bishops and Regulars.

[255] Vaughan never published an Italian version of his pamphlets, nor is there in the archives of Propaganda Fide an English version of the same. As for 'modifications' to the texts, in 1879 Vaughan wrote to the Bishop of Clifton: "Will you kindly have laid before Card. Simeoni the following fact[s]. Having been desired by Propaganda to lay my case before the Bishops in Low Week 1875, I did so in the form of two pamphlets, containing the correspondence between Fr Gallwey and myself and a statement of the case. After reading over one of the pamphlets, I found I had introduced matter, reflecting on the efforts alleged to have been made by the Manchester priests to get penitents of other priests. This was not necessary for my case. I therefore within a week of our meeting reprinted the pamphlet, suppressing that matter etc., and sent corrected copies to the Bishops. I also took some copies to Rome and kept a few by me." AAW, V.1/7, Vaughan to Bishop of Clifton, 27 May 1879. The letter is marked 'copy to Bp of Clifton.' For full text see below, Vaughan to Bishop of Clifton, 27 May 1879.

I shall write again when there is news of anything. No letter from me means no change. Archbishop Stonor has arrived in Naples with Fr Shea.

Ever yours sincerely in J[esus] C[hrist],
A. Weld
P.S.
The above was written yesterday, but by a mistake was not posted. I open it to add a few lines. It appears that Cardinal Antonelli spoke to the Pope just in the nick of time, before the Bishops went in a body to him; no doubt this helped to put him on his guard. A day or two before that, Vaughan told Fr Maxwell that he did not mean to go back till he had beaten us. Yesterday Nardi gave Vaughan a long talk and told him not to join Bismarck[256] and other things in that style. Vaughan told him that all the Bishops agree with him. They did not mean to disturb the Colleges we had but did not mean us to have more or to that effect. Nardi advised him to come to me and come to terms. He said no, I will go to Fr General, he is in Rome. We have put Fr General well up, and there is no hope of his being soft. On the whole I think he is getting shaky, but will fight hard yet, he will be satisfied with nothing but stopping our scheme altogether. It will be a dreadful humiliation for him to go back beaten. I think his connection with Manning does not help him much now, but rather to the contrary. Please do not name Nardi, he begged me particularly not to, I do it to you not to appear to conceal anything from you. He is not liked here, and some of ours do not trust him, but I believe he is sincerely friendly to us.

Porter to Gallwey
Manresa House,[257]
6 May 1875,

Dear Rev. Father,
I saw and read Dr V[aughan]'s pamphlet; it is a very objectionable document. Fr Weld should be instructed to *demand* its production at Rome; it could not fail to help our cause by the obviously dishonest and malevolent tone in which it is written. Some assertions as to fact and some omissions require comment. The *Agreement* is much insisted on, also *the vested interests*. On the agreement: 1) it should be brought prominently forward that only one condition was named, *viz* the purchase of Canon O'Toole's [sic] plot of land for £1,500, at a time when it was

---

256 Otto von Bismarck was particularly harsh on the Jesuits; he expelled them from Germany in 1872 as part of his anti-Church decrees (*Kulturkampf*).
257 ABSI, RX/5, Porter to Gallwey, 6 May 1875.

not worth the price. 2) From the day the church was commenced, we constantly looked out to buy land for a college, without the smallest doubt in the mind of Fr Weld or Fr Whitty[258] or in my mind![259] I was then the Superior of Manchester and I may add Fr Birch and my brother [*sic*]. This shows we never understood that we had bound ourselves not to open a college.

As to the *vested interests*: can you get good reliable evidence from the Xaverian Brothers as to their financial condition?

I asked Dr N[oble] to let me have the pamphlet, I said I wanted to show it to your Rev[erence]. He would not allow me to carry it out of the house, but said I might read it and you might go and read it at his house. My opinion is that that the reading will repay you for the journey. Ask Dr N[oble]'s leave to copy extracts, or if you like, take Fr Norris as your secretary, or send for me, I will meet you at St George's and do the scribe. Dr N[oble] informed me also that Dr V[aughan] has printed a second pamphlet,[260] an answer to yours. Dr V[aughan] wrote that he had sent a copy to Dr N[oble], but Dr N[oble] never received the copy.

Pamphlet No 1 is bad enough, it ought to be studied and carefully answered. It lends itself to a triumphant answer.

Yours very truly in Xt,
George Porter.[261]

Waterworth to Gallwey
Worcester,[262]
6 May 1875.

My dear Fr Provincial,
Bishop Vaughan has I fear printed two violent diatribes against us, and not one only. The occasion of the second can be told in a few words.

Shortly after your Reverence's interview with Bishop Ullathorne, Bishop Ullathorne had a long talk with Bishop Vaughan. Likely enough it regarded Oxford before we gave up that mission, and the complaints urged against us since our return to that mission. But this is all conjecture.

At all events Bishop Vaughan took occasion from it to write a first and 2nd pamphlet and my informant who is a dignitary and most

---

[258] Robert Whitty SJ, 1817–1895.
[259] In *Facts and Documents*, Gallwey claims that during the lifetime of Bishop Turner, "Fr Weld had secured a plot of land adjacent to the site of our church expressly with a view to a future College: so far was he precluded by any compact from ever establishing a College." p. 6.
[260] *The Bishop's Reply*.
[261] George Porter, SJ, 1825–1889; later became Archbishop of Bombay.
[262] ABSI, RX/5, Waterworth to Gallwey, 6 May 1875.

intimate with the Bishop and a singularly exact man, tells me that the 2nd pamphlet is, he fears, more violent than his first.[263]

The Bishop is quite indignant at thus being made a Cat's paw of Bishop Vaughan, and dragged into a disagreeable controversy. He has written to remonstrate I hear; but with what success I have not heard. I write this to show that your Rev[erence] must not look out for one but two pamphlets.

Ever your Rev. obedient servant
W. Waterworth.[264]

Kerr to Franchi
Bournemouth,[265]
9 May 1875.

Your Eminence,

I dare to hope that your Eminence, will forgive me if I allow myself once again to approach your Eminence about a matter which at the moment deeply interests the Catholics of Gt. Britain.

As a lay member of the Catholic Committee for Poor Schools, I have been obliged to study the question of education in its present state, and I can say that there has never been a moment when the future of the Faith has been more in danger. Only the greatest energy and unity of Catholic action can deliver the children of our days from the irreligious influences of State Education. So it is with deep affliction that we hear of the unfortunate intention clearly determined in certain dioceses of closing schools of the middle class conducted by the Jesuits according to their ancient privilege.

Your Eminence knows that the state here, following the example of the [illegible] is trying to take over the education of the poor and the middle class in England and in Scotland by means of state schools established everywhere at great expense.

Armed with all the prestige that position and money provide to advance this secular system, the state [aims] to make their schools attractive, through the superior education but [also] *via* salaries and the [illegible] of value will make it impossible for Catholics to rival it. Even

---

263 This is not accurate as far as the first pamphlet is concerned: *The Claim* was, according to evidence at Propaganda Fide, written on 17 March 1875 (APF, Anglia 20, f. 331); the second pamphlet: *The Bishop's Reply*, was, according to the same evidence (f. 428), written on 7 April as a reply to Gallwey's memorial to the Hierarchy. For Vaughan's reasons for publishing the pamphlet see below, Vaughan to Bishop of Clifton, 27 May 1879.

264 William Waterworth SJ, 1811–1882.

265 APF, Anglia 20, Kerr to Franchi, 9 May 1875.

young schoolmasters and schoolmistresses, brought up by Catholics, are tempted by the salaries to accept positions in schools without religion.

In this crisis it is a matter of great importance that the Society of Jesus must not be excluded in the general call which is being made in England for the creation of centres of education. It is not only important for the future of the Society of Jesus but also for the future of the great question of Catholic education in Gt. Britain.

There is only the teaching of the Religious Orders which can face up to state education in the new schools, called 'Board Schools', where the state is putting education without religion within reach of all classes.

I confess to your Eminence that it is for me an unbelievable matter that, with the enemy thus at the door, the ecclesiastical authorities can hesitate to see the help of the religious orders, and especially of the Jesuit Fathers. I am convinced that the Sacred Congregation of the Propaganda is perfectly *au fait* with the present situation of these matters, and so I limit myself to expressing to your Eminence my feelings, and those of a large number of lay Catholics.

With regard to the future of the Catholic cause in this country, I repeat that we need all our strength and unity of action in the crisis in which we find ourselves.

With the greatest respect, and highest consideration I am your
Humble and devoted servant,
(Lord) H. Kerr[266]
(Of the family Lothian)

Porter to unknown
Manresa House,[267]
10 May 1875.

... Can you get any reliable evidence from the Xaverian Brothers that they have not succeeded? Or is there any truth in one speech I heard *viz* that they had thought of withdrawing from Manchester altogether?

Yours very truly in Xt,
George Porter

---

[266] Henry Kerr, 1833–1900; diplomat; in 1870 he succeeded in the marquisate to become the 9th Lord Lothian; Secretary for Scotland 1887–1892.
[267] ABSI, RX/5, Porter to unknown.

Weld to Gallwey
Collegio Romano,[268]
Rome
11 May [1875]

My dear Fr,

I have not written these two days because I had nothing very clear to tell you, and still less that was good. I can now tell you more distinctly the state of things. Fr General's presence is as you guess a great comfort. He takes matters into his own hands, and has had two interviews with Cardinal Franchi and one with the Pope. The state is this: Franchi says still that as to our rights there is no doubt, but Vaughan is as obstinate as an animal which however he does not name and will listen to nothing. The Holy Father is annoyed at the dispute and wants it ended,[269] and there we are. It is clear Cardinal Franchi will do nothing. It is hoped the Pope will not act. The Bishop wants the matter to go before the congregation. We shall not oppose it. Though as the Cardinal Prefect is opposed to this course it may be referred to a committee of Cardinals. In the mean time we are preparing a memorial which will be printed in Italian, and will give us a fine opportunity of a good defence and may open eyes here in Rome. The result as to this particular case we must leave to God. To tell the truth I feel more anxious now about the effects of scandal and irritation which will be caused. We must in any case do what we can to allay it.

The extract[270] you sent me is chiefly against you and you can answer it better than we can. If you will do that part that concerns your actions in English Fr Armellini will put it into Italian and work it in. I would make it strictly defensive and such that a copy could be given to Vaughan himself. From the portion you send, his pamphlet is very weak and he does not shew a single sound argument. It will do us good, except with a certain red; but I fear scandal very much.

We have had already two consultations with Fr General on this business.

Yours ever sincerely in J[esus] C[hrist]
A. Weld

---

[268]   ABSI, RX/5, Weld to Gallwey, 11 May [1875].
[269]   See Vaughan's Diary, 7 May 1875.
[270]   From Vaughan's first pamphlet, *The Claim*.

Weld to Gallwey
Osservatorio,[271]
Collegio Romano,
Rome.
12 May 1875

My dear Father,

I took a good run out of Rome yesterday with Fr Raniera and Fr Shea, went to Monte Cavo and the Passionist Convent on the site of the ancient temple of Jupiter Triumphant, a magnificent position; the view from which effectively put B[isho]p Vaughan out of one's head for the day, which was a great relief to me. There is no change in the position, nor is there likely to be immediately. Fr Armellini is working at the memorial. We think that it is better to make our statement of the Manchester Case distinct from the answer to Vaughan's accusations. The latter should be in English and should be done chiefly by you. The other must be in Italian and had best be done by Fr Armellini with whatever material we have and you may yet send. I say this in the supposition that he has not printed anything in Italian. I have not found out as yet that he has, I think we can make our case very strong, and that he has nothing solid to bring against it.

You are quite right about his power of bully, but there was not much fear of him bullying me as we do not meet. I have only seen him once and I thought it better not to discuss the matter with him so as not to enable him to prepare answers to our arguments. He has however succeeded in bullying Cardinal Franchi who has become painfully sensible of his obstinacy and determination to listen to nothing. This is becoming so evident that I am beginning to think the cause can hardly go entirely against us. We are now trying to make the Cardinal sensible that if he yields to V[aughan] in this way against reason he will find him quite unmanageable a little later, and that he will do him a great service if he will insist on the Canon Law now and make him bend. We have several Cardinals very favourable to us, and try to get them to strengthen the Cardinal Prefect, but it is a delicate thing for them to interfere. This is a strange world!

Ever yours sincerely in J[esus] C[hrist],
A. Weld

---

[271]   ABSI, RX/5, Weld to Gallwey, 12 May 1875.

Weld to Gallwey
Collegio Romano,[272]
13 May 1875.

My dear Fr,

I have received yours of May 7th this morning. I had yesterday spoken with Fr General about the London question. We both thought it better to keep it distinct and only to throw in enough into the memorial to show that Manchester is only a part of a system. London is so long a story that it would take attention too much from Manchester at least so we think.

I suggested yesterday that you should answer Vaughan's pamphlet, but there are some points which I must answer and which I can do well; I will send you the notes to work in. I think the answer should be dignified avoiding recrimination.

I had these for when Mr Palmer called on me, and we discussed the question for a little time. He had seen Stonor and opened his eyes considerably on the impossibility of Catholics meeting the Board Schools without the help of the religious. He confirmed the idea I got from the extract you sent me that they have no argument except destroying our right and accusing you and me. On the whole our position seems to me stronger everyday. I am principally afraid now of Vaughan boring the Pope till he is tired and sends us an order to give up. Mr Palmer quite laughed when I shewed him the map and our relative positions, and how he wanted to come close to us. What you say about the effect of prayer I feel very much. I can pray more with great composure that God will do what is best for the Church and the Society and am free from that feverish anxiety which used to spoil all my prayers and my sleep too. If it comes to a compromise, I think I would propose that we should help the Xaverians to move elsewhere. It would be the most honourable way out for the Bishop. He would have all the credit of having fought their battle bravely.

Mr Palmer is leaving Rome next Monday so letters must not be addressed to him. Whoever they are written to had best be told to bring them to me. They are only of use [illegible] to work into a memorial.

I saw Cardinal Monaco[273] last night he is a sincere friend of the Society, and promised to do all he could to strengthen Franchi. He is also a friend of Vaughan's and took him to task for opposing us, saying "this won't do" etc. It has occurred to me, and Mgr Nardi made the same suggestion to me this morning, to suggest to you to ask Bishop Danell[274] to let you have a College in Southwark. There must be as many

272   ABSI, RX/5, Weld to Gallwey, 13 May 1875.
273   Raffaele Monaco la Valletta, 1827–1896; secretary of Petitions and Memorials.
274   James Danell, 1821–1882; Bishop of Southwark 1871–1882.

Catholics there as there are in Manchester and it would not interfere with a College in London proper later. Is the ground already occupied? We should secure positions before the ground is occupied if we can.

I heard a report this morning that an unanimous petition has come from the Bishops that no philosophers are to be received in any College except Capel's, I had heard something of it before, but not in the form of a petition from all the Bishops. It is incredible that they could succeed, but I have written to Dr Smith to ask him to look it up as it concerns us all. They would certainly give us notice at the Propaganda before treating such a question; and fortunately Manning is not as popular [as] he was, and that in certain questions is useful to us.

Ever yours in J[esus] C[hrist]
A. Weld

Weld to Gallwey
Collegio Romano,[275]
14 May 1875.

My dear Fr,

Nardi had a consultation with Fr General today. I can hardly say there is any important change in affairs, but I must say they do not look as bright. The Cardinal Prefect always acknowledges our right, but seems more and more to wish us to yield. The Holy Father says "agree". Fr General is gone this evening to the Cardinal to press on him that coming to an agreement does not mean that we are to yield etc.

Our best friends among the Cardinals say that the question must not go before the Congregation and Fr General is so much impressed by this that I think he will follow their advice. In the mean time Fr Armellini is preparing the memorial for the Cardinal, in which he will have all our points together.

Vaughan told Mgr Nardi yesterday that the Pope had settled the question himself, but as this was after his audience, and he is said to have looked very weary and silent afterwards, I suspect the Pope said nothing more than that we must come to an agreement. As Cardinal Franchi also had his audience yesterday we shall soon know if anything has been done. In the mean time the affair is becoming the talk of Rome. We have made good friends near the Pope but it is necessary not to bore him. They do their best for us. I shall write again tomorrow to let you know the result of the General's visit.

Ever yours sincerely in J[esus] C[hrist]
A. Weld.

---

[275] ABSI, Weld to Gallwey, 14 May 1875.

Weld to Gallwey
Collegio Romano,[276]
Rome.
15 May 1875.

My letter of yesterday will have prepared you for the news that Fr General would accept terms if he can get decent ones. In his conference with the Cardinal yesterday he agreed to a compromise on the following basis: that we should close our school and that the Bishop should be bound not to come so near as to render a school of the Society impossible. The distance was not settled. We shall stand for a mile; our rights and privilege to remain intact. The Cardinal promised Fr General that he would oblige him to keep at a sufficient distance not to prevent a school of the Soc[iety] later.

If this is secured, I think we have gained all we care much about. We shall certainly have our school later. The time will depend on the extent of his failure to supply the wants and the demand of Catholics for education of the Society. In fact it will be very soon seen that there is no gain in our closing the school except to [save] the Bishop's honour, and not much more, but a real loss for religion, so that I think if we can insist on his keeping his side we shall soon have our school.

It has become evident that the petition of all the Bishops against us rendered it impossible to hope for a complete triumph and I am not sure that this will not put us with a more favourable position than if we had got it. The school will be delayed, but that does *us* no harm. The ground will be secured and we shall gain sympathy, besides the Pope would not have us fight it out.

Ever yours sincerely in J[esus] C[hrist],
A. Weld
P.S.
The other party think they have got a complete victory. They do not know yet of the clause about distance. The Cardinal assured Fr General he would insist on it. We shall not agree without it. Part of the agreement is for Vaughan to write a letter to Fr General *asking* him to close the school to let him carry out his plan.

---

[276]   ABSI, RX/5, Weld to Gallwey, 15 May 1875.

Vaughan to Manning
15 May 1875[277]

SJ have brought up all their artillery. The present is a crisis on which all depends. The only hope is in Pius IX and Cardinal Franchi. The Pope allowed me nearly half an hour to explain the whole case to him.[278] A few days after he said, *Quell, affare dei Gesuiti è una vera porcheria* [*sic*].[279] The Pope sent for the General to come from Florence, and the only question was as to the mode of desiring them to close the colleges.

Vaughan to Beckx
The English College,[280]
Rome,
Whitsunday 16 May 1875.

I am obliged to call attention of your Paternity to the case of the college which has been opened in Manchester by the Provincial SJ. It is not, I trust your Paternity will understand, from any want of appreciation of the eminent services rendered to the Church by the Society, still less from any indifference to the services which it is capable of rendering to the cause of Religion in the diocese of Salford in the future that I have been unable to sanction the establishment of a college of the Society in Manchester.

Circumstances altogether independent of any such considerations have left me no alternative in the matter. If I touch on some of them, in the briefest possible way, it is simply to point out to your Paternity that no other conclusion was open to me than the one I actually came to, unless indeed I was to abandon an important work begun and carried on at great pains and cost by my Predecessor.

The chief duty of a bishop in these days, as it appears to me, is to provide for the education of his flock. Acting upon this principle, the first resolutions I came to, in conjunction with my Chapter, immediately after my consecration were 1) to found a seminary in Salford, and 2) to develop the work begun by my Predecessor in Manchester into such a college as should not only meet all the educational needs of the better class among the Catholics of that city, but should also be fostering vocations and to increase the number and raise the character of the future

---

[277] See Shane Leslie, *Henry Edward Manning: His Life and Labours* (London, 1921), p. 302.
[278] See Vaughan's Diary, 30 April 1875, p. 171.
[279] 'This business with the Jesuits is a real mess/a pig's ear.' See Vaughan's Diary, 3 May 1875, p. 171.
[280] ARSI, Anglia 1/4 – IV.4, Vaughan to Beckx, 16 May 1875.

diocesan clergy, which ought to be formed not of strangers from various lands, but of men sprung from the soil, agreeable to the actual requirements of the country.

These two resolutions were published in a Pastoral Letter dated 30 November 1872. Many thousand copies of it were circulated throughout the diocese and it was read on Sunday from the pulpit of the various churches, including the four parochial churches served by the Fathers of the Society. Indeed at that early date I was able to announce, after tracing an outline of the project, that I had "already taken certain preliminary steps (towards the development of a college in Manchester) though the time for public action had not yet arrived", the erection of the diocesan seminary claiming my first attention. Within a short time of the publication of this Pastoral I had arranged for the purchase of a valuable plot of land and buildings, which will serve to double the accommodation of the school begun by my late Predecessor in Manchester, and now under the care of the Xaverian Brothers.

If the site of this school, or 'Collegiate Institute' as it is called, is within ten minutes distance of the church of the Holy Name, it should be observed that the school occupied its present site – which is the best in Manchester for its purpose – some years before the Jesuits returned to Manchester, and that consequently it was the Society that settled itself down near the school, and not the Bishop who planted his school in the neighbourhood of the Jesuit church.

These Resolutions which I adopted after mature deliberation with the Chapter and then canonically published in the Diocese, are not only in perfect harmony and sequence with the line of conduct entered upon by the late Bishop, and essential in my judgement to the due organisation and full development of the Diocese and to the good of Religion, but they were publicly announced before the Fathers had expressed to me any desire to found a new college of their own in Manchester and before even its nomination of the present Provincial and his plans had taken place.

Having now laid the whole case before the Sacred Congregation of Propaganda, it appears more clearly than ever to be my duty to adhere to those Resolutions and thus protect and develop the various interests both of the Diocese and of the Brothers, which are confided to the care of the Ordinary.

And here without entering into the question of privileges (the exercise of which ought to be advantageous and not prejudicial to the interests of the Diocese) I would beg your Paternity to observe that as the establishment of another college of the Society in Manchester would create an obstacle in the way of my plans for the organization and due development of the Diocese and would be injurious to the interests of another teaching Community, I have no alternative but to ask of your Paternity to be good enough to desire the Provincial to close the college in question. If on the one hand the Society has several flourishing colleges in England, especially the splendid establishment of Stonyhurst in my Diocese for the education of the higher classes, I venture to hope on the other hand that it will not be taken amiss that the Bishop should reserve to himself the education of the middle class in his own city of Manchester and should adopt such measures as he may think necessary and most advantageous for the good of his clergy and of his people.

At the same time, I trust that your Paternity will see that the course which I pursue in begging your Fathers to attend exclusively to the parish work entrusted to them by the late Bishop, far from being an indication of want of esteem for the Society, to which I am united by many public and private ties of duty and affection, is the only one that conscience permits me to follow and is laid down for me by circumstances which I can neither control nor ignore.

Nevertheless I hope as time goes on to have many and various occasions of availing myself of the services of the Society for the spiritual advantage of my flock just as (and I have much pleasure in saying it) I have already done on many occasions in the past.

I can assure your Paternity that after my ardent desire to promote development and perfection of our recently established hierarchical diocesan organization, I desire nothing more than to behold a similar development and perfection among the Religious Orders, which form the strong auxiliary force of the Church. And if these are my feelings toward the Religious Orders in general, they are certainly realized when I think of the Society of Jesus – and this not only of the zeal, learning and virtue for which it has been everywhere conspicuous and of the service which it may continue to render to Religion in my Diocese but also on account of my intimate relations with the Fathers of the Society from my very youth.

I cannot close this letter without an expression of sincere regret that our respective sense of duty should have occasioned a temporary divergence in our views.

Meanwhile I beg to remain with great respect, Right Rev Fr General your humble and obedient servant.

+ Herbert, Bishop of Salford.

Weld to Gallwey
Osservatorio,[281]
Collegio Romano.
16 May 1875.

My dear Fr,

I told you yesterday that we should have to close our school, and that we should insist on the condition of Vaughan opening no school within a mile. Nothing is yet concluded. I saw the Cardinal this morning on the subject of the distance and ascertained a point which we have really known all along, but was able to shew the deceit lurking behind. You know he has all along put forward the two incompatible arguments – the interests of the Xaverians, and his own intention of a school to form his own clergy etc. These two are combined in the expression of "developing the Xaverian school." I told the Cardinal that if we close it must be on the condition of his establishing no school within a mile. He said "Oh that is quite safe for he is only going to develop the Xaverian." I then explained to him what that meant i.e. putting in Priests and other teachers etc. so as to alienate the Xaverians. He could hardly believe me and said, "if he does that he will have broken his word".[282] He has written a letter to the General in which he says he only wishes to *develop* the Xaverians etc. I insisted that he meant quite a different thing. The Cardinal said that he must have nothing but Xaverians pure and simple. Fr General will sign nothing till he gets this in writing from the Cardinal. The question is what terms or expression would satisfy you. Perhaps this – 'no teachers except Xaverian Brothers within a mile, or no school except of Xaverian Brothers'. I suppose that *bona fide* Xaverian Brothers we cannot complain of because they are there already and moreover I suppose we should not fear them, as they have not got educated men and are not likely to have them, and if he is confined to these Brothers there will be a clamour for our teaching Society. In fact the Cardinal speaks of this agreement proposed as only a settlement for the moment and what we insist on is that nothing be done to prevent our having our school later. This point will not be given up unless a command comes from the Holy Father. If his grand school for reforming his clergy and to receive South Americans who come to Manchester to study commerce etc. is to be entirely in the hands of the Xaverians, he has not gained much and in the mean time has written a letter, the draft of which Fr General has seen, and thinks it very beautiful, he is full of the highest praise of the Society and the gratitude he himself owes to it especially in England, in which he asks as a favour without prejudice

---

[281]   ABSI, RX/5, Weld to Gallwey, 16 May 1875.
[282]   See Vaughan's Diary, 20 May.

of privilege that Fr General will give instruction for the closing of the school in order that he may *develop the Xaverian College etc.* He must have felt some humble pie in writing this after what he has done and pointed against us. Words do not cost much. All will depend on our being supported now. The Cardinal is willing but weak. I told him we must have the pamphlets to be able to explain as Stonor and others, but chiefly the Italians, have talked all round Rome against us. He said we would have them. I have talked with Dr Smith who thinks that as times are, if we can make a sacrifice of fact without giving up a principle we shall be wise in doing so, but I think that if we can succeed in keeping him to no school except *bona fide* Xaverians within one a mile we have gained a triumph, and have fought a fight of great importance, as the necessity of a better school will be apparent at once. In the mean time Fr Armellini is going on with the memorial.

You had better telegraph what declaration you would insist on about the Xaverian school and what you would be satisfied with as to distance and wording.

Yours ever sincerely in J[esus] C[hrist],
A. Weld.

Birch to Gallwey
Manchester,[283]
46, Ackers Street,
17 May 1875.

Dear Fr Provincial,

We will concoct as short and pithy an answer as we can to the Bishop's wild, vague and inconsiderate charges. How odd that he never made any such before. As regards myself personally, it is certain that he has expressed himself (to his uncle Fr Vaughan) in exactly an opposite sense. I hear Fr Gadd has done the same.

I hear that Dr Vaughan is to be made coadjutor Archbishop and to be replaced by Dr Weathers.[284] An idle report I suppose.[285] I wish you could see and have a talk with Revd. Mr Ramsey now at Ashton near here, our fast friend. I hear it reported that Canon Cantwell of St Patrick's has said that we have more friends amongst the clergy than we are aware. I ought to add, that the good Canon has not distinguished himself by his devotedness to his Bishop since Dr Vaughan has been at Salford. What

---

[283] ABSI, RY/2/2, Birch to Gallwey, 17 May 1875.
[284] William Weathers, 1814–1895; on Manning's specific request he was consecrated auxiliary Bishop of Westminster in 1872.
[285] See below, Vaughan's Diary, 7 May 1875.

he may say must be received with caution, and I think, kept *mum*. He is a great friend of the Nicholson's[286] and speaks his mind there very freely.

Obediently yours in Xt,
Henry Birch.

Vaughan to Manning[287]
18 May 1875

I read my letter to the General, corrected or softened by Franchi, to Cardinal Cullen[288] and the Redemptorist General.[289] They all thought it would do very well, and considered it a good piece of gilding for the bitter pill. I saw the General SJ yesterday. Was very open about Gallwey and Weld, and he did not defend them. He wished not to close the Manchester school till the midsummer holidays. This I refused absolutely to allow. He said he would consult Weld, and I went off at once to the Vatican. The Pope, meeting me asked *Tutto è finito?* And said, *Deo Gratias; mi ha piaciuto il vostro foglio.* I replied, *Purché non mettano un indugio.*[290] When he was sitting down in the library he called me up to him and asked me the meaning of the *indugio*. I told him fully, and said it would be keeping the wound open for two or three months. He seemed displeased at it, and I have asked Cardinal Cullen to put in a word for me. I have announced that I don't return till the school is closed. I shall remain here till the Day of Judgment if need be, and the heat begins to suggest that the day is approaching.

Vaughan to Franchi
The English College,[291]
18 May 1875.

Most Rev. Eminence,

May I forewarn Your Eminence of the probability that a proposal will be made to Your Eminence as has already been made to me from the Father General, not to close the school before the July or August holidays, and that for the sake of their dignity.

---

286   Edward Nicholson, architect, acted as agent when the Jesuits bought land in Ackers Street on which to build the Holy Name church.

287   Leslie, *Manning*, p. 302

288   Paul Cullen, 1803–1878; Archbishop of Dublin 1850–1878.

289   Nicolas Mauron, 1818–1893; Superior General 1855–1893.

290   This may be translated as: "The Pope, meeting me asked 'Is everything finished'? And said, 'Thank God; I liked your paper.' I replied, 'As long as they do not make any delay.'"

291   APF, Anglia 20, Vaughan to Franchi, 18 May 1875.

But this delay cannot be allowed as I have not failed to point out to the Father General:

1) Because the complaint would remain unsettled for some time, and is increasing in violence and in scope, even when there be goodwill on the part of some. During which period the little game of the Fathers in Manchester may develop further; and who knows what might happen when the people are urged on by persons in the background.

2) This ungenerous way of prolonging the agony, both by the Jesuits and their friends, and by others, will make impossible that concord and confidence that I would like to see speedily re-established between the Bishop and the Society.

Better therefore for the Jesuits, better for the Bishop, better for all that they should shut the school this same week of the Pentecost holidays – which is the time of main holidays for the whole population of Manchester.

I have already told the Fr General that I am not coming back before the closure. Yesterday the Holy Father asked me if everything was finished.[292] I answered Yes, as long as they do not make a delay. He spoke to me rather at length about this new proposal of a delay, and showed himself to be unhappy. I gave him the reasons indicated. I have taken the liberty of writing these lines to warn Your Eminence and meanwhile I take the opportunity of kissing the Sacred Purple.

I am your most humble and most loyal servant.
Your faithful and obedient servant [*sic*],
+Herbert, Bishop of Salford

Birch to unknown
46, Ackers Street,[293]
19 May 1875.

[No name]

With respect to the charges brought against us by the Bishop, it is obvious to remark, that they are now made by his Lordship for the first time, and come upon us in the nature of a surprise. Whether complaints may have been made by the clergy during the past two or three years, his Lordship has never notified them to us before. With respect to the charges of seeking to exercise undue influence in the parishes of the secular clergy, I believe that it is quite groundless, and that his Lordship

---

292 See above, 18 May 1875, Vaughan to Manning.
293 ABSI, RX/5, Birch to unknown, 19 May 1875.

has been misled.[294] I know nothing of any devices such as are alluded to. If members of the laity outside the district of the Holy Name have frequented either the services or the confessionals of the church of the Holy Name, it has been their own act, and they have exercised a liberty in these respects, never denied to the laity anywhere, and equally open to them in respect of any other church of the Diocese.

I know nothing of the employment of young ladies to collect money or people from the missions of others further than this: that the collectors for the Altar Society call on a few bench holders of our church, for the small monthly subscription. I am equally ignorant as to the boasting in respect of London, Liverpool and Manchester,[295] but it would surely have been a great disgrace to the Society if its advent had *not* brought new life and an accession of strength. It is however true, that the laity have not been slow to bear witness to the satisfactory results in this behalf. As to the charge of spreading injurious reports against the Bishop, I believe it to be wholly baseless. I never heard of any such reports, and I do not believe that such have been spread – on the contrary it has been the endeavour of the FF [Fathers] throughout this business to exercise great reticence in their intercourse with the laity, to be most tender of the Bishop's good name, and in a word, prevent the scandal which they feared might accrue, as far as possible. On the other hand, it is unfortunately true, that they have found during their intercourse with the laity a knowledge amongst them of the facts of the present case which has caused them much surprise, but which are certainly not acquired from the FF. From what source was it obtained? Equally must I deny the charge of attempting to raise a party, of making lamentations, of informing a number of the laity beforehand of intended open opposition etc.[296]

294   Vaughan had accused the Jesuits in Manchester of having "sought in the past to increase the wealth of their congregation by invading the districts of the Secular Clergy, just as they now seek to invade and carry off for their own use the educational plan of the Bishop, in spite of his protest, and to gather round themselves all the best classes of Manchester and the surrounding districts. It is such conduct as this which has led some people to speak of the Society as animated with the self-seeking spirit of a 'sect.'" *The Claim*, pp. 16–17.

295   This is in reply to Vaughan's complaint "of the boasting that the Society in London, Liverpool, and Manchester, has created a life or wrought reforms which were needed among the Bishops and Secular Clergy – [these] have impaired the ecclesiastical peace and goodwill which existed before their advent in Manchester." *The Claim*, p. 16.

296   Vaughan claimed that after he had refused, in writing, to grant the Society permission to open a college, "injurious reports were spread against him abroad, and an attempt made at home to raise a party by making lamentation in the houses of some of the laity." *The Claim*, p. 13. And "… a number of the laity were informed beforehand of the open opposition it was intended to offer the Bishop." *The Claim*, p. 14.

In a word, I believe that his Lordship has been misinformed, and that he will surely see on reconsideration that he has been misled in respect of the actions of the FF of the Society in Manchester, who are not conscious of having entertained any other than a desire to promote his authority, his wish for the good of souls, and the interests of the clergy.

Henry Birch

Greenan to Gallwey
Holy Name,[297]
Manchester.
20 May 1875.

Very Rev. and dear Father,

I was very much grieved and hurt the other day on hearing the extracts you sent from the Bishop's pamphlet. Nothing can be more unfounded I think than the allegations therein contained. I write to say for myself that I have never invaded any other parish, nor enticed people to come and live in ours, nor tried to allure them to our church, nor spread reports against the Bishop. On the contrary, I have frequently been the means of the Bishop getting money; I have often told people who seemed to prefer our church to their own that the absolution of a secular priest was quite as good as a Jesuit's and the like. In cases where I have been sent for in a hurry and have had to administer the Sacraments to a person in danger of death I have asked permission before acting.

Whereas, on the other hand, I have cases noted down in my book when the Sacraments have been given in our parish by the priests of another parish without their having either asked leave, or notifying to us that they had done so. Moreover, it is quite a common thing for us to hear of a secular priest nearby having said the most bitter things of us to the great disedification of those to whom they so speak, and lastly I can bring forward instances in which it is *alleged* that a Very Rev Canon has persecuted people who thought well to come to this church of ours.

In spite of all this, I have always endeavoured to defend the priests and the Canon mentioned. It is almost impossible the while not to be indignant and to show it.

I remain,
Very Rev. and dear Fr Provincial,
Your obedient son in Xt,
T. A. Greenan SJ.

---

[297]   ABSI, RX/5, Greenan to Gallwey, 20 May 1875.

Greenan to unknown
Holy Name[298]
[no date, no name]

The Bishop's allegations are nothing more or les than the common anti-Jesuit Ushaw slang. Canon Carr of Formby – the epitome of that sort of thing, made just the same complaint of our Society, and curiously enough in almost the self-same words. Had I not been told that I was hearing the Bishop's pamphlet, I should have said "all that is from Canon Carr". I remember distinctly … his use of the words 'invasion,' 'aggrandisement', 'respect of the bp' – the very words used by Dr Vaughan.[299] I don't think I ever felt so much disgust in my life, for two hours I felt really sick. The invaders and enticers will be chiefly Fr Jackson and myself – and that for two reasons. First, our districts are contiguous to St Wilfrid's (Canon Toole). Secondly, a good many both of his penitents and mine come from St Wilfrid's and St Chad's (Canon Sheehan). Hence it follows that we are not infrequently sent for to hear the Confessions of penitents that are sick. I have never been in that capacity into St Chad's – yet I have no doubt that Canon Sheehan has me down for a very black sheep indeed. He is intensely annoyed because some of his people come to me for Confession and he has been most rude to them in consequence.

There is a case now in hand which most likely will be reported to the Bishop as one of Jesuit enticement. A lady close to St Chad's, who has been used to coming to confession to our church for some time, says the Canon has shown her great despite [*sic*] for this. Anyhow, she is going to be married, and she communicated to me her wish to have the ceremony at the Holy Name. I did my very best to dissuade her from even thinking of it, and she promised to say nothing about it. But woman-like, to tease the big Canon, she got her sister to go ask him if the marriage might take place down here. He refused her most un-courteously and intimated moreover that no Jesuit should go there to do it either. Nobody had asked, nor was going to. The lady and the gentleman too, are indignant, not at the refusal so much, as at the way in which it was given. They say that their liberty has been interfered with, for the Canon said he could "compel them" to be married at his church, and that "he did not approve of the lady's associations of late" – meaning, as the context shows, her coming down to the Jesuits. I tell your Reverence this, as I have no doubt this will be brought as an instance of our interference.

[298] ABSI, RY/2/2, fragment of a letter, handwriting is that of Thomas Greenan.
[299] Vaughan described the establishing of the college in Manchester, done without his knowledge, "as an invasion made in the night unknown to the Bishop." *The Claim*, p. 15, see also p. 7.

Your Reverence's news this morning has greatly afflicted us. Anyhow, if we are beaten so much the worse for the Bishop, it will be an unlucky day for him.

Weld to Gallwey
Collegio Romano,[300]
20 May 1875.

My dear Fr,

I wrote to you yesterday in such bad spirits that I did not send off the letter hoping that Fr General's visit last night to the Pope would bring better news. It has not brought much. I told you a few days ago that our best friends among the Cardinals advised us strongly not to carry the question to the Congregation. I know this was the opinion of some, but it was one Cardinal of the Propaganda who chiefly produced the impression on Fr General. I now find that they do not all think so, and as on the other hand it is becoming quite clear to me that we shall get nothing any other way, I am urging Fr General to do all he can to carry the question before the Cardinals. My chief fear is that the Holy Father has already some time since decided that we are to yield and that the Cardinal is only playing with us in true diplomatic fashion so as gradually to lead us into a complete concession. His proposal for Vaughan to write a letter to Fr General which Fr General accepted on condition that nothing should be done to render a school impossible later has so far come to nothing and has opened my eyes very considerably. The Cardinal had read to Fr General a draft of the letter, some changes were demanded which the Cardinal undertook to have made; finally the letter came just as it was containing a clear declaration that we were to confine ourselves to parish work while he [Vaughan] would provide for education. The letter was sent back to the Cardinal as inadmissible. The Cardinal answered that he had done his best to make him [Vaughan] change it, but he would not. This shews us what is to be expected there. The Pope does not enter into details with Fr General, but seems glad to get to another subject. In Rome, we hear it said that the question is settled, but unless the Holy Father has really interfered with authority, it is as far off as ever. We are on the right side of the wall and time makes no matter to us, but I fear very much an order from the Pope. It is hard to get anyone here to speak to him for us. The Cardinals do not like to go out of their office because he does not like it. I have called on the Marquese Taluppi but failed to see her. I am going again tomorrow morning. I understand it is quite true that an unanimous petition from the Bishops has come to

Propaganda praying that no young men of 15 or so be allowed to go to any College except Capel's. Dr Smith has enquired at the Propaganda but was told that there was no fear. He will however watch it.

Ever yours sincerely in J[esus] C[hrist],
A. Weld.

Weld to Gallwey
Collegio Romano,[301]
25 May 1875.

My dear Fr,
    You must be resigned to hear that the worst anticipations of my last letter are verified. Yesterday the Cardinal called Fr General to a conference with the Bishop (he would never meet me) and after a discussion of our right which neither could deny they went on to all the little reasons against our school which had been already answered, but the answers to which were never alluded to and finally the Cardinal told Fr General the substance of a letter he was to write by which he unconditionally closes the school, without however removing any principle or acknowledging any fault, and so the matter ends.
    It was a forgone conclusion, and the Cardinal has been playing with us, as I believe meaning us to yield all the time. Fr General could not shew the shadow of disobedience to the will of the Holy See, and had nothing to do but acquiesce.
    I feel sure God will bless his humility and obedience and help us to save more souls elsewhere.
    Fr General himself will speak to the Cardinal about the division of the district and I will get a copy of the pamphlet if I can, but if Vaughan refuses to give me one I do not believe that anyone here will make him do so – if words were of value we should long since have had all we want. Fr General will no doubt write to you on the matter in a day or two. I need not say, do all yourself and tell the Manchester Fathers to do all they can to prevent scandal. This we owe to God. I shall return to Fiesole at the beginning of next week.

Ever yours in J[esus] C[hrist],
A. Weld.

[301]   ABSI, RX/5, Weld to Gallwey, 25 May 1875.

Beckx to Vaughan
Rome,[302]
25 May 1875.

Right Illustrious and Right Rev. Monsignor,

In your letter written on Whitsunday Your Rt. Rev. Exc[ellency] asks me to close our school in Manchester, and makes clear at the same time that you are not moved in this by any hostile feelings towards our Society, but only by the opinion that this school would be an obstacle to the carrying out of one of your plans supported by the advice of the Chapter and made public to the whole Diocese. You declare, further-more, that in this you do not intend to deny any of our rights or privi-leges, nor to exclude the Society forever from the education of children in the said city. On the contrary that, if in the future the need or useful-ness should arise, you would call us to help. Awaiting these special circumstances, and the expressions of good will from Your Exc[ellency] towards the Society, I consent only too readily to your request, because working in the Lord's vineyard in full harmony with the R[igh]t Rev. the Bishops is of the utmost importance, and because I know for sure that it is His Holiness's desire that perfect concord should reign among the clergy in these difficult times, and that any occasion that might disturb it in any way should be avoided.

To that end I shall write to the Superior of the Society in England that the school is to be closed at the end of this month, and to close, I am, with deepest respect,

Your Illus[trious] and R[igh]t Rev. Excellency's
Most humble and most devoted servant
Peter Beckx
Prov. Gen. of the Society of Jesus

Vaughan to Manning[303]
25 May 1875

Yesterday the General and I had a long *abboccamento* [preliminary talk] in the presence of Cardinal Franchi.[304] He complained that the Pope had told him to *combinare* [cooperate] with me and that I would not enter into that view. Both of them proposed that the motive for closing should be for the sake of peace. Against this I strongly protested, inas-much as justice was the real ground for closing, and that the motive of

---

[302] APF, Anglia 20, 18775–1877, f. 309, Beckx to Vaughan (copy at ABSI, RX/5).
[303] Leslie, *Manning*, p. 303.
[304] See below, Vaughan's Diary, 24 May; also Appendix 6, Franchi's notes taken at the meeting.

peace would perfectly well accord with the title of Bismarck, which the Jesuit party has applied to me. Franchi saw this.

Beckx to Gallwey
Rome.[305]
27 May 1875.

Reverend Father in Christ,

After all the deliberations and discussions about the school set up in Manchester have been unfolded, I must give to Your Reverence, by the present letter, the mandate to suppress this school and return the children to their parents.

We have been unable to obtain that a definite period of time should be specified after which it will be licit to reopen this school. It is necessary that, in a spirit of obedience and trust, we subject ourselves to the Divine Will, and commend the whole matter to His Providence.

From the letters of the Very Rev Dr Vaughan and from my answer to them Your Reverence will better know our situation.

When, God willing, the matter reaches that stage, I desire and earnestly command that (if and when the occasion offers itself) all our Own [*sic*] should not speak of this matter unless in a spirit of patience and charity, and that they should diligently avoid speaking ill of the Bishop or Bishops, or display a negative attitude privately or publicly; for that would harm us more than it would the Right Reverend Prelates: wherefore (mindful of the Apostle's warning) let us conquer evil with good, and may God turn our humiliation, if such it is, into His glory and our good.

To Your Reverence I commend myself your servant in Christ,
Peter Beck SJ.

Vaughan to Beckx
English College,[306]
Rome.
29 May 1875.

Most Reverend Father General,

After having received your letter, I am very happy that our differences have come to an end, in a manner satisfactory to both parties. Moreover, in further clarification of what I declared to you during our

305   ABSI, RX/5, Beckx to Gallwey, 27 May 1875.
306   APF, Anglia 20, f. 310, Vaughan to Beckx, 29 May 1875.

conference in the presence of the Cardinal Prefect, I take the opportunity to repeat what I said in my letter of the 16th of this month – that I did not issue a decree to exclude forever the Society from education in Manchester; on the contrary, I did not have the faculty, nor much less the will to do so; but that I wanted to give full freedom to the Ordinary to make any future deliberations that he might deem most appropriate for the good of his flock.

I make this correction, which is perhaps a matter of very small significance, solely for the purpose of greater exactness and honesty on my part.

Most respectfully yours,
with the assurance of my most profound respect, [*sic*]
Your devoted and obedient servant
Herbert, Bishop of Salford

Weld to Gallwey
Collegio Romano,[307]
1 June 1875.

My dear Fr,

I find that everyone here considers our rights perfectly safe as far as the present transaction is concerned i.e. they remain just as they were. I think a little better than they were, notwithstanding the opposition to the Bishop.

Fr General only consents to close the school on account of special circumstances. Our friend at the Propaganda considers Fr General's concession as an act of *summa prudentia*, and that it will do us great good in other matters. We are advised to remain quite quiet now both as to Manchester and London, but Fr General approves of your going on with the memorial about London to be presented at an opportune time. I think that for the general good we should do all that is possible to keep down discontent, calm our friends and make the best of the situation of opening a school where we can. Southwark if you are allowed, if not, try Fr Holmes. There must be lots of boys there more capable of a better education. If you sent the two scholastics from Manchester there, and opened a middle school taking the best boys out of the poor school, you would get some good subjects and immensely benefit the Catholics of the town. It would not be as brilliant a thing as Ackers Street[308] would have been, but in the circumstances it would do more for religion. You have the whole town to yourselves and there must be much good mate-

---

307 ABSI, RX/5, Weld to Gallwey, 1 June 1875.
308 The site of the Jesuit College in Manchester. The identity of Fr Holmes is unknown

rial; I think you would get more boys than in Preston if you do not put the pension too high.

I suspect from what you say about Capel's College that it will be wise to take no step about moving the Theology till we see further how his establishment shapes.[309] I have got both Vaughan's pamphlets and given him yours. His are very bitter against you and me. His last shows how much of his case consists of accusations, indeed I might say of deformation, a great deal of the rest of it is special pleading, though to one who does not know all the case it is very telling. I am writing a complete statement of our case which will be deposited in Propaganda.

Yours ever sincerely in J[esus] C[hrist],

A. Weld.

P.S.

You shall have the pamphlets. I shall send my answers to what concerns me.

Globe Evening Newspaper[310]

'The Bishop of Salford and the Jesuits'

'The intelligence that the Pope, at the request of the Roman Catholic Bishop of Salford, had suppressed the new school which had been established by the members of the Order of Jesus in Manchester, has, says the *Manchester Guardian*, created considerable interest in Roman Catholic circles. It has been known for some time past that a serious question had arisen between Bishop Vaughan and the Jesuit Fathers in Manchester with regard to the opening of a school which the latter has established in connection with the Church of the Holy Name, for the education not only of lay pupils, but also of those who were destined to become members of the Order. The Jesuits carried their plans into effect during the absence of the bishop in the United States, and a number of pupils had been obtained when Dr Vaughan returned to his diocese. The Bishop, who has founded, after great exertions, a diocesan seminary in connection with his cathedral, found himself unable to acquiesce in the plans of the Jesuits, and a very animated and even embittered controversy arose at once. The Jesuit school or seminary would, of course, have been beyond the control of the Bishop, and it was thought desirable to carry the appeal to Rome. The Bishop's case was laid before the other members of the Roman Catholic hierarchy in England and Ireland, and it is said that Cardinal Cullen was one his active supporters. However that may be, the contest at Rome was long and severe. The Bishop laid

---

[309] See above, 16 November 1874, Weld to Gallwey.

[310] ABSI, RX/5, *Globe Evening Newspaper*, Thursday 4 June 1875.

his case personally before the Pope, and he has been successful. The Jesuit Fathers in Manchester received a communication from Rome a day or two ago, and yesterday their school was closed. It has been said, though apparently without authority, that Bishop Vaughan felt the question at issue to be so momentous that if it had been decided adversely to him he would have resigned his see.'

Fragment of a letter accompanying the above[311]

This is tolerably accurate, and is very temperately put for Protestant papers. It is not contradicting of [*sic*] my original version. At *first*, all went well for the S.J., but the Bishop proved a more subtle diplomatist than the Fathers, and instead of enacting the impetuous *role* on which he started, he subsided into the blandest and meekest of men, winning over the General by professions of devotedness to the Order whose pupil he was, and pointing out an [*sic*] *inexpedience* of the Provincial's plan of acting in the letter of his instructions and up to the full powers conferred by the Bull which authorises the Order to open schools wherever they have a church, without needing the permission of *any* prelate. The General for the sake of peace, or what he was persuaded to regard as such, agreed to permit the rights of the Order to remain in abeyance for some time, so that practically the issue is not that the Provincial has any way exceeded his powers, but that the General consents to the non-exercise of those powers for the present. The Bishop on the contrary very greatly exceeded his powers, and showed a total ignorance of canon law and ecclesiastical precedent by threatening to suppress the S.J. when it is notorious that he could do nothing of the sort as long as they had been guilty of no canonical offence, and after all it is from the General in the first instance and not from Propaganda (who are really powerless in the matter, without a new Bull explicitly framed to meet the case) that the Bishop got the favour he sought, not having the right he supposed he possessed, for the right was and is entirely on the side of the Order. I do not suppose we shall have much light thrown on the mystery by the *Tablet* tomorrow, for the cue of his Lordship's journal will be to preserve the directed silence. As to the talk of his intended resignation in the event of failing at Rome, that is, of course, the merest nonsense and it only [would] have entered a Protestant head to mention it, though it is highly probable the informant of the paper is some local representative of the Bishop, who has a passion for appearing in print. I believe his *amour propre* was much stung by the Provincial's going on with the school without waiting for a promise of definite authority to [*sic*]

---

[311] ABSI, RX/5, no names, date or place. The handwriting is that of Fr A. Greenan.

Episcopal consent or non-consent, but all reasonable time had elapsed and the Bishop took advantage of his own wrongdoing as groundwork for doing further wrong. Moreover, it was flagrantly contrary to all the usages of honourable controversy, or disputation of any kind, to withhold from the accused a statement of the accusations, and this the Bishop did in respect to his pamphlet.

Vaughan to Manning[312]
5 June 1875

Having received a telegram to announce officially the close of the SJ school, I set my horses' heads towards England. I am surprised – we are all surprised – to find how completely beaten the SJ is in Rome.

Weld to Gallwey
Collegio Romano,[313]
Rome.
13 June [1875]

My dear Fr

I send you a copy of the *Osservatore Cattolico* of Milan and of the *Voce della Verità*. They contain notices of Manchester. It would be well I think if some one sent them to the *Weekly Register* unless you think them too strong. They are written by Nardi.[314]

Fr General thinks it would be well for you to write to B[isho]p Vaughan something to the effect that there are in his pamphlets assertions injurious to us, and not according to fact and that for the sake of charity and mutual confidence they ought to be rectified and at the same time point out to him the chief things.[315] We shall then see what he says, and if he gives no satisfaction it will be necessary to write an answer.

The Cardinal Prefect has written a letter to Fr General which you will have in which he says the matter is settled *indipendentemente dai principi* [independently of the principles].

He also says that Vaughan has pledged himself to have nothing but Xaverians in Grosvenor Square (he repeated this to me again this

---

312   Leslie, *Manning*, p. 303.

313   ABSI, RX/5, Weld to Gallwey, 13 June [1875].

314   Vaughan commented on these articles, "Father Weld got Nardi to write a very misleading article in the *Voce* after I left Rome, which besides making Howard, Stonor and O'Callaghan furious has had the good effect of making the Pope and Cardinal Franchi very angry. I have written an answer with my name, and let a good deal of the cat's body out of the bag." Leslie, *Letters*, p. 268.

315   See below, 31 August 1875, copy of Gallwey's letter to Vaughan.

morning) and it is really contained in his letter to Fr General where he pledges himself to protect them. We shall see what he does. I shall be glad to know what goes on in Manchester. Fr General thinks we had better be quiet at present both as regards Manchester and London, but I have told the Cardinal we shall present a memorial about both. I have had a good letter from Barry [?]. I told the Cardinal of it, and shall have it translated and put in with the other letters.

He told me to study the question of the University and to propose a project, and he would write to Manning. My idea would be that the best thing that could be done would be to sell the premises and buy others a little out of London, where we could cooperate, and best of all near Roehampton, if you move the Noviciate. He wanted me to ask Manning to let us have our Scholasticate at Kensington. I told him he certainly would not grant it, and that if he did, land is so dear, it would be very difficult. I think a good memoir might be made showing the way in which that place was chosen without consulting religious, as it is said, to satisfy Capel, and its unfitness for youth who will not afterwards be able to live in London, and how inevitably he has divided Catholics by excluding us. This would be useful as a document, but we all think here that at present we shall get no decision against Bishops. I believe the Catholic University will break down to such an extent that they will have to make terms with us, and so we have only to be quiet till the day comes. I cannot believe the Bishops will gain their point about young men going to other Colleges, but Dr Smith promises to watch the case. He has been told on good authority there is no fear of that. If you have anything to propose about the Catholic University let me know. We ought to be able to work together some how, and not against each other.

Fr General has no objection to your contradicting false statements in the newspapers, but I would be careful not to get into a controversy with the Bishop. The two articles I send you are good ... Nardi has done his best for us in all this affair.

Ever yours sincerely in J[esus] C[hrist],
A. Weld

Vaughan to Furniss
Bishop' House,[316]
Salford.
18 June [1875]

My dear Mr Furniss,[317]

I will look in, if I can, before I leave next week and I have no doubt I shall be able to remove the trouble from your mind. Meanwhile there is one consideration of a fundamental character, which ought to satisfy every good Catholic layman – *viz.* that the whole matter in dispute had been fully brought by both parties before the Holy See and has been decided. Would it be fitting or loyal in laymen, who have been informed only of one side of the question, to seek to reopen it, or to declare themselves dissatisfied with what has been done by Supreme Authority?

Wishing you every blessing,
I am your faithful and obedient servant,
+ Herbert, B[isho]p of Salford.

Vaughan to Noble
Enniscorthy.[318]
30 June [1875].

My dear Dr Noble,

Mr Furniss has sent me a letter from you which I presume was intended for my perusal. I shall be happy to read any statement you may wish to make in case the substance of it has not already come to my knowledge. Reading is better than listening where the object is not all oral discussion, but rather implication. I shall be home by the end of the week.

Wishing you and your family every blessing,
I am your faithful and devoted servant,
+ Herbert, Bishop of Salford.

---

[316] ABSI, RY/2/2, Vaughan to Furniss, 18 June [1875].
[317] James Furniss JP, leading member of the Manchester Catholic laity.
[318] ABSI, RY/2/2, Vaughan to Noble, 30 June [1875].

Noble to Vaughan
Ardwick Green,[319]
Manchester.
2 July 1875.

My dear Lord,

I am in receipt of your letter written from Enniscorthy. I hardly know that I have any statement to make beyond what is comprised in my letter to the Jesuits. I have been over forty years in Manchester, but have never interfered in Catholic politics, consequently I have had but little acquaintance as to what goes on; nevertheless I was quite prepared to accompany a few gentlemen in any interview your Lordship might have conceded, thinking that your Lordship was probably unaware of the breadth and depth of feeling on the subject of instruction for Catholic children. I thought moreover with others that the feeling in question could be brought out advantageously only by 'oral discussion'. As however, your Lordship thinks differently, I have too much respect for your sacred office as well as esteem for your person to obtrude any argument upon your assertions.

I remain, my dear Lord,
most faithfully yours
Daniel Noble.

Noble to Furniss
32, Ardwick Green,[320]
Manchester.
[no date]

My Dear Mr Furniss,

Many thanks for letting me see the Bishop's letter. I can but regret that his Lordship has ignored the request for an interview, and treated your letter as though it had been personal on your part.

About a "decision" of the Holy See, that is precisely the point upon which there may be a misunderstanding, which an interview might have cleared up. I have myself information from a very high quarter, not Jesuit, not local, not even clerical – that at Rome they were anxious to preserve peace and did not know the extent of the inconvenience it would be to the laity who are only claiming a right the Church readily concedes. They therefore adopted an expression of acquiescence, saving all the rights of the Society, not in the slightest degree admitting anything

---

319   ABSI, RX/5, Noble to Vaughan, 2 July 1875. The letter is marked 'Dr Noble's reply to Bishop's letter from Ireland'.
320   ABSI, RY/2/2, Noble to Furniss, no date.

but that the Provincial had done what he had a perfect right to do, but for the sake of peace, begged the General to waive that right.

I cannot see any disloyalty (from a Catholic point of view) in dissatisfaction with things as they stand. There may be some misapprehension which might have been removed, had the personal conference been granted; at any rate, we fail to see how one can be disloyal to the Holy See in preferring as instructors for youth those whom the said See has always favoured and encouraged.

The question now disturbing Catholic minds does not affect me practically, my sons having completed their scholastic education; but I grieve most sincerely at the wide spread sense of dissatisfaction that has been brought about – dissatisfaction most intense and, as far as I can learn, all but universal amongst the laity, who feel, justly or unjustly, that practical rights have not been respected, rights which include the privilege of choosing instructors for their children.

I suppose many feel the present complication, as I do, mixing largely with Protestants, Free Thinkers and Infidels, against whom one has had to defend the Jesuits, ever since the renewed persecutions have been set up. From a Catholic point of view this has been easy enough against the enemy. But *et tu Brute* what can one say here where one is vaunted? I can devise no answer in explanation that does not make matters worse.

Here again, something might have been obtained from the declined interview. You may make any use you like of this letter.

Yours truly,
D. Noble

Stutter to Furniss
15, Shakespeare Street,[321]
31 July 1875.
Feast of St Ignatius

My Dear Mr Furniss,
Some little explanation may not be an unfit accompaniment with the Requisition which is to be sent to *de Propaganda Fide* respecting the schools of the Jesuit Fathers which have been already closed.

The names, which were obtained in the few hours' labour which I could devote to it, do not shew the almost universal regret[322] which is

---

[321] APF, Anglia 20, 1875–1877, f. 159, Stutter to Furniss, 31 July 1875.
[322] Louis Charles Casartelli, 1852–1925; fourth Bishop of Salford 1903–1925; at the time of the petition he was a student for the priesthood; he would later become the Prefect of Studies of Vaughan's commercial college. Casartelli commented in his diary for 4 October 1875: "Called at Nobles; discussed the Bishop and Jesuit Question. Saw

felt on the part of laymen in Manchester at the result which has deprived them of the advantage of a College, where a high order of mental culture would have been imparted to their children.

All but *two* out of a large number to whom the document was submitted for their signature expressed in strong tones their regret that Manchester had been deprived of the teaching powers of the Jesuit Fathers, in whom they had confidence, and they acknowledged the benefits conferred upon Catholics by the establishment of the Church of the Holy Name in their city.

They refused their names, because they had been told, and they believed, that 'Rome had spoken', a reason commendable as faithful and obedient children of Holy Church. In the *absence* of such a decision, their names have all the force which attaches itself to the requisitionists who were not so misled.

Although [*sic*] those who have signed are the parents of boys who were being sent to the Jesuit College[323] and of others who would have sent their children thither, if the school had not been suddenly closed.

In my experience of nigh a quarter of a century amongst the Catholics of Manchester, and amongst educated men, not of the 'household of faith,' I never observed a more demonstrative display of regret for the cause which has deprived this City of a valuable Catholic educational establishment.

I remain my dear Mr Furniss yours faithfully.
W. E. Stutter[324]

Noble to Franchi
Manchester.[325]
31 July 1875

Most Eminent Lord,
     As the first to offer my signature to the accompanying memorial, I am requested to inform your Eminence that it has originated in the

---

Cardinal Franchi's letter, which distinctly says that the question should be resolved on a friendly and independent basis rather than as a matter of principle, or words to that effect. Certainly Dr Noble makes a plausible case. He also read me the petition to Propaganda wherein it is disinguously stated that the laity are almost unanimously in favour of the Jesuits." SDA, Casartelli Diaries, vol. 2, 24 August 1875 – 25 February 1876.

323 Comparing the names of the pupils who attended the college (see above, n. 236) and the names on the petition of the laity to Propaganda Fide (see Appendix 8), only two match.

324 W. E. Stutter, a Catholic journalist.

325 APF, Anglia 20, 1875–1877, f. 154, Noble to Franchi, 31 July 1875.

spontaneous action of the laity of Manchester[326] and that in procuring signatures, the object has not been to obtain numbers but only a few from those who have given thought to the whole question and also in their spheres exercise a certain measure of influence and some of whom feel themselves practically inconvenienced by a closure of the Jesuit schools in their city.

I have the honour to be your Eminence's humble servant,
Daniel Noble

Petition from the Manchester laity to Propaganda Fide[327]

"The undersigned, representatives in some measure of the Catholic laity resident in Manchester and the neighbourhood, beg most respectfully to memorialise the College *de Propaganda Fide* with reference to the following facts and consideration.

"They have long been cognisant of, and some of them have practically experienced, the need of efficient Catholic instruction for middle class youth in this city.

"It has for upwards of 30 years been earnestly hoped that arrangements might be made whereby this duty might be performed by members of the Society of Jesus, but difficulties have always arisen to interfere with the successful realization of this wish; difficulties upon which they deem it expedient to observe a respectful silence.[328] It was thought, however, that these had happily been at length overcome when lately the Jesuits opened a school in connexion with their Mission in this locality; a School which in a day or two had secured the attendance of some twelve or thirteen boys the parents of three or four of whom were on the one side Protestant. And the numbers would certainly have been increased very largely in a very short time, but that additional boys were refused admission when it was made known that the Bishop was unfavourable to a continuance of the School in question; and when it was finally closed, the boys already under instruction were scattered, and there is reason to fear that some will be sent to Protestant schools,

---

[326] See above, 27 April 1875, Greenan to Gallwey.

[327] APF, Anglia 20, 1875–1877, f. 162. The petition was taken on 31 July 1875. For the list of names see Appendix 8. For Vaughan's reaction to the petition see below, Vaughan to Franchi, 28 October 1875; Vaughan's Diary, pp. 28–29.

[328] For the opposition of Bishop Briggs and the Manchester clergy to a Jesuit church in the 1830s see ABSI, 14/2/9 Transcriptions, f. 183, J. Bird SJ to T. Glover SJ, 5 May 1839; also Leeds Diocesan Archives, Bishop Brigg's Papers Old Series, doc. 462, William Turner to Bp. Briggs, 1839, regarding a laity request to the Jesuits for a church in Manchester. For a general overview of Catholicism at the time see also G. P. Connelly, 'Catholicism in Manchester and Salford, 1770–1850' (unpublished Ph.D. thesis, University of Manchester, 1980), vol. 3, pp. 61–128, 437–479.

wherein they will hear no mention of their religion otherwise than for the purposes of calumny and derision.

"The Memorialists can have no reasonable expectation that any adequate supply of the existing want can be obtained by agencies outside the Society of Jesus. They have considerable acquaintance with the circumstances of this district, and look in vain for the necessary teaching power. Lay teachers and Belgian Brothers have been extensively tried, but the result has not been the production of a high type of Catholic youth, who in the secular battle of life have in consequence been placed at a great disadvantage, in comparison with boys educated in Protestant schools. Lay teachers, so far at least, have been found unreliable; and parents can hardly be expected to approve of primary education being conducted for English children by foreign teachers who can but rarely master the idiomatic niceties of the language and still more rarely are they enabled to secure the desirable purity of accent.

"The Memorialists have observed with a keen sense of humiliation a very different state of things in the sister-town of Liverpool, wherein the Society of Jesus has a most flourishing and successful establishment. This fact has made them all the more lament the recent extinction of what they believed would have constituted the germ of a corresponding state of things in this City of Manchester.

"Finally the Memorialists would urge upon the College [*sic*] *de propaganda fide* in a spirit of due submission to ecclesiastical authority the desirableness of re-opening the whole question in view of the earnest and all but universal wishes of the Catholic laity,[329] and of what they deem to be the best interests of their children."

Greenan to Gallwey
Holy Name.[330]
3 August 1875

Very Rev. and dear Fr,

The enclosed will explain itself.[331] I cannot learn for certain whether the Bishop has printed a new pamphlet. Certain is it, that it is not in the hands of the Priests generally. Six weeks ago Canon Rimmer showed a pamphlet to one of our Manchester priests, but he could not give any

---

[329] See above, n. 322.
[330] ABSI, RX/5, Greenan to Gallwey, 2 August 1875.
[331] There is no evidence as to what the enclosure consisted of, other than Wilding's reproaches to Stutter. See below, Stutter to Wilding, 2 September 1875.

information as to its date.[332] I will at once forward any information I may obtain.

Your Rev.'s obedient servant,
T. A. Greenan. SJ.
PS
    The first part of Stutter's letter refers to some stern reproaches made by Canon Wilding concerning the petition sent lately to Rome in our favour. The poor Canon was pale with rage and threatened all manner of future penalties against poor S[tutter] for having gone against "his Bishop."

Waterworth to Gallwey
8 August 1875[333]

My Dear Rev Fr,
    Having two rather difficult dispensations to procure, as well as permission to be absent on a Sunday, I called on B[isho]p Ullathorne yesterday. Fortunately the Bishop had just returned and seemed immensely glad to meet me. He granted at once all my requests and further volunteered faculties to any Father who might take my place.
    He said something about the Manchester business. He said that had the Bishops been distinctly informed of our privileges, we should have been spared a good deal of trouble.[334] Naturally, he observed, a new hierarchy is jealous of its rights and guards itself against any interference with those rights, until claims are canonically established. He added you might for our instruction append to your constitution documents explanatory of your actual position as ratified by Rome. The Dominicans have done this and with them we have no difficulty.

Ever, dear Rev. Father,
Yours sincerely,
W. Waterworth.[335]

---

[332]   According to a note at APF, Anglia 20, 1875–1877, f. 428, the first pamphlet is dated 17 March 1875 and the second pamphlet 7 April 1875.
[333]   ABSI, RX/5, Waterworth to Gallwey, 8 August.
[334]   See Bishop Clifford's later comment in Snead-Cox, *Life of Cardinal Vaughan*, vol. 1, pp. 275–276.
[335]   William Waterworth SJ, 1811–1882.

Greenan to Gallwey
Holy Name,[336]
25 August 1875

Very Rev. and dear Fr Provincial,

The pamphlet you spoke of is not in circulation among the priests generally. If it exists all, it will be only among the Canons. A Rev Wood[337] has been appointed to All Saints – formerly of St Wilfrid's, a convert, – I suspect he is to take charge of the chapel there and to be head of the school. I hear that the Brothers are up in arms – but I have no reliable information. I will set out this evening and put a friend or two "on tracks". The said Mr Wood is a most zealous, energetic little priest, but when he was at St Wilfrid's he used to speak so vilely of the Jesuits that he disgusted even some of his best friends. I was told this by the "friends" themselves. Our congregation and parish are daily increasing in numbers.

I remain,
Your obedient son in Xt,
T. A. Greenan SJ.

Gallwey to Vaughan
London[338]
31 August 1875

I have a natural disinclination to approach a disagreeable subject I have deferred as long as I could – a question which I felt must probably sooner or later be put to your Lordship. I cannot now delay any longer as Fr General has written to call my attention to the subject and ends with the words: *haec res est maxime presento momento et differeri sine prejudicio non potest.*[339]

The question is whether there is any likelihood of your Lordship publishing any correction or modification of certain statements in your Lordship's pamphlets on our attempted college in Manchester which seem injurious to the Society or some members belonging to it.

I would be very glad to spare your Lordship the trouble of entering in the question but I see no means of avoiding this duty.
P. Gallwey

---

[336] ABSI, RX/5, Greenan to Gallwey, 25 August 1875.
[337] Charles Walter Wood, 1838–1905; converted to Catholicism at the age of thirteen; curate at St Wilfrid's 1866–1870.
[338] ABSI, RX/5, copy of Gallwey's letter to Vaughan, 31 August 1875.
[339] "This is a serious matter especially at this moment and cannot be deferred without prejudice."

Armellini to Franchi
Rome,[340]
2 September 1875

Most Reverend Eminence,

The pamphlets published by the Bishop of Salford, on the occasion of the Catholic school opened by us in Manchester, contain slanderous affirmations that cannot be tolerated either according to justice or according to charity. St Ignatius did not refuse the offences that were bestowed on him personally; but with regard to slander that concerned the Society, he could not find peace until the damage caused was repaired. This is why, in accordance with the wish expressed by Father General, I dare to beg your Most Reverend Eminence to take a look at the slanderous phrases that I enclose;[341] (ignoring those concerning Father Weld and the English Provincial, that also require reparation).

The wish of Father General would be that Your Eminence, by your authority, might convince the Bishop to repair the unfortunate effects of these false accusations, in other words, he must reconsider his views, to allow us to defend ourselves in the Press.

Please forgive the nuisance that I must, with utmost discomfort, cause you.

Please consider me most respectfully yours,
Your most devoted servant
Torquato Armellini

Stutter to Wilding
Manchester,[342]
2, September 1875

Very Rev and dear Sir,

I called last night to see you purely on business matters for Father Nugent's paper, the *Catholic Times*,[343] with the object of obtaining an advertisement and also for the best information about the decorations, etc. of the church, requisite to giving a report on the following Saturday. I regret indeed, that I obtained no response to my application and I

---

[340] APF, Anglia 20, 1875–1877, Armellini to Franchi.
[341] See Appendix 7.
[342] ABSI, RX/5, W. E. Stutter to Canon Wilding, 2 September 1875.
[343] James Nugent, 1822–1905; founded the *Northern Press* in 1865, which became the *Catholic Times* in 1872. See John Furnival, *Children of the Second Spring. Father James Nugent and the Work of Child Care in Liverpool* (Leominster, 2005).

feel that the newspaper, which I represent, may have suffered from a supposed error which I think I have committed in connection with a certain memorial to Rome to which I appended my name. I am sorry if that be the case.

In your remarks to me you used a strong expression, *viz.* that I had been engaged in "dirty work" by some persons who you supposed had made "a tool of me", and coming from you, whom I have ever held in the highest respect, I feel it acutely; and when I recollect the generous welcome you gave to the Jesuit Fathers, on their second advent in Manchester, I am sincerely astonished.

I have been nearly a quarter of a century connected with one or other of the Catholic newspapers (the *Tablet* more especially) and not many weeks before the death of the late beloved Bishop, I received a special commendation from him for the way in which I conducted my newspaper correspondence, having never presumed to give advice in ecclesiastical affairs, and being very careful and judicious in my reports. These were the words of dear Dr Turner to me, and I can conscientiously say I merited it. Is it likely then that I would be guilty of doing "dirty work" against our beloved Bishop, whom I love with an enthusiasm inspired by his chivalrous character and his zeal for Holy Church? Certainly not. There are reasons why I should especially be devoted to the Jesuit Fathers: by them, more than thirty years ago, I was received into the Church, and I can but be grateful to them. *They would never sanction,* nor would I perform, any "dirty work" on their behalf. Indeed the Jesuit Fathers had nothing to do with the "Memorial". It was the spontaneous work of laymen, in which all alike took their part, and on their own responsibility, and their sole motive a disinterested one – exercising a parental right respecting the education of their children. Indeed so far from opposing the Bishop, it was helping him as they believed, out of a *false position in which he had been placed by others.* This may have been a misconception, but it was the true motive of the committee of laymen. They saw that the Jesuit Fathers were especially acknowledged by the Catholic world to be the most competent teachers of youth; and they saw that *without any expense to his Lordship or any liability,* this would be accomplished in the highest degree; therefore in seeking a greater power than their own to influence his Lordship *to yield what had been conceded by the General of the Society,* appears to me to be an act of filial duty becoming obedient children.

Besides it had not escaped the notice of those who have taken a part in "the Memorial" that there were many Canons, who were not like you in giving a welcome to the Jesuit Fathers, or who lacked "emulation" as you expressed yourself to me on one occasion; *but also for years have been adverse to their coming to Manchester at all, and have looked with a jealous eye upon them. They were not considered to be the best advisors to the Bishop in a matter in which parents had an equal right to be heard.*

I do not desire to enter into the question of privileges which have been accorded to the Jesuit Fathers in matters of teaching, but the *prestige* of 300 years is a good credential to parents for receiving them with open arms as the tutors of their children. My conscience tells me that I have done nothing wrong – certainly no "dirty work" – and as Dr Newman says conscience before all things in your actions. As far as my poor abilities are concerned I have employed them in behalf of Holy Church, and I believe no wealth which the world could give, would tempt me to be unfaithful, She has been my *sole solace*, and however unworthy I may have been in not corresponding to the graces which She offers, I love her with an intensity which my heart and intellect tells me I should, and I venerate her Hierarchy and love her priesthood too well to commit myself to any "dirty work". I hope, however mistaken you may consider me, you will recall terms which might diminish the affectionate regard in which I have ever held you.

I remain Very Rev and dear Sir,
Yours faithfully,
W. E. Stutter

Stutter to Greenan
Danl. Lee & Co.,[344]
Fountain Street,
Manchester.
3 September 1875

My Dear Fr Greenan,

I enclose a copy of a letter which I sent to Canon Wilding for I felt it a great insult he had passed upon me. Whatever he may think of it I know he deserves what I have said as well as to the Canon to whom I allude. I just saw one of the Xaverian Bro[ther]s and I learn from him – (what I heard that they had had notice to quit) – that it is true. This is confirmed by his asking me what I supposed was *the value of their property*. I replied I thought it would be worth 30 per cent more than when they came to Manchester – I find from authority the value has increased 100 per cent. I shall take care to inform them of it. I think a storm is brewing which will not be confined to a teapot!

Yours affectionately,
W. E. Stutter

Vaughan to Gallwey
Bishop's House,[345]
Salford
4 September 1875

My dear Fr Gallwey,

Your note of Aug. 31 has followed me about the country and come to hand only today. I shall be happy to hear from Fr General of any specific corrections or modifications he may think are required and to give them my best attention.

Wishing you every blessing,
I am, your faithful and obedient servant,
+ Herbert, Bishop of Salford.

Gallwey to Vaughan
111, Mount St., W.[346]
London
20 September 1875

My dear Lord,

As we are very busy sending out missioners to S. Africa, I have not been able to attend to the business to which I referred in my last note; and as I hear that your Lordship is suffering somewhat in health, I am even now very late [*sic*] to trouble you with a disagreeable subject. As Fr General however wishes me to lay before your Lordship some of the passages which seem to us to need urgent correction in the pamphlets or statements printed by your Lordship with regard to the Society, I will of course endeavour etc.

His Paternity – directs – [*sic*] if for that purpose your Lordship will kindly furnish me with copies of the two statements originally laid before the Bishops.

Very much regretting the trouble I am causing and begging a blessing,

I am very truthfully your Lordship's servant in Christ,
P. Gallwey.

345   ABSI, RX/5, Vaughan to Gallwey, 4 September 1875.
346   ABSI, RX/5, Gallwey to Vaughan, 20 September 1875. Letter is marked 'copy'.

Weld to Gallwey
San Gerolomo,[347]
Rome.
23 September 1875

Dear Fr,

I write a line to say that a letter has been written to Fr Armellini telling him to see Cardinal Franchi and to tell him that it is quite necessary either for him to write a formal letter condemning the pamphlets and ordering him to withdraw them (of which letter we should have a copy) or we must be allowed to defend ourselves. I have sent him all the accusations which he can read to the Cardinal. Find out what he (the B[isho]p) is really doing at the Xaverians, and if it is *certain* that he has reprinted one of the pamphlets.

In haste.
Ever yours sincerely in J[esus] C[hrist],
A. Weld

Vaughan to Gallwey
Beaufort Castle,[348]
Beauley [*sic*].
27 September 1875.

My dear Fr Gallwey,

Your note has followed me about Scotland – hence a delay. I regret that I cannot send you the printed statements till I return to Salford, where they are locked up – this will be in the second week of October. In return I shall be obliged for a copy of the statements made by yourself.

As I declined the responsibility of the consequences which followed the step you took on the 15th March, so now I must decline all responsibility for the consequences which may follow from the course you are pursuing. While I am willing to give your objections full consideration, I think it well to say that I do not engage to enter with you upon a discussion or controversy, which might be indefinitely protracted, and cannot affect the question which has been intractably closed.

Wishing you ever blessing
+ Herbert, Bishop of Salford.

347   ABSI, RX/5, Weld to Gallwey, 23 September [1875].
348   ABSI, RX/5, Vaughan to Gallwey, 27 September 1875.

Stutter to Birch
Danl. Lee & Co.,[349]
Fountain Street,
Manchester
12 October 1875

My dear Father Birch,

I think it is said in Shakespeare that if a thing is to be well done do it quickly, and I think I have accomplished my task with the speed of a faithful Mercury. I have been at the fountain head for information so upon this you may depend *as true*. We wanted a boy for the counting house and this afforded me the opportunity of paying a visit to Brother Mathias – as I have often done before for a similar purpose, so he could not suspect my real object – or rather the *greater one*. I gathered from him to this effect – the Brothers would not *submit to be under the Bishop* as to their school – and the money wanted for the Institute was much too large for his Lordship to purchase. Therefore a compromise has be affected [*sic*] – and the Brothers are to stay in exact position [*sic*] they have been since they took the school – but promises are held out that the Bishop will rather help them with scholars – that is with scholars for an *inferior school* – (no compliment to the Brothers) and that a high school will be opened on the other side of All Saints (at Cockshoot[350] as I told you) – to which then are to be appointed *Oxford Men*. To make the matter sure I called at Cockshoot under the pretence to [*sic*] hiring the large room – when he told me it was *let to the Bishop for a high school*.[351] Thus the matter is clear and definite. The church that is the new St Alphonsus (already I see in the Catholic Directory) will not hold more than 400 people – and this church will, Brother Mathias thinks, greatly affect the church in Granby Row.[352] But if you look at the skeleton kind of map you will see that St Alphonsus has *been brought from the midst of your Catholics* – and if they come to the church they

---

[349] ABSI, WF/2, Stutter to Birch, 12 October 1875.

[350] Cockshoot was the name of a Manchester-based coach building company.

[351] This was the beginnings of Vaughan's proposed commercial college, known as 'St Bede's'. Within a short space of time two houses in the south-west area of Manchester, facing Alexandra Park, were secured and the college continued its existence there. Brother Plunkett CFX, in a retrospective of the English Province of the Xaverian Brothers entitled 'Historical Sketch of the English Province', in *The Ryken Quarterly* (n.d.), commented on this development: "The irony of the situation was that the following year [1875] the Bishop did exactly what he had forbidden the Jesuits to do, open a rival school to the Collegiate Institute, and that immediately next door in property which the Institute had decided not to purchase." p. 14. For a history of the founding of St Bede's see Snead-Cox, *Life of Cardinal Vaughan*, vol. 1, ch. 8, 'The Founding of St Bede's'; also Martin John Broadley, *Louis Charles Casartelli: A Bishop in Peace and War*, pp. 22–27, 29–31.

[352] St Augustine's.

will have *as far to go as to St Wilfrid's itself.* So much for the zeal and love for the poor. My opinion is they will build *a high school* – as they call it on the *vacant ground bought by Canon Toole*[353] – *if thy can get the money to do it* – and then if *they can drain the Catholic Institute*[354] – and get the whole education into their own hands – the property of the Brothers will be rendered *worthless as a paying school* and the property will then by *force* be sold to the conquerors. I have no doubt the Brothers are being cajoled into the belief that the premium of the scholars *will be so high*, that the parents of the present pupils will not be able to send them to the high school – a false assumption as there are no Catholics who can give *a high premium that is very little above the Brothers themselves. By a process of induction*, I arrived at a conclusion from *half-expressed words – from the manner etc.* of Brother Mathias – that he is not quite certain he will not be "sold", as the cant expressive word is, I have no time to say more now – and you must excuse the hasty wording of this note – but if I get from the meeting in good time after the Cardinal's speech I will call at the house when I can better explain. But if [*sic*] all I have said as to facts you can act upon.

With affectionate regard
I remain dear
Father Birch
Yours faithfully,
W. E. Stutter

Richard Brindle to William Brindle
Oldham[355]
15 October 1875,

My Dear Brother,[356]
    When you and yours friends have read the pamphlet sent to you please return it not later than Wednesday or Thursday, and say nothing whence you got it, as it might compromise me if known … I heard from Thomas this morning he scarcely knew of your serious illness. Are you improving? Did your efforts at dinner last Thursday do you harm? Will Dr Turner allow you any good Champagne? If he will let me know as I will try to get a few pint bottles, which you may take from time to time. They will perken [*sic*] you up. Let me know how you feel.

---

353   Canon Toole had purchased a site near to All Saints for the purpose of building a chapel-of-ease for St Wilfrid's, Hulme.
354   The Xaverian Brothers' school.
355   ABSI, RX/5, Richard Brindle to William Brindle, 18 October 1875.
356   William Brindle SJ, 1824–1880.

Your brother,
Richard[357]
P.S.

Since writing this note I have received this morning the document from you. I had two Belgian clergymen here yesterday – they say that the Bishop's argument in behalf of their brethren the Xaverian Brothers is in truth worth nothing, as they would gladly have given up all to the Fathers SJ on being compensated.[358]

Birch to Gallwey
Portsmouth St.,[359]
Oxford Rd.,
Manchester
16 October 1875

Dear Fr Provincial,

The enclosed letter from Mr Stutter gives, I presume, satisfactory information except as to the question whether the church has already been opened by the Bishop. I had to wait a little before I could find this out. The church is not as yet actually opened. I will report at once when this takes place.

It is reported, I fear truly, that the Bishop has returned home invalided for the present, and forbidden by his medical man to do any work at all, but to give the brain careful rest.[360] Lady Londonderry[361] was here the other day, and told Fr Anderdon[362] that the Bishop when out driving with her in Scotland called himself half jokingly, a poor persecuted Bishop, and seemed disposed to reproach "some of your great ladies".[363]

---

[357] Richard Brindle.
[358] See *The Claim*, p. 11 for Vaughan's declaration of support and defence of the Xaverians.
[359] ABSI, RX/5, Birch to Gallwey, 16 October 1875.
[360] Casartelli wrote in his diary, 10 October 1875: "To Salford to see Bp., who has returned from Scotland no better: his head is bad; needs six months absolute rest." SDA, Casartelli Diaries, vol 3. Shane Leslie notes how, "Manning found Vaughan prostrate, and wrote to Ullathorne (October 15, 1875): '*Private*. I was at Salford and saw the Bishop. He has overtaxed himself for ten years, and since he went at Salford very severely. This last wretched contest has been the last strain. An interval of rest will, I believe, restore him.'" Leslie, *Manning*, p. 303.
[361] Mary Cornelia Edwards, 1829–1906; married George Vane-Tempest, 5th Marquis of Londonderry.
[362] William Anderdon SJ, 1816–1890; nephew of Cardinal Manning; served on the staff at the Holy Name, Manchester.
[363] Vaughan wrote from Beaufort Castle (18 September 1875), where he was recuperating, "Eating, walking, talking and sleep, in fact the leading the most animal of lives seems to be suiting me very well and except a certain weakness in the head when I work

The other day, I saw Mr Nicholson, and he begged me to say that he should wish to see your Reverence next time you come to Manchester, and added some such phrase as this, "one wants to go straight through life, as one goes along." Whether or no this points to compunctious wishing, I cannot say, but I half suspected so.

He then told me he had lately seen the Bishop's pamphlet, and spoke of it with indignation – could not believe that it was the work of the Bishop – that no one knew better than he (Nicholson) the facts connected with the first coming of the Jesuits to Manchester, and he half thought of going to see the Bishop himself.

All this sounds friendly, but words don't cost much, and no one knows better than Edward Nicholson, the difference between the value of friendly profession, and hard cash. If we can manage to work upon his religious scruples, perhaps we shall bring him to, but he is no easy card to play.

Obediently yours in Christ,
Henry Birch.

Brindle to unknown
St Beuno's,[364]
N. Wales
21 Oct., [1875]

Revd and dear Father,

My brother Richard sent me two pamphlets a few days ago edited by Dr Vaughan. I returned them immediately after reading them as he wished them to be returned to Canon Wilding who had lent them to him. He wrote me the enclosed letter today with information he had from the Xaverian Brothers which Fr Jones[365] considered important as regards Dr Vaughan's publication.

Yours truly in Xt,
Wm. Brindle

---

the brain I am feeling very well. Lady Londonderry is staying at some house between this and the Marjoribanks, and we lunched with her and we had it out in part on the Jesuit affair." Leslie, *Letters*, p. 269.

[364]   ABSI, RY/2/2, Brindle to unknown, 21 October 1875.

[365]   James Jones SJ, 1828–1893; succeeded Gallwey as Provincial in 1876. "During his Provincialship he was busily engaged and intensely interested in protecting the exemptions and various rights of the Society and other Religious Orders in England." *Letters and Notices* 22, p. 143.

Birch to Gallwey
Portsmouth St.,[366]
Oxford Rd.
Manchester
22 Oct. 1875

Dear and Rev. Provincial,

Fr Jackson returns from Stonyhurst tomorrow, on the conclusion of his retreat. I must not omit to mention that Fr Fitzsimon on going to see the Bishop's new Seminary, met his Lordship there most unexpectedly, and the Bishop opened up the whole subject of our dispute, and Fr Fitzsimon says that however unwillingly, he was obliged to speak his mind to the Bishop very frankly. He will tell your Reverence details next time he meets you, should you desire it. The Bishop after beginning by saying that Card[inal] Franchi had just written and was displeased at the memorial of the Manchester laity, added, that he hoped there would now be peace.

He also explained his intention of sending you his pamphlets. Perhaps he has already done so.

Obediently yours in Christ,
Henry Birch.

Vaughan to Gallwey
Bishop's House,[367]
Salford
22 October 1875

My dear Fr Gallwey,

I have been delayed a little beyond the time I mentioned. I now send the two pamphlets which you asked for. I will give your observations my best attention.

I may take this opportunity of saying that the mission to be given in the Manchester churches will begin on the first Sunday of Advent, and that, counting on your promise to supply three Fathers for the occasion; I propose that they should go to S. Joseph's. This mission has an estimated population of 4,700 souls.

Wishing you every blessing,
I am,
your faithful and devoted servant.
+ Herbert, B[isho]p of Salford.

[366] ABSI, RX/5, Birch to Gallwey, 22 October 1875.
[367] ABSI, RX/5, Vaughan to Gallwey, 22 October 1875.

Vaughan to Franchi
Bishop's House,[368]
Salford.
28 October 1875.

Your Reverend Eminence,

I am sorry to have yet again to trouble Your Eminence on the subject of the College in Manchester. I have just received a copy of the petition which has been put forward in Propaganda.[369] I think I should make the following brief observations, which could be made in considerable [*sic*] more detail if the matter were to call for it.

1. The signatures to the Petition cannot be considered as representative of the Catholics of Manchester, being persons involved in the matter. A number of the signatures have been surreptitiously obtained, and some of those who have signed regret having done so. Many names are of persons of no standing whatsoever. The great majority of respectable Catholics refuse to sign the petition and the supporting material. It has been carried round by the minor agent of a trading firm, to the great disappointment of his employers.[370]

2. The paragraph of the petition referring to the opening of the Jesuit school is misleading or untrue in almost all its particulars. Your Eminence has a note of the children who attended the Jesuit school – not one of them came from Protestant schools. They are all known to the clergy and are not liable to lose their faith or be sent to Protestant schools. Some of them have returned to the Xaverian Brothers, others are waiting to enter my select (top-grade) school at Christmas.

The paragraph on the Xaverian Brothers is also misleading and untrue. Some of the petitioners who have signed would like to have it believed by the S[acred] Congregation that the Xaverian Brothers are foreigners, with foreign accents and are incompetent teachers and that the population is dissatisfied with them. The facts are, on the contrary, as follows.

1. The Xaverian Brothers are a community of 30 employed in teaching. Of the said community *only three* are foreign, the others being English or Irish. Of the foreigners a Prussian teaches German, a Belgian teaches French in the middle school of the Brothers, and a Prussian teaches in a school at the Cathedral.

---

[368]   APF, Anglia 20, 1875–1877, 28 October, Vaughan to Franchi.

[369]   Vaughan later wrote to Lady Herbert of Lea (24 November 1875), "I hear from Rome that the Petition has not been presented and I am told here they are ashamed of it. I also hear that they won't reopen the question at all in Rome." Leslie, *Letters*, p. 272.

[370]   This was W. E. Stutter; his employer was Daniel Lee, a calico printer and one of the most prominent members of the Catholic laity in Manchester.

2. The Brothers are not such incompetent teachers they are made out to be. They are almost all appointed to teach on a professional and scientific level and they possess Government diplomas conferred for the examinations they have passed. As elementary teachers they should be considered more competent than the young scholastics who have not had this special teacher training.[371]

3. The Middle School to which allusion is made, which the petitioners wish to supplant with a College run by the Society, far from falling into disfavour, is in fact expanding. This time last year it had 76 pupils; at the moment it has 90. The nationalities of the teachers in that school are: 4 English, 1 Irish, 1 Prussian, 1 Belgian.

4. I have undertaken to supply everything necessary that could be needed, adding to the school of the Brothers a *select school* (top-grade) for the few who require it. By acting thus I have myself had to make an outlay of 125,000 Italian lira. An excellent priest is at the head of this school; and I have presently a community of 20 priests in the Cathedral seminary, who will render some excellent teachers, and in the meantime I have taken on teachers who have diplomas guaranteeing their suitability awarded by English and Prussian authorities respectively.

This school will be opened on the 1 January and will as I have said be run by Clergy of the Diocese.

I believe I have already informed Your Eminence that two or three months ago in response to a circular sent out to all the Rectors in Manchester and in which it was asked how many Catholic children there were who were asking for a better education than the one currently given, I learnt that the overall number in the population is not in excess of 26. The Rector of the Jesuit church said that he knew of no more than 19 in the entire city. For these there is ample provision as I have said above.

The other paragraph refers to the humiliation felt by the petitioners when they think of the Jesuit College in Liverpool. They make no mention of the fact that the late Bishop of Salford gave the Jesuits permission to open a College of the Society in Manchester when there was none – they opened it and that after a few years they abandoned it voluntarily because, in the words of the Provincial (see his letter of August 20 1874) "it threatened to not turn out to their advantage." The Jesuits missed the opportunity then, and they have no reasonable cause for complaint.

---

[371] Vaughan is here referring to the Jesuit Scholastics who taught in the Ackers Street school.

Without wishing to detract from the reputation of the Jesuit College in Liverpool I must say that this is a side of this question of which the petitioners are perhaps unaware, and to which they make no allusion.

I do no know whether Your Eminence intends to take account of such a petition or to transmit a reply through my hands.[372] Your Eminence has fully appreciated, in the course of the year, both sides of this painful question, through Frs Gallwey and Weld, and through letters sent on the one hand by Propaganda, on the other hand by me. It seems an impertinence on the part of those who have been led by a few ill-informed persons to ask Your Eminence to re-open a question which was formerly closed. I dare to believe, considering the inferior social and intellectual standing of the greater part of the petitioners and the way in which the petition has been drawn up and signed, that it would be injurious for Episcopal authority if the question should be re-opened due to their influence. This would give to these persons a position and a claim to which they have no right. The general feeling among the Catholics in Manchester is that the Petitioners have behaved badly and forgotten their duty and that a rebuke is needed.

Submitting myself in all and through all to the authority and prudence of Your Most Reverend Eminence, I kiss the Sacred Purple and have the honour to sign myself.

+ Herbert, Bishop of Salford.

Vaughan to Gallwey
Bishop's House,[373]
Salford.
26 November 1875

My dear Fr Gallwey,

I wrote to you on the 15th asking for the names of the Fathers you propose to send to Manchester for the public mission and expressing some anxieties on the subject. Tomorrow we inaugurate the Mission and I have heard nothing. I am pained at neither having received a letter in reply nor a visit from yourself when you were preaching in Manchester a few days ago and might easily have satisfied me. I am informed that the names of two of the Fathers whom you intend to send to the Holy Name were given out from the pulpit on the Sunday you were here. Would it not have been proper to have told me also of the names, as I had asked for them, before you announced them to the public? If all this has been the result of accident or want of thought I shall think no

---

[372]   For Franchi's response to the petition, see below, Vaughan's Diary, 10 February 1876.
[373]   ABSI, RX/5, Vaughan to Gallwey, 26 November 1875.

more of it, if it has been done on principle I must beg of you to inform me that it is so.

Wishing you every blessing,
Your faithful and devoted servant,
+ Herbert, Bishop of Salford.

Gallwey to Vaughan
Lowe House,[374]
St Helens,
Lancashire
29 November 1875

My dear Lord,

I have only today received your Lordship's letter of the 26th inst. The note which I posted on the same day will, I hope, have explained that my silence was not the result either of thoughtlessness or accident nor maintained in any principle. The wish uppermost in my mind at present is, thank God, to avoid causing pain or giving offence. The fact was simply that up to Friday last, I could not complete my list of names. For a fortnight I had been busy everyday writing letters or sending telegrams to secure a staff. I had three Fathers ready but could not be sure of the rest, and I did not wish to send in a list which could not be depended on.

Even now I must ask your Lordship to make a correction in my list and to grant faculties to Fr Corcoran instead of Fr Hayes. At the same time I will ask your Lordship to add or send to Fr Birch to say that the faculties granted in the Cathedral extend to such Fathers as could not be then granted. I had mentioned to Fr Birch the names of the Fathers on whom I could rely and he without reference to me wrote the announcement to which your Lordship alludes. But as I have already said, it never occurred to me to send in any names to your Lordship till I could send or complete a list. It would have been a pleasure to me to have called on your Lordship when I was in Manchester last week but I took it for granted that a conversation would neither be agreeable to your Lordship nor perhaps prudent until the difficulties about your Lordship's pamphlets are cleared up. I think I can say truly that no ill feeling guided me, but simply a wish to avoid indiscretion.

Very truly,
your Lordship's servant in Xt,
P. Gallwey.

374   ABSI, RX/5, Gallwey to Vaughan, 29 November 1875. Letter is marked 'copy of letter to Dr Vaughan.'

Georgiana Fullerton to unknown
27, Chapel St.,[375]
Park lane. W.
[n.d.]

My dear Father,

My friend Madame de Salvo, a cousin of Cardinal Manning and Father Anderdon sends me the following extract from a letter of Cardinal Chigi she has just received. "The Holy Father is very sorry that Cardinal Manning opposes the opening of a Jesuit College in London. He needed the Fathers to give way (about Manchester) in order not to irritate Cardinal Manning. It is these miseries which impede the progress of Catholicism in England."

Your obedient child
G[eorgiana] F[ullerton][376]

Beckx to Gallwey
Fiesole,[377]
20 September 1876

Rev Fr Gallwey Provost Provincial,

By this letter I remind your Reverence of what has been mentioned several times before. It is about the circular regarding our concerns in Manchester, which the Most Reverend Lord Vaughan has written and broadcast throughout the Diocese, at home and abroad. In that letter many things are said that are not true and that are injurious to our Society, and especially to Your Reverence[378] and the Rev Fr Assistant.[379] We have protested against this unfair manner of proceeding, which remains a truly unjust slander, and we have insisted several times that your Reverence undertake the written justification and refutation of the malicious accusations broadcast against us. I well understand that Your Reverence in your time as Provincial, has not found the necessary space to write our justification; but now that your Reverence is free of that burden, I desire and earnestly beg Your Reverence to take this task upon yourself: we believe there is no one better to get this job done than Your Reverence, and I know that in Your Reverence's term of office

---

[375] ABSI, RY/2/2, Georgiana Fullerton to [?], no date.
[376] Georgiana Fullerton, 1812–1885; daughter of the 1st Earl Granville and Harriet Cavendish (daughter of the 5th Duke of Devonshire). Outspoken on political matters, she was a figure to reckon with.
[377] ABSI, RV/2/2, Beckx to Gallwey, 20 September 1876.
[378] Peter Gallwey.
[379] Alfred Weld.

documents have been transmitted that will help justify us and reveal the truth. Hence, I beg Your Reverence again and again to assume this defence of our mother the Society and vindicate her honour and innocence against the hecklings of her adversaries: to this end I pray God to assist and bless Your Reverence.[380]

P. Beckx.

Johnson to Coleridge
111, Mount Street, W.[381]
London.
8 April 1878.

Dear Rev. Father,
   I find that the school in Manchester was begun in 1853. It was conducted for 18 months. It may therefore have been closed in 1854. I am however disposed to think it was closed in 1855.

I am, dear Rev. Father,
yours sincerely in Xt.,
Joseph Johnson

Harper to Coleridge
Blackpool[382]
23 April 1878,

My dear Father Coleridge,
   Father Johnson has requested me to supply you with information touching the points mentioned in your letter to him.
   There were two entrances of the order into Manchester, separated by some interval of time, much as it would seem though you had confounded [*sic*]. The first (about which I know nothing save what has been gathered from reports and conversations as among our own), began with the opening of a School. I think Fr Strickland had to do with it, if he was not the head man. In consequence of the then Bishop (Dr Turner) declining to grant us permission to open a chapel, we retired from Manchester, the Bishop continued the School; and this was the origin of the present school at present carried on at the Crescent, Salford, under

---

[380]   Gallwey did not undertake this task; perhaps this is as well given his volatile temperament and combative instinct. It was Henry Coleridge who drew up the Society's response to Vaughan's two pamphlets. This was published privately in 1879 as *The Case of the Bishop of Salford and the Society of Jesus*. Copies are to be found in ABSI and SDA.
[381]   ABSI, Johnson to Coleridge, 8 April 1878.
[382]   ABSI, RX/5, Harper to Coleridge, 23 April 1878.

the head-mastership of the Rev Mr De Clerc, who has been its life, I believe, since the Bishop took it into his own hands.[383] This is not St Bede's; indeed, *as I know*, the preference shown by the present Bishop (Dr Vaughan) for the latter, has been an occasion of serious war, and has caused that [*sic*] the Belgian priests at Manchester are now among our staunchest friends. Whether Dr Turner did, or did not stipulate, on this *first* occasion, that a chapel should not be opened, I cannot say, but, I dare say, you will agree with me that it is improbable he should have done so; otherwise, why did we retire, as soon as we were informed that we could not open one?

But I now come to our *second* entrance into Manchester, after a considerable interval of time. And about this *second* entrance I have every right to speak; for Dr Turner, the then Bishop, made this second offer to the Society in the person of the *then* Provincial, solely and exclusively through me. I can further guarantee the substantial accuracy of the account I am about to give you; since I have had occasion once before to detail it at the then Provincial's request; and, though the account was written years after the occurrence, Father Moore said that it was an accurate repetition of what I had previously told the community at St Beuno's *immediately* on my return from Salford. Moreover, Canon Wilding would be a witness to some of the most important statements in the ensuing narrative, which could be practically confirmed by Mr Nicholson.

While Professor at St Beuno's, I was invited by Canon Benoit to preach at Salford Cathedral during part of the Advent and the Christmas of 1865. The sermons, as you know, are in print (vol. ii of Sermons by Fathers SJ). The year 1866 is given in the Preface. It is, I think, a mistake; and I have corrected it in pencil in my own copy. On this occasion, I stopped at the Crescent, and the Rev. Mr De Clerc (then, as before, head master of the adjoining school), gave me up his room. One day (as I was about half way through my labours), and I was writing in the room assigned me, there came a knock to the door, and, on my saying, "come in", the Bishop (Dr Turner) entered; and sat himself down at once (for he always condescended to treat with me on the most familiar terms) on an arm-chair on the other side of the table where I was writing at the time; and, offering me a pinch of snuff, said, "Father Harper, I have called to know if you could manage to take a drive with me tomorrow, and what time would be most convenient?" I replied that I should make his Lordship's convenience my own. He thereupon fixed a time, and then he said as follows: "I tell you why I want you. I have long

---

383   This is a mistake. The Salford Catholic Grammar School, to which Harper here refers, began in 1862.

desired to have your Fathers in Manchester, but I have been unable to do so, in consequence of the opposition of my Chapter.[384] But I am now resolved to have you here. I want priests who can treat of the subjects of the day; and you are the only people who can do it. And I want experienced directors for my clergy. There was only one of my Chapter favourable to you; and it is the same now. But I am determined to have it; and I authorise you to make the offer to your Provincial. I will show you the district which I propose for you tomorrow."[385]

I expressed my astonishment at what Dr Turner had just said. "For", I said, "I cannot pretend ignorance, my Lord, of the Canon to whom you refer. It is Canon Wilding. But I should have thought Canon Benoit would have been our friend; since I came here to preach at his special invitation." "You are wrong," replied the Bishop; "there is not a member of my Chapter more opposed to your coming here than Canon Benoit." After this, he added that Canon Wilding knew more about the district he intended for us than he himself did; and that I should do well to apply to him for information. He then left.

On the morrow he came again, and took me in a cab to Burlington Street where we got out, leaving the cab to wait for us. We came to the property which had been bought in that street by Canon Toole, and he said to me, "You will have to buy this property from the Canon. I must stipulate for [sic] this, as a condition *sine qua non*." I think he added that he had been obliged to promise Canon Toole this much. The Canon had originally bought it, I believe, as the site of a chapel-of-ease to his own St Wilfrid's. He then took me round the boundaries of the proposed district; and we re-entered the cab; the Bishop again authorizing me to communicate his offer to Father Weld. He next invited me to dine with him. But we had just arrived at Piccadilly (the corner); and I said, "I am sure you will excuse me, my Lord, for I am anxious, after what you have said, to write to my Provincial by tonight's post, giving him all the information I can. You have referred me to Canon Wilding for information. We are close by Granby Row; and it is just the Canon's dinner-hour; so I shall be sure to catch him in." "Go, by all means", said the Bishop, "and dine with me tomorrow."

---

[384] See ABSI, Letters to Bishops and Cardinals, Turner to Etheridge, 4 January 1853; Turner to Weld, 27 September 1866.

[385] This was in Chorlton-upon-Medlock. Vaughan claimed, in the 'Summary' which he sent to Rome in December 1874, that the Society "chose out for themselves the richest and best locality in Manchester." *The Claim*, p. 26. The evidence Harper presents clearly shows that the district was assigned to them by the then Bishop. This is further buttressed by the following letter from Weld to Turner on the subject of a suitable district: "I feel little doubt the neighbourhood proposed by your Lordship is one in which we shall be able to do good service and I shall [sic] think it will suit us very well." ABSI, Letters to Bishops and Cardinals 1840–1891, Weld to Turner, 2 January 1867.

Accordingly, I got out, went to Granby Row, and dined with Canon Wilding; after dinner we had a long conversation about the affair, the particulars of which I do not remember, and at dusk, I borrowed a black neckerchief and gills [*sic*], and went with the Canon in a cab to Burlington Street again. A large vacant site, directly opposite the property which had been bought by Canon Toole, had attracted my notice when I was out with the Bishop. I left Canon Wilding in the cab; and, in my disguise, sought for the information, and after some trouble obtained the information I wanted, *viz.* that the plot of ground in question was for sale. I then left Canon Wilding, returned to the Crescent, and wrote by that night's post to Father Weld, exposing all that I had been commissioned by the Bishop to say, as well as all the information I had collected. In particular, I called attention to the particular plot of ground towards which my inquiries had been directed. I have never ceased to regret that this site was not chosen in place of the one we now occupy. In my judgement, it was a gigantic mistake, and subsequently events have only tended to confirm the judgement I had first formed.

Here my evidence ceases. I believe that the Provincial came down to Manchester with Fathers in his confidence and accepted the Bishop's offer, determining at the same time upon the present site. But of all this I have no personal information. The next I knew of the matter was my preaching in the temporary chapel, and becoming a sort of supernumerary on the staff connected with it. I wish to subjoin certain notes to this narrative

1) You will see that some parts of this narrative are confidential. I have never given the whole story so fully before.

2) As regards our *first* entrance into Manchester, when the school was established, FF Wm. Brindle, Noble, Brother Cranke, would give you full information.

3) The Bishop never mentioned *to me* the question of a school, either for or against. The proposition was to give us a mission. What may have occurred afterwards in the final arrangements with the Bishop I do not know, because my presence was not wanted at the final deliberations.

4) I forgot to add, that on the morrow after writing to Father Weld, I called on Mr Nicholson, to beg him to procure information as to the terms of sale in connection with the plot of ground in Burlington St.

I hope that the above information may be of service, and remain, with my best Easter wishes,

Yours most sincerely
in the SS Heart
Thomas Harper

Johnson to Coleridge
Catholic Church,[386]
Blackpool,
28 April 1878

Dear Rev. Father,

I think I should be perfectly justified in saying that when Provincial I did not beg that the Society should be in Manchester and promise the Bishop that we should spend £5,000 on the College and having this soon in hand for that special object.[387]

It is impossible for me at this distance of time to answer for every letter which I wrote. I left copies of all important communications with Bishops and others whilst I was Provincial, but I fear that since that time, they may have disappeared.

It may be true that I might have said that there was in our hands a sum of £5,000 which *could* be applied to a College but such a statement if made would not be a promise to spend that amount nor could it imply that it must be directed to a college. I write cautiously as my letter to Dr Turner may be in the possession of Bishop Vaughan.

I am dear Rev. Father,
Yours sincerely in Xt.,
Joseph Johnson

Etheridge to Coleridge
Stonyhurst College,[388]
7 May 1878.

Dear Fr Coleridge,

In answer to your letter of May ... I have to state that while I was Provincial I asked the Bishop of Salford, Dr Turner, for his consent to our opening a school of the Society in Manchester and he granted it without any difficulty. Leave for a parochial church was not asked for because at that time it was proposed not to increase the number of our parochial churches. The £5,000 is a fable and so is the promise to spend that sum on the College. For the reasons for giving up the Manchester school I must refer you to the provincial who succeeded me, Fr Johnson.

Kindly pray for me, yours ever in Xt.,
John Etheridge SJ.

---

[386]   ABSI, RX/5, Johnson to Coleridge, 23 April 1878.
[387]   In *The Claim*, Vaughan alleged that the Jesuits assured Bishop Turner "they were going to spend £5000" on the College they were about to open in 1853 (p. 12); here also Vaughan gave further reasons as to why Turner imposed a compact on the Jesuits' return to Manchester.
[388]   ABSI, RX/5, Etheridge to Coleridge, 7 May 1878.

Porter to Coleridge
St Margaret's,[389]
Edinburgh,
15 August 1878.

Dear Father Coleridge,

I hear you are drawing up a statement of the Manchester College question and I venture to send you my contribution. I was in Manchester the very day Dr Turner gave his final assent to our entrance into Manchester. I was soon moved from Liverpool, where I was Rector, to meet Fr Weld, the Provincial and Fr Seed, the Rector of St Beuno's. Neither Fr Seed nor I saw or spoke with Dr Turner: Fr Weld saw him alone. We all three went to Mr Nicholson's office and examined the proposed district. I remember distinctly that Fr Weld mentioned that the Bishop wished to attach two conditions to the admission of the Society into Manchester. One was that Fr Weld should take over a piece of land purchased by Canon Toole in Burlington Street and refund the Canon the £1,500 he had paid for it. The other was that the new church should be built on Canon Toole's piece of ground.

About the purchase of the land Fr Weld made no difficulty; but he told the Bishop he would decline the offer of entering Manchester if he were to be saddled with the condition of building the church in Burlington Street. His Lordship then withdrew the second condition and left the Provincial free to build his church anywhere he pleased within the limits of the district he had offered him.[390] That same day the site in Oxford Street was fixed upon and the agent was instructed to effect the purchase.

So little idea was there in our minds that his Lordship had made any condition that there should not be a college, that the very same day Fr Seed and I went all round the district several times to look out for a suitable piece of ground for the future college. We decided in favour of what then was a large open field, near the Armenian church which was in process of erection, on Clarence Grove, if I remember the name of the thoroughfare. I urged Fr Weld to secure the purchase, I remember well saying to him, "I do not think the college will be wanted for many a long year, but this plot of ground you should secure now, even if you are obliged to leave it idle and pay a rent upon it." The house and church at Manchester during their erection and for some years later were made dependent on the district college of Liverpool; and as rector I several times urged on Fr Weld and his successor, Fr Whitty, the advisableness of purchasing the piece of ground for a College.

---

389   ABSI, RX/5, Porter to Coleridge, 15 August 1878.
390   ABSI, Letters of Bishops and Cardinals, Turner to Weld, 3 January 1867.

It is needless to point out that neither Fr Weld nor Fr Seed nor myself on that day had any idea that we were entering Manchester under any express stipulation that we were never to build a college.

The first time I heard of such a condition was during the correspondence between Dr Vaughan and Fr Gallwey. It is quite possible that Dr Turner intended to impose the condition and he may have spoken as though he had actually imposed it. But I can testify that Fr Weld never understood such a condition to be imposed and I think the fact of our looking out for a suitable plot of land will be taken by all fair minded persons as a proof Father Seed and myself did not understand the existence of the condition.

The one condition on which the Society entered Manchester was the purchase of Canon Toole's land and about that condition there was not the smallest doubt or room for doubt either on the part of Dr Turner or of Fr Weld.

I remain,
Yours very truly in Xt.,
George Porter[391]

Vaughan to Eyre
Bishop's House,[392]
Salford.
23 September [1878]

Dear Father Eyre,

I told you at Glasgow that I should not undertake the *Dublin*; I have since been persuaded to accept the proprietorship of it, and as I have today succeeded in getting Bishop Hedley to accept the editorship (subject to the assent of the B[isho]p of Newport) I have consented finally to take it. I hope you will kindly continue your connection with it as Censor. I desire this for a further reason, *viz* I do hope that a means will be found to heal the disagreement which exists between the Bishops and the Regulars, or rather should I say to bring about a spirit of conciliation among all parties, and everything which can unite us more together is of a double value in this direction. I am anxious that the *Dublin* should be as careful for the honour of the Society and of the Regulars as you could wish. There is suicidal danger of a repetition of the troubles of former days, unless great care is taken. I should like to have a conversation with you upon the subject, and see what can be done to prevent them.

[391] George Porter SJ, 1825–1888.
[392] ABSI RY/2/2, Vaughan to Eyre, 23 September [1878].

Yours faithfully,
+ H[erbert] B[isho]p of Salford.

Vaughan to Jones
Ince Blundell,[393]
4 October [1878]

My dear Fr Jones,

I owe you an apology for not having yet acknowledged the receipt of your two notes. I have been unusually held at work since my return home.

I beg to assure you that your letter telling me that the Bishops were not meant in that note perfectly satisfied me, more especially as I had heard that you were the writer of it.[394] I may add in justification of the interpretation of the *Tablet* that no less than 8 Bishops took the same view.[395] I do not know what the other Bishops may have thought or whether they had seen the *Month*. I still very much wish to see you. I think we should understand one another well if we met and spoke together openly. We have in our hands to do a good deal together for peace and for religion. I think it only needs a full conversation in the mutual and friendly good relations which I am happy to believe have always, since I had the pleasure of knowing you, subsisted between us soon to put a stop to a danger which really threatens the peace of the Church in England, and help to a better understanding.

There is an article in the current *Month* which cannot fail to do harm and which the *Tablet* would not fail to reply to. There are 4 or 5 things which I could point out as calculated to do harm and to provoke domestic controversy, and which are therefore I think to be regretted.

---

[393] AAW, V.I/7, Vaughan to Jones, 4 October [1878]. Letter is marked 'copy'.

[394] The 'note' here referred to was appended to an article by Coleridge in the *Month* 15 (1878). The article deals with 'The Tractarian and Ritualist Views of the Episcopate'. The note was occasioned by the Jesuits, in L'Estrange's words: "[having] decided at this time to insist on the independence of religious orders in the work committed to them by the Holy See." The note, written by Jones, runs thus: "The danger of laying profane hands on the rights and functions of the Holy See, by an undue exaltation of Episcopal authority, is fully exemplified by the theory repeatedly put forward within the last few years, that to the Bishops of a country *exclusively* belongs the authority to regulate and control measures affecting Catholic education. We do not assert that those who propound this theory mean to call in question the immediate authority of the Holy See; but they most assuredly have used it to strike at the independence and efficiency of those by whom that authority is locally represented; and in doing so they have directly though unconsciously assailed that authority itself." p. 12. Quoted in Peter L'Estrange, 'The Nineteenth-Century British Jesuits, with special reference to Their Relations with the Vicars Apostolic and the Bishops' (unpublished D.Phil. thesis, University of Oxford, 1990), pp. 175–6.

[395] The *Tablet*, 14 & 21 September 1878, p. 331 & pp. 357–8.

If it is not convenient to you to come North, I should be very happy to meet you anywhere half way, if we could thus get a couple of hours together quietly and uninterruptedly. I shall be preaching at St Austin's, Preston, on Saturday and shall remain there till after post time on Monday. I then go to Leagram for a couple of days.

Believe me to be,
Your faithful and devoted servant
+H[erbert] B[ishop of] S[alford].
PS I asked Fr Eyre to continue as Censor of the *Dublin Review*.

Jones to Vaughan
111, Mount Street,[396]
Grosvenor Sq. W.
5 October 1878

My dear Lord,

I fear very much I should be unable to leave London before the 13th. Anytime after that that will suit your Lordship I shall be happy to call on you at Manchester or elsewhere if more convenient.

I am very sorry your Lordship finds motive of complaint [*sic*] in the *Month*. It speaks of matters that have been before the Catholic and protestant public over a long time and in the treatment of which the Society has suffered all kinds of indignity. Our reputation has been grievously injured and the bad name that has been attached to us in *odium filii* is now made use of to alienate the faithful from us. We have put up with this for a long time and now it is, without attacking anyone, without obtruding our special grievances, we but open our mouth to plead for some consideration, we are met with personality [*sic*] and insinuation. I cannot repudiate the *Month* nor advise it to be suppressed that [*sic*] it is not one with the Society in this affair. We all wish for peace. We shall do nothing to endanger it, but I am sure that no one who really desires it will see in our desire to assert the truth an incitement to discord.

I thank your Lordship very much for your kind expressions towards myself. You have always shown me great kindness and consideration. I trust I shall continue to deserve this privilege which I value very highly.

I have the honour to be,
Your Lordship's very faithful servant,
J. Jones.

396   AAW, V.I/7, Jones to Vaughan, 5 October 1878.

Jones to Vaughan
111, Mount St.,[397]
Grosvenor Sq., W.
10 October 1878

My dear Lord,

I thank your Lordship very much for your letter of the 7th. It encourages me to offer a few remarks that may further clear the way for the good understanding we both so earnestly desire.

I fully accept the principle that it is always a duty to forgive and that it is often the best to bear in silence injurious accusations. But a person placed, as I am, in a public and responsible position, may sometimes be bound to vindicate the character of others or of the body to which he belongs, and I conceive that this is my case in the present state of our affairs. In undertaking this it was never my intention either directly or indirectly publicly to refer to the question between us and the Bishops *sub lite* in Rome. Nor did I mean to introduce your Lordship's pamphlets in public discussion. I intended to confine my remarks to such topics as had already been treated of in the public press, and to do this merely in so far as was necessary in self defence. What I have already written to your Lordship and what I now add is intended to show the necessity of this, as I am fully confident that my plan if fairly met it [*sic*] will not lead to discord or scandal but will be a remedy for both.

Your Lordship cannot have failed to notice the reckless way in which questions of theology and Canon Law are frequently dealt with in the publications of Catholics. It is moreover notorious that this last impropriety represents the ignorance and confusion in the minds of some priests and laymen on such subjects; witness for instance, mischievous nonsense written by Mr Petre[398] in his last letter to the *Tablet* on the subject of the immediate authority of the Holy See.[399] In perfect ignorance of what he is saying, he distinctly denies the ordinary jurisdiction of Bishops in his eagerness to depreciate the exemptions of Regulars.

If what Petre says is true, we may with perfect justice be stigmatised as aggressors, schismatics and rebels in withstanding for instance, the claims of a Bishop who wishes canonically to visit our non-parochial churches or Colleges. These terms have been repeatedly applied to us in similar cases, and at present we certainly lie under this serious imputation. Who will say that it is beyond our right or our province to resist such intolerable propositions? What scandal or discord can follow from

[397] AAW, V.I/7, Jones to Vaughan, 10 October 1878.
[398] The Reverend the Honourable William Petre, founder of the school at Woburn Park.
[399] See the *Tablet*, 28 September 1878. Petre claimed that the bishops were the immediate and only representatives of the Holy See's authority to the secular clergy and the laity; religious orders enjoyed exemptions only for their own members and autonomy.

doing so? We do not want to have any correspondence or personal alter-
cation with Petre; we will not plead before the tribunal he has set up for
us. We do not notice his theological exploits as coming from him, but
as [illegible] a place in the Catholic press and representing a peculiarity
as to the mode in which some Catholic priests can dispose of several
questions.

I must refer to one more matter before ending. Your Lordship says
you have been troubled and much discord has been brought into your
diocese, and I cannot but infer that you attribute this to some members
of the Society, I must content myself with saying that if any member of
this Province of the Society has acted in this way it will be my duty to
offer to you the fullest and most public reparation in my power, and I am
determined come what will, singularly to discharge this duty.

I have the honour to be your Lordship's faithful servant,
J. Jones.

Jones to Coleridge
111, Mount St.,[400]
London, W.
12 October 1878.

Dear Fr Coleridge,

I leave this tomorrow for Manchester and on Monday I am to see
the Bishop. I will tell him what I have to say in one interview and as
I do not expect to return to him there will be no need of sending the
pamphlets. I do not mean to debate merits with him. I will only say what
I think about them and what I have a right to expect. I look upon his
late writings in the *Tablet* as a confirmation and aggravation of his past
conduct and you may be perfectly sure I will enter into no hot headed
treaty with him.

You have by now seen Petre's letter in the last *Tablet*. I hear he said
some time ago, "I will sting the Jesuits into an answer." He is now trying
to do so by palpable untruths. What pains me most in the whole affair
is this that I am so far sheltered against the personal abuse which I have
brought on the Editors.

I am most anxious to prove to yourself and to every body else that
I am determined to back the *Month*. I have made this particularly clear
to Vaughan and he has dropped, at least for the present, his request
respecting the *Dublin*, until he makes reparation for his conduct. I don't
see how we can help him in any way.

---

[400]   ABSI, RX/5, Jones to Coleridge, 12 October 1878.

I take the following from a letter from Fr Weld – "I have just read the note in the *Month* (October). I think the *Tablet* has got more than it bargained for: but there is (to me) an unmistakable hit at the Cardinal in the first article p.137, which I think it better to have avoided. It is not a question of doctrine but of personal conduct and I think we should not put our grievances before the public."

Perhaps I am not doing right in giving you Fr Weld's name. The "hit" is not against the Cardinal than [*sic*] against several others and it is not merely a question of "conduct" but a matter touching our rights. I have a few notes almost prepared on the subject of our exemptions, but I cannot send them by this post.

Yours faithfully in Xt.,
J. Jones.

Jones to Coleridge
Manchester,[401]
15 October [1878]

Dear Fr Coleridge,

I had three hours yesterday with the Bishop. I think it did some good for I opened my mind to him with great freedom with regards to the conduct of the Bishops and chiefly as to his own pamphlets. I told him I could not allow our fathers to have anything to do with the *Dublin Review*, first on account of his treatment of the *Month*, and secondly because as we had to deal with his pamphlets and obtain reparation for the injury they had done to us, I could not with sincerity make a compact to [*sic*] which he asked as a sign to all men that we are at peace etc.

I only received Fr General's instructions when I returned here after the interview. As far as the Bishop is concerned I acted exactly as the General directed. I give the passage as it seems exactly to reproduce the Bishop's remark about the *Month*. On second, thoughts I send you Fr General's letter.

I told the Bishop you attributed to him the personal attacks on you in the *Tablet* which you thought very unfair and that I shared your opinion. He denied emphatically that it was personal. In the course of the argument that followed on this I pointed out one expression 'Is it honest'? 'Is it manly'? I said the ground on which these terms were used was admitted to be [illegible] but that so far from any apology being offered the whole article in which they were used was confined [*sic*] and reported in the later paper. He answered that he had withdrawn them on saying that whatever had been written in the supposition that this interpretation of the note was true, "now fell to the ground."

There is a leading article in the *Glasgow Herald* of the 12 on the *Month* v the *Tablet*. I have not seen it, there is also a letter in today's *Manchester Guardian* by Canon Toole in which he goes into the question of our exemptions. He says some things which I underline in the papers I send you and which it may be well to note.

Yours sincerely in Xt.,

J. Jones.

Jones to Vaughan
111, Mount Street,[402]
Grosvenor Sq., W.
9 November 1878

My Dear Lord,

Shortly after the interview I had with your Lordship on the 14th of last month I wrote to inform our Father General of what had passed between us as to the Manchester school pamphlets.

I told him that I had said to your Lordship that I regarded those pamphlets as grievously injurious to the reputation of the Society and that we felt bound to provide that reparation should be made where the injury had been done. That you replied to this that you were not conscious of their being injurious, but suggested that such statements as we considered injurious should be sent to you for consideration.

The Fr General in reply desires me to intimate to your Lordship that we sincerely desire to live in peace and charity with you and with all ecclesiastical superiors. Nevertheless we are bound to conserve the good name of the Society to which those pamphlets, not in one or a few places only but almost throughout, have done grievous injury. It remains therefore quite useless for us to indicate any particular passages to which we object. Our objection extends almost to the whole. We claim reparation commensurate with the injury done, and if your Lordship does not see your way to provide for what it is our duty to claim, the only way open to us is to lay the case of the Society before the tribunal of the Holy See as we are prepared to do.[403]

I have the honour to be your Lordship's obedient and faithful servant,

James Jones.

[402]   AAW, V.I/7, Jones to Vaughan, 9 November 1878.
[403]   L'Estrange notes that Gallwey had already pointed out to Vaughan the parts of his pamphlets which were found objectionable. The Jesuit consultors therefore suggested that the matter might be represented to Cardinal Simeoni in Rome. L'Estrange, p. 177.

Vaughan to Jones
6 December 1878[404]

My dear Fr Provincial,

I have only been back some 10 or 12 days and have been so busy that I have failed to acknowledge the receipt of your note of November 9. I do so now.

I am obliged to you for intimating the desire of the Fr General that we should live in peace and I entirely reciprocate the good wishes. I should not have placed in the hands of some of my Clergy the two pamphlets you refer to had there not been a grave reason for doing so. Nor did I do so till finally I found there was no other way of meeting the reports that were circulated. Had I not earnestly desired peace I should not have enforced upon myself the restraint and limitation which I did, when I gave away a few copies of them. I do not see what I can say in reply to your note. I believe the pamphlets to contain the truth, but I have no desire to circulate them.

Wishing you every blessing,
I am your faithful and devoted servant,
+Herbert Bishop of Salford.

Vaughan to the Bishop of Clifton
Bishop's House,[405]
Salford.
27 May 1879.

My dear Lord,

I am much obliged to you for the information you gave me. Will you kindly have laid before Card[inal] Simeoni[406] the following facts.

1. Having been desired by Propaganda to lay my case before the Bishops in Low Week 1875, I did so in the form of two pamphlets, containing the correspondence between Fr Gallwey and myself and a statement of the case. After reading over one of the pamphlets, I found I had introduced matter, reflecting on the efforts alleged to have been made by the Manchester priests to get the penitents of other priests. This was not necessary for my case. I therefore within a week of our meeting reprinted the pamphlet, suppressing that matter etc., and sent corrected copies to the Bishops. I also took some copies to Rome and kept a few by me. I have printed nothing more upon this case since the Easter of 1875.

---

[404]   ABSI, RX/5, Vaughan to Jones, 6 December 1878.
[405]   AAW, V.1/7, Vaughan – 'copy of letter to Bp of Clifton', 27 May 1879.
[406]   Giovanni Simeoni, 1816–1892; Prefect of Propaganda Fide, 1878–1892.

2. Respecting the circulation of these pamphlets, I have used studied precaution to prevent their publication or extended circulation. a/ I printed on the copies of both of them the words *"Strictly Private and Confidential"* and *"Printed for Official Use"*. b/ Before going to Rome I had not shown them to any persons in the Diocese, except the Chapter. c/ On my return from Rome (1875) I found that the Jesuits had circulated a pamphlet of their own on the case (in Italian), giving only selections from the correspondence with comments of an extremely hostile character. I found that all kinds of false ideas had been spread among the clergy as well as among the laity as to my conduct. I thought it necessary therefore to put some 10 or 12 of the principal Priests in possession of the case and gave them for the first time copies of the pamphlets. d/ So far from endeavouring to circulate the pamphlets I have always declined to give copies of them to the laity. I may have shewn them to three laymen on account of their close personal relations with myself – but to no more. e/ I have again and again during the last 4 years declined to give the pamphlets to priests and laymen, saying that the question was at an end. I have occasionally given copies to Bishops who specially asked for them. f/ Since the beginning of 1876 I do not remember to have given a copy to any Priest, – certainly not to more than 2 or 3. g/ The dozen copies or so given to my clergy in 1875 and the few copies given to Bishops have no doubt been shewn to persons who had been altogether prepossessed [*sic*] against me, and they have done much to modify or change the opinion they had been led to form.

I have now these remarks to make: the first is that I gave Fr Jones in writing last autumn the substance of the above facts, in order to shew him that I had not been circulating the pamphlets within the last three or four years, but on the contrary had used great forbearance under a good deal of provocation. It is therefore acting against my deliberate assurance, when he writes to Card[inal] Simeoni that I am circulating pamphlets against the Jesuits, or carrying on any hostile measures.

My second remark is that I have on three separate occasions asked Fr Gallwey in 1875 and Fr Jones last year to point out to me any statements which they consider to be false, assuring them that, if I admit them to be so I will correct them.

They have always declined to attempt to do this. Fr Jones in his last reply said: "It seems quite useless for us to indicate any particular passages to which we object. Our objection extends to the whole."

I do not see how I could have made any fairer offer.

The third remark refers to Fr Jones' letter to Card[inal] Simeoni. Last October Fr Jones was full of an intention of publishing an answer to these pamphlets, and told me to expect his reply in print. A few weeks after I received a letter from him saying that he had related our conversation to the General, and that "Fr General in reply desires me to intimate to your Lordship that we sincerely desire to live in peace and harmony with you." And he ends by saying not that he is about to carry out his intention and publish but that "the only way open to us is to lay the case of the Society before the tribunal of the Holy See."

It appears then that the General disapproved of the Provincial's intention to publish and said that "the only way open was appeal to the Holy See". The Provincial in now writing to Card[inal] Simeoni is apparently striving to get a plea on which to carry out his intention of publishing. The proceeding I fear is somewhat tortuous.

I conclude by assuring you that I have made every effort and every advance to bury the original case, and to ignore the reports which have been circulated to my disadvantage. It is much to be regretted that a certain number of the Jesuits continue so aggressive a policy.

A public controversy is much to be deprecated on account of the disturbance to peace within the Church, the scandal it will give abroad and the injury it will do to the Jesuits themselves. I shall certainly not incur the responsibility of provoking or beginning it; but if I am bound to speak it will be necessary to make a very plain, full and uncompromising statement, leaving the consequences to those who have evoked it.

I confess that the [illegible] conduct of the Jesuits adds considerably to one's anxieties, and that I have only just strength to get through my regular work.

BISHOP VAUGHAN'S DIARY[1]

Rome, April – June 1875

April 25

Arrived in Rome. Early next morning Fr Weld called to say he wanted to have a long talk with me about the Manchester affair. I replied it is too late; the matter is before Propaganda; I suppose you will obey? "Yes" [He replied]. "But you have not done so in closing the school". "Never ordered to close; but are taking no new scholars" [said Weld].

April 30

Audience with the Pope; I told him that I am being sacrificed by S.J. Explained: 1) My published intention to form a college or develop. 2) S.J. had had a college before and retired. 3) The compact as prohibition. 4) The Jesuit claim to a right (the Pope here said *i diritti sono i miei*) [the rights are mine]. 5) That the Bishop of Liverpool wrote and that the boys in S.J. College[2] are crying victory over Bishop of Salford; and that S.J. and friends boast that they are always triumphant in Rome. (The Pope here said that they had not been to him.) I urged that if S.J. have their College in Manchester it would be like confining the Bishop to Trastevere and giving Rome to them. (The Pope said he had not known the relative position of the two towns, but had thought them separated.) 6) I said I could do no good in the Diocese if I do not form clergy; that my college should be in Manchester; that S.J. had Stonyhurst and other colleges in England etc. 7) The Pope said *vedremo ciò che dirà S. Pietro, ma mi pare che il vescovo dovrebbe esser maestro in casa sua* [we will see what St Peter shall say, but it seems to me that the bishop should be master in his own house]. Said he would send for the General S.J.

May 3

Pope said at the *passeggiata* [an afternoon walk] to Cardinal Franchi, *quest' affare dei Gesuiti è una vera porcheria* [this business of the Jesuits is a real mess].

---

1   AAW, V.1/30, Vaughan Diaries.
2   St Francis Xavier's, Liverpool.

May 6

Mgr Nardi said Fr Weld had told him that I had not forbidden S.J. to have a college in Manchester until they actually established one.

Cardinal de Luca said that in pointing out to him the position of Salford and Manchester and saying that the Bishop might be satisfied with Salford, Fr Weld had not mentioned that Salford was a poor quarter and the middle class and wealth were in Manchester.

May 7 [see the Pope's words, p. 181 below]

Cardinal Franchi says he had 1½ hours with General S.J. who was *montato* [had a high opinion of himself]. The Cardinal gave him the alternative of a *lotta* [a struggle/fight] with all the Bishops or of closing the college at my request. He said he did not wish the first, and would reflect on the second. Franchi mentioned this to Cardinal Patrizi, who exclaimed *macché riflettere, non c'è bisogno di riflessione in una tale proposta!* [Reflect, you must be joking! There's no need for reflection on such a proposal!] Cardinal Franchi told him that the Bishop of Salford was *inflessibile* [inflexible] in the matter, and that if I could not organise the Diocese I would send in my *rinuncia* [resignation]. Cardinal Franchi suggested that I must write [to] General S.J. a letter, requiring him to close; said he had come with the Pope to the conclusion that this was the proper way to let the S.J. withdraw with honour and *decoro* [dignity] from their position. I still urged that it should be closed on the ground that in the dispute between the Bishop and S.J. the Pope had settled the matter. He replied, "No, the Pope does not wish to be brought into it;" he had said, "This business annoys me; see that it is settled so that the Jesuits close the College." I objected that S.J. would now say that they closed on a *petition* from the Bishop. He replied, "You are not to make a petition, but to insist on the closing – *un intimo* [*sic*; an order] – but avoid the question of 'privilege.'"

May 12

I wrote my letter; and today, May 12, read it to Franchi. He said it was *un programma degno, magnifico, parole d'oro* [a dignified, magnificent statement, golden words]; that he would read it to the Pope; that if General (who had not called on him since his conversation on Sunday) did not accept it, *daremo corso all' affare* [we'll get matters moving], "you may consider the matter as settled etc". I told him – and repeated it – that the sentiments of good will expressed in the letter were common to the whole Hierarchy; and that the struggle arises from the facts: 1) That for 300 years the S.J. have been independent all over England without Bishops or a Hierarchy. 2) That they originally had opposed the nomination of bishops and then that of the Hierarchy. 3) That having now 13 centres[3] which are forming their institution, they (S.J.) are necessarily diminished and reduced to a secondary position as an auxiliary body. Human nature rebels against this, and hence we are subject to some such trials and rebellion. Cardinal Franchi says the story is spoken of all over Rome. S.J. is everywhere, and I am pointed out as the enemy of the Society. Princess Chigi on hearing my name announced asked him if I were not the enemy of the S.J.; Franchi said he replied that I was very good etc., and not an enemy etc.

Cardinal Franchi expressed a hope that all was settled; that S.J. did not wish their privileges to be discussed etc. I told him that they now felt their hands were not clean; they want to wash them and to return later to their plan of acquiring the use of the rights and privileges they claim.

May 13
The Holy Father

At the Vatican this morning the Pope spoke to me on coming out of his room. Fr Raneira S.J. was behind me and says he heard it all. The Pope said, *mi rallegro con voi di tutto cuore. Vengo da leggere il vostro foglio magnifico, mi ha dato un vero piacere. Questo va bene un bellissimo programma.* [I congratulate you with all my heart. I have just read your magnificent paper; it has given me great pleasure. This is a very fine statement]. Two or three Cardinals, Oreglia, de Luca and Chigi spoke to me as though they had heard or seen the letter with much pleasure. De Luca said he had read my pamphlet and thought it ought to be translated into Italian.

Fr Ranini was present and heard the Pope use these words and went off and spoke about them to Howard.

May 14
Cardinal Franchi

Said he understood our position in England and went through as though it were his own what I had said to him on the 12th. The other Cardinals did not see it so clearly. He read over my letter, asked if he might show it to General S.J. next day, which I agreed to. Asked if I would mind meeting General S.J. at Propaganda, I said most willingly; or I would call upon him myself provided always he first agreed to close the college. I said I had refused Fr Weld a conversation on the subject when he called on me the morning after my arrival until the college was closed. Franchi said I was quite right.

---

3   Vaughan is here referring to the thirteen dioceses created at the restoration of the Hierarchy in 1850.

Franchi objected to an expression in my letter that: "privileges to limit jurisdiction of Ordinary etc. need be clear without doubt etc;" suggested the correction I have adopted *viz* that this cannot interfere with the interests of the Diocese, which he said was a stronger general principle. I urged that it would not be enough; that they should close upon the letter if Propaganda did not urge the principle he had just referred to; more especially as Rome was unwilling to examine and pronounce on the privileges in question. He said they were unwilling on account of the public use that could be made of such a discussion. But that he would give them as a rule in his answer to their letter that they are to attempt nothing but in accord and agreement with the Ordinaries.

I again insisted on the necessity of this. He said the General complained that while they were persecuted by enemies of Church [*sic*] the Bishops were becoming unwilling to use them and were opposed to them. He was afraid that Gladstone[4] would get hold of this Salford affair and bring it as proof that not only Protestants etc. but the Bishops were opposed to S.J. But the Cardinal seemed to have pointed out to him that they were themselves answerable for what had happened; and indeed he said that the General did not attempt to defend what had been done in England by the Provincial. Franchi asked whether I should object to meet [the] General at Propaganda I said oh no, nor anywhere else. If he had agreed to close the College I would call on him myself and deliver the letter as I have no ill feeling. But before meeting any of them they must agree to close. This he said had been agreed on.

May 16

Conversation with Cardinal Franchi about draft of my letter, which he had read to General S.J. and Armellini. They both ended by expressing satisfaction with it. Franchi took out all the parts in which 'prohibition' and other words indicative of dual authority came in but without saying that it was on this account but urging that the S.J. wished for a sentence that I would, if population increased and circumstances changed, give them leave to have a College. Franchi urged this. I refused unless every Bishop were to be called on for a similar declaration. I shewed him how falsely I had been charged with saying they shall "never" have a College in Manchester and read from my *Reply to Fr Gallwey*.[5]

I observed that his goodness might be deceived by his mild words – that I had to deal with S.J. in Salford. That I did not make any promise which might be misunderstood, that one S.J. had spoken to me about

---

[4]   William Ewart Gladstone 1809–1898; Prime Minister 1868–74, 1880–85, 1886 (Feb.–July), 1892–94. He wrote a number of anti-Catholic works after 1870.
[5]   Vaughan's second pamphlet: *The Bishop of Salford's Reply: Uncanonical Reopening of the Jesuit College and Summary of the Whole Case.*

making war with Bishops and talked of Bishops as of enemies etc.
I would not mention his name; that this was not the first instance of
aggression. There was that of Brompton and others etc. They had a plan.
I urged that his letter to S.J. and the one to Bishops should be most
clear and unmistakeable, that it was on this condition that I consented
to softening down my letter, that all depended on it etc. He assured me
again and again that he would say they could not act but in harmony
with Bishops; that their privilege does not apply to England, that it is
not opportune to exercise the privileges, but that it is certain that if they
exist they do not apply to England. He said I should see what he wrote
before it was sent. He said that both General S.J. and Fr Armellini, who
was with him, said to him that they were perfectly satisfied with the
draft of my letter read to them by His Eminence, that the General took
him by the arm and cordially thanked him.

Cardinal Cullen. The same day, being in doubt as to the strength and
sufficiency of my proposed letter to S.J., I read it to Cardinal Cullen
and Mgr. Marty. They were both much pleased, said *ponti d'oro per
il nemico che fugge* [take full advantage of an enemy on the run] is
the rule. Cardinal Cullen said he had just seen Franchi who had told
him all about it, and had said S.J. wanted a letter they could publish
or shew. Cullen laughed at the idea of my preferring S.J. to any other
Order, which the word *specialmente* in last but one paragraph implied.
I have since changed the word to *certamente*, which withdraws the idea
of preference. He said the withdrawal of the words *ripetute proibizioni*
[repeated prohibitions] made no matter, and so of other withdrawn
phrases, but said that the sentence that *l'esercizio dei privilegi deve
essere a vantaggio non a pregiudizio della Diocesi* [the exercise of privileges should be to the advantage, not the prejudice of the Diocese] was
very important and left the Bishop judge.

General C.SS.R. In the afternoon, being anxious as to the sufficiency
of the letter in respect to the position of Episcopal authority maintained
in it, I read it to the General C.SS.R.[6] and Fr Douglas. They like my
first draft best, but would suggest the addition of the word *permettere*
before *sanzionare* [sanction], but finally thought that *sanzionare* was in
one respect sharper, in as much as the want of Episcopal sanction was
to be the reason for closing the College. The General gave it credit for
being *molto moderato* and well argued. I suggested that in my reply to
the answer of S.J. I might add such expression as I might think necessary. They both advised me to be quite satisfied with the letter.

6   Nicolò Mouron.

May 17

<u>The General S.J.</u> Said Mass over body of St Ignatius, as I have done several times during the last week, and carried the letter[7] for the General on my heart under cassock at the time. Saint Ignatius will whip his own sons if they need it – if they don't deserve it, then I am mistaken, and should not wish them to catch it, as they are doing. Took the letter to the General. He began by saying do you wish us to leave Manchester; I said you have a parish, I have not asked you to leave that. I spoke to him from my notes, made on a visiting card, as follows. 1) We have suffered much from imprudence of the Society in Manchester – great injury done – (he thought the Society also had suffered much.) I replied it was by their own act; they were aggressive, their penitents and pious women had chatted all over England; called me the Bishops' Persecutor of S.J. etc. That I had avoided speaking to most of the clergy in my Diocese but the Chapter and priests living with me and had spoken to none of the laity, whereas S.J. had been most imprudent. (He thought others besides S.J. had spoken – he was told so.) 2) I said it arose from two persons principally: Gallwey, of whom I said at his appointment that he would bring the Society into trouble, he was *irruente* [impetuous] imprudent, full of piety, work and mortification, but *irruente* [impetuous] etc. (*Ah, è Irlandese, gli falta un poco la calma*) [Ah, he's Irish, he lacks calm a little] – but I don't know him, never saw him" etc. [said General]; Weld, was "*troppo fino*" ['too refined']; I described his way of acting etc. Said I was sure these things would not have happened in the Italian Province, or if he had known them all; I was certain he had been deceived. He said that Weld was very good, to which I assented, but added *è troppo vivo, ha troppo zelo* [he is too animated/lively, he has too much zeal] and repeated several times *troppa fretta* [in too much of a hurry] adding *non in commotione Dominus* [the Lord's not in a hurry]. 3) I then began by the fact that they had once been in Manchester and had left it. (He knew that and condemned their leaving; there had been something with the late Bishop that they were not to have a Church; though this was not according to their rights, they had yielded and then left, but had done wrong to leave.) I then explained how the Bishop had taken up the abandoned school; that it was under the Xaverian Brothers (he asked who they were; knew nothing of them); I told him they were much respected; a teaching body; had Government diplomas or certificates for teaching; that if they could not teach everything I could supply the deficiency; that a Jesuit College established close by would injure them seriously. (He represented that a College S.J. would give them many vocations; spoke of their need of *English* subjects for colonies etc.

---

[7]   His letter dated 16 May 1875 (Whitsunday). ARSI, Prov. Anglia 1014–IV.4

and that it would supply the Diocese with vocations.) I answered at length: 1) That the Diocese with one third priests not of it, needed priests; that on this account I had determined in beginning of my episcopate with Chapter [*sic*] to develop the Manchester school, that if their [*sic*] were vocations for S.J. they should have them. (He replied *questo è un argomento a pari* [this is an equally valid argument] and admitted its force.) I then went on to say that Fr Gallwey had urged this, and quoted his letter, and said that one of the secular priests he named had been a boy at Liverpool College [*sic*] had had influence brought to bear while a boy to go to a Jesuit College, and when a sub-deacon had been offered by a Jesuit facilities for getting rid of mission oath if he wished to join S.J. (The General said he could not approve of that) I said these are the difficulties made by imprudent though zealous members of your Order, and you suffer on account of them. I said I was not able to withdraw in the least from my final resolution to have the education of the Manchester middle class. (He thought the class might increase with time etc.) I said it may increase or decrease with trade, it is mainly all Irish (here he interposed, expressed surprise, said he was not aware of that, and seemed to refer to his former statement that they wanted *English* subjects). I said S.J. should be content with Stonyhurst (but he said at Stonyhurst *sono forestieri*) [they are foreigners] I said he was evidently mislead [*sic*] and said many foreigners among the philosophers, but the great mass of the boys were our best class English; you have there most of the rich of my Diocese etc., should be content with your share and not covet Manchester. (He asked whether Stonyhurst was in my Diocese) I replied it was, and added you have within ¾ of an hour by rail Liverpool where you have another great College. (He said he did not know *non mi hanno detto*) [they have not told me] that Liverpool was so near to Manchester – he then spoke of the number of vocations supplied by their College in Liverpool to the Secular Priesthood. I replied that the Bishop of Liverpool[8] was far from satisfied with the result; the S.J. takes all the best; some few may become seculars but the effect of your College is to take all the best for S.J. (he again said *non mi hanno detto* that Liverpool was so near Manchester.) He said they had told him that I should not make much difficulty about their founding a College in Manchester, that after a time I should be glad of it, when I saw the good it was doing. I replied it is quite evident that you have been *ingannato* [deceived]; you never would have acted, as the persons about you have done – they are exposing the Society to great evils by their conduct etc. He replied that they had told him, but of course he did not know otherwise, that I should yield and not make much difficulty, and added *vi è*

---

8   Bernard O'Reilly, 1824–1894; Bishop of Liverpool 1873–1894.

stata troppa fretta) [there's been too much hurry there]. He then spoke of their privilege to found colleges; said Fr Weld had consulted some of the Cardinals; that before Paul III they had received the privilege, and that Fr Weld told him that Pius [VII] in [the] Bull of Restoration had revived that privilege, but he added *bisogna avere molto riguardo ai vescovi ed alle necessità della Diocesi* [it's necessary to pay great attention to the bishops and to the needs of the Diocese]. I then referred to the second opening of the College; that Fr Gallwey had informed me that he had received a telegram from Rome which cancelled his promise to me about closing and empowered him to reopen. He said that he had not heard of that, that Fr Weld was in Rome for three weeks, [and] very active; but he had not heard of this. I added that Propaganda had not sent the telegram, and that I had demanded to see the evidence, that had it been from Propaganda I should have bowed, but not otherwise. He said "you had a perfect right to see the evidence, *ma io non sapevo*") [but I was not aware] etc.). I again said you have been deceived. I professed my good will to the Society; that I would act with them if they would behave well with me. He said it was very necessary to show mutual signs of good will. I urged much the necessity of his recommendation of prudence to his subjects, that peace would depend on their good behaviour, etc. That if they gave no reason for complaint I would act towards them as though there had been no breach. I said that I wished for a speedy answer to my letter, as my movements would depend on it. He said this was natural and he would see Fr Weld, but urged that the school should remain open till [the] holidays. I said, "till today, then, because these are the Whitsun holidays." He did not know that, but asked when the longer holidays would be. I said in two or three months. He wished it to remain open till the mid-summer vacation. I said I could not consent, that it was imperative to close at once and finish with the whole subject, that it would now be a three days' wonder, and that otherwise a wound would be kept open and increase for three months; that I could not return to the Diocese till I had heard from Salford that the college was actually closed; that I should act to S.J. with all kindness, as I had done in the past, but that I must insist, if we were to have peace, upon immediate closing – that this week was a good opportunity. He said he would not answer then, but would reflect and consult Fr Weld who was *tanto fino* [so refined]. I then left saying it was essential to close at once.

The Holy Father.

The same day (17 May) went to the Vatican. The Holy Father coming out said *dunque tutto sta concluso, ho letto vostro foglio. Deo gratias.* [So then, everything is over, I have read your paper. Deo gratias.] I replied, "yes, Holy Father *purchè non mettano un indugio*" [as long as they don't make a delay] etc. and he went on. Afterwards in the library when he had sat down he called me and said *che vuol dire l'indugio?* [what does a delay mean?] I replied "I fear from what I have heard this morning they wish to delay closing for some months till the vacation". *Perche?* [why?] Because *pensano ad un certo decoro, ma questo sarebbe lasciar la piaga aperta per tutto quel tempo, seguirerebbe partiti, farebbe parlare per tutto quel tempo. Meglio per mi, meglio per loro di chiedere adesso subito – parlerà la gente per tre giorni invece di parlare per tre mesi e allora sarà tutto finito.* [Because they are thinking about some dignity, but this would be to leave the wound open for all that time, factions would follow, it would make people talk for all that time. Better for me, better for them to close now straightaway – people will talk for three days instead of three months and so everything will be over.] The Holy Father said *capisco, va bene, vedremo, vedremo,* etc. [I understand, that's good, we'll see, we'll see.]

    Cardinal Oreglia during *passeggiata*, spoke of hostility of Bishops to S.J. and Regulars. I denied it, but spoke of their encroachments – necessity to found works of the Hierarchy; position of S.J. [and] its conduct in Manchester. He referred to the University question in London; I said the Cardinal had publicly invited them to found their own colleges in other parts of England; that Kensington was a college of the Bishops – just as the Apollinare was a secular priest's college; and the Jesuits might found theirs and have it to themselves, like a Collegio Romano only not in London because it was preoccupied. England large enough, but they wish always to be first, in best places etc. Oreglia said London was as big as a Pontifical State; but I observed the population was not Catholic – then said he it must be converted; very well, when it is converted there may be parity and then S.J. may have a College. Sacconi spoke of hostility to Regulars, or S.J.; need of peace, etc.

    The fact is so long as Weld is allowed to go abroad as an *imbroglione* [a cheat/trickster] he will do no end of mischief. All these reports etc. he is pushing, he and his friends.

18 May
Mgr Agnozzi.

    Called on Agnozzi about the Jesuit proposal of delay. He was at once all against it. I said it looked like a *arrière pensée* to keep the College; he would tell one of them it must be closed at once, this week. [I] told him I had found the General had been *ingannato* [deceived]. He spoke of my letter as *magnifico* etc., and as counteracting the impression made that the Bishops are opposed to Religious Orders. I then went into the whole subject with him as I had done with Cardinal Franchi [on] 10 May. He said, but Religious have not enough to do sometimes. I represented that if they would take the poor and help the Bishops they would have plenty to do. That the Bishops complain only seldom, are very patient, but some things they must disapprove and feel.

As an instance, I said S.J. exclusive and selfish, e.g. the effect of Farm St., is to draw from the parishes all the rich; notorious that the Jesuit followers cease to care much for the Diocesan works. They had done little or nothing to help the archbishop in rescuing and maintaining 2,000 poor children, described the contact with board – the monthly correspondence etc. etc. But Farm St had no special friendliness to this. Compared Farm St with Horseferry Road – the wealth and attractiveness of one and the squalor of the other – a Jesuit had said they did not improve or build because it belonged to Diocese. This Agnozzi took up and said he would speak to General about it. I then told him of their asking names of penitents in Confessional: of which work place, club, at church at Manchester. He said this used to be true against S.J. years ago, and spoke strongly against it. Wondered that the General did not take it up, said he should speak to them etc.

20 May
Cardinal Franchi and Pope.

Went to the *passeggiata* at the Vatican; before the Pope came out Cardinal Franchi said that the General S.J. had had an audience the night before. The Pope had asked him if he were pleased with my letter; said it was very good, that he had himself read it. The General said he was pleased with all but one point, which he wished modified – *viz* the permanent exclusion of the Society from teaching by Bishop saying that he reserves to himself the teaching of the *mezzo ceto* [middle class] in his own city. The Pope said *ma diamine, mi pare che il vescovo dovrebbe* [? illegible] *per qualche cosa e giudice* [but goodness me, it seems to me that the bishop should be (illegible) for some things and the judge] – in other words the Pope and Cardinal Franchi quite agreed with him in thinking that the Bishop might reserve this to himself if he thought fit.

Franchi said Antonelli (who had taken up the matter) and [illegible] who was with him, with whom he had just been speaking, were both pleased with the letter and said the actual solution was the only way out of the difficulty, and thoroughly accepted the solution as the best and only one. Franchi said they [S.J.] had told him that the Xaverians were incompetent to teach the higher classes, and said they understood I would found another college besides that of the Xaverians and that close to their parish. I said that was as it seemed to me no matter of the Jesuits (which he admitted) and added that my intention was to supplement the Xaverian teaching with that of my own students or young priests and with that of others as might serve. He added you reserve to yourself to judge the question whether S.J. may ever in the future have a college or part in the education of Manchester. I said certainly, and that I must retain the same right and position as any other Bishop. Franchi thoroughly supported my reserving *mezzo ceto* of Manchester, while S.J. had Stonyhurst; and both he and [the] Pope referred to the fact of their having Stonyhurst. Afterwards I called on Antonelli who said he was quite satisfied with the solution. I explained to him that the necessities of the Hierarchy had limited S.J. etc; this he understood as inevitable and said it must be so. And I spoke of peace and union.

Pecci[9] spoke of the subject and I told him of the position; he also accepted the position and spoke of peace. Monaco[10] also implied that he was satisfied, and he also as usual spoke of the advantage of the Religious Orders – which I also admired when they were in their place. Franchi said that neither Armellini nor the General had spoken to him about a delay and that he therefore had not suggested it. I said they will perhaps put it into their reply to me. He asked whether I had told Cardinal M[anning] of the solution, I said yes, that it was near solution and that all the Bishops would be equally glad – yes said Franchi because they see that this was a plan of attack – it will make S.J. more careful in future.

The Pope. (**May 7**) [see also p. 201 above]

The Pope coming out of the room said, *il suo Vescovo di Salford sta sub iudice, colla spada di Damocle sopra la testa* [The Bishop of Salford is *sub judice*, with the sword of Damocles over his head] to which I replied, *Questo va bene, S. Padre, perché sta nelle mani di Pietro.* [That's good, Holy Father, because it is in Peter's hands]. This showed how he was interested in the question and understood its importance.

20 May

Cardinal Patrizi.

Told him of the Jesuit affair, of which he had been informed; he agreed that I had been quite right in the line I had taken, and that I had a right to have a college in Manchester. He was glad the matter had ended without it going before the Protestant public; said Jesuits should act in harmony with Bishop.

Walked with Mgr Rinaldini.

1) He said was [*sic*] pleased with the *mezzi termini* [the compromise.] Of course, what Roman would not be! Said that when S.J. had the Roman seminary all the best vocations went to S.J. and Roman clergy was being left without subjects. 2) Said that Church could not be dedicated to Sacred Heart theologically. All the Consultors at Congregation

---

9   Cardinal Vincenzo Gioacchino Pecci, 1810–1903; the future Leo XIII..
10 Cardinal Raffaele Monaco La Valletta, Propaganda Fide.

of Rites, with one exception, so decided; Cardinal Patrizi strong in the
same sense. P. Ramini (unknown to Rinaldini) urged the others that "we
have not been heard" – "but who are you"? he said, and then found out.

3) He said the *missa pro populo* is not binding on Bishops as on
parish priests; Congregation of Council praised a certain abbot Mullino
– a friend of Rinaldini – for saying it on Sundays and feasts, but added
that *de obligatione non constat.* Rinaldini told Barnabo,[11] who was
equally surprised, and ordered him to make a formal enquiry of the
Congregation of the Council. The Council gave privately several reasons
why Bishops not so bound as PPs; set all the Consultors to work – and
never gave a final decision. So that the obligation stands now as *a non
constat.*

May 21
Fr Weld.

He said there is room in Manchester for five or six colleges; that
there would never be peace until there was a Jesuit College there –
not by action of S.J. but in spite of them on account of the desire the
people have for a college S.J; that no one in Rome had said S.J. had
been wrong in the matter of a college in Manchester, their conduct had
been rather approved; they had their rights and privileges; that he never
had any contact with the late Bishop, but would never have founded a
college during his lifetime on account of his expressed wish upon the
subject; that the fact of their having Stonyhurst, a college at Liverpool
¾ of an hour distant and many other colleges in England had nothing to
do with their having one in Manchester; that the Bishop could have his
two miles off in Salford; that S. J. did not chose their district but it was
assigned to them; prophesied that I should regret it etc; did not know
that my letter to General was to end the question; said it excluded them
forever from Manchester.

22 May
Cardinal Franchi.

Told him the General S.J. had not answered, that he will probably
leave Rome after Sunday; that Fr Weld had told me that nobody had said
that S.J. were in the wrong; that he was not aware that my letter was to
end all; that there is room in Manchester for six colleges – that in spite
of their good will to prevent it there will be no peace in Manchester till
the S.J. has a college there etc. I asked him to get a speedy answer and
the closing of the college; that I would not leave Rome till it was closed.

Franchi said I was quite right not to leave till all was finished; that
I was to tell Rinaldini of the facts, send him to him and that he would

11 Vaughan is here mistaken. Allessandro Barnabò died in 1874.

send this evening to the General to ask him to send an answer and close. He said Fr Armellini had been to him objecting to the statement in my letter that I reserved the education of the middle class to myself. "What", said Franchi to him joining his hands, "do you think the Bishop in his own Diocese is of so little account as not to be able to reserve to himself the education of his own city"? etc. etc. He said he reported this conversation to the Pope and referred to the sentence in question. The Holy Father said *non cambiate una parola della lettera, sta molto bene.* [Do not change a word of the letter, it is fine.] I told him of the effect produced in Liverpool by the Jesuit school, that good vocations to the secular clergy are got of it either by chance or by scheming etc. Told him I had other accusations – a long paper from Liverpool, but did not wish to do more than settle the case in hand.

He said I was to tell the Bishop of Liverpool from him that he might present his case against the S.J., and that it should be considered etc. He again insisted on the necessity of S.J. entirely closing down their college in Manchester and that without delay. Mgr Nina told Fr O'C[12] that the General S.J. had received a sharp reprimand from the Pope, who reproached him thus: *perché venite aumentare le mie amarezze con questa imprudenza* [why do you come to increase my hardships with this imprudence] – speaking of the Salford case.

24 May
Cardinal Franchi, General S.J. and Self present.

General said he would close for sake of peace, but that they had the right to open colleges.

The Bishop replied if that motive alone were put forward he should protest and say that justice came in as the chief motive, i.e. to wants of Diocese, to plans published, to X[averian] Brothers; and that these had all been provided for by the condition imposed by the late Bishop on re-admitting S.J. into Manchester.

If the right was claimed he should appeal to Holy See to determine the right, because he and others held it to be doubtful. Also, the exercise of rights is suspended when they occasion injury or conflict with needs of the Diocese. The General quoted Pius VII; the Bishop pointed out that Pius gave power to *regere seminaria et collegia* and did not speak of founding them independently of Bishop and the existing interests; that Pius restored the Constitutions but not the privileges. Cardinal Franchi said the privileges did not come under discussion, and that the Bishop did not say he intended to exclude S.J. forever from education in Manchester. General said the Bishop's letter appeared to him to be a

12 Henry O'Callaghan.

perpetual exclusion. Bishop replied that he did not intend, and could not had he so intended, to make a decree excluding S.J. or any Order from education in Manchester. As circumstances might change, so he would leave the Bishop of the time free to invite S.J. or any other to coop-erate in education in Manchester, he could promise nothing but to try and act for the best. The Bishop pointed out Stonyhurst, Liverpool and Chesterfield as places where they could send boys to; but that Bishop wanted Manchester to carry out his own plans for Diocese and for the development of Xaverian College. General thought there was room for several colleges; Bishop replied that the Chapter and himself decided otherwise and that unanimously. He added that a further proof was that S.J. having come to found a college voluntarily left it because as the Provincial writes, "it threatened to be a losing concern;" that the Bishop and Brothers had found difficulties to be great. The General replied that the S.J. had done wrong in retiring, but had done so because they could not carry on the school without aid of a church. The Bishop replied that this was proof of the difficulty of establishing a school in Manchester; but that nevertheless the X[averian] Brothers had no church and had to contend therefore against that difficulty also. Bishop said that Cath-olic Manchester was poor; that within the memory of living men there was but one Catholic church in it; that it had grown only by the Irish immigration. That it may decrease; that there is not a Catholic family in Manchester proper with a carriage and pair; that there is not room for more than one school of the kind. Cardinal Franchi added that the Xaverians and the Bishop were first in the field etc. The Bishop said that they would never have been readmitted but for the condition; a condition which had not only been accepted but acted on in their first coming to Manchester – and which he was justified in believing would be observed and acted on if he readmitted them.

General said Fr Weld denied the condition; Bishop replied that the Secretary to [the] late Bishop, who really governed the Diocese and had advised the reintroduction of S.J., asserted it, and it was well known to [the] Chapter that the Bishop would never have readmitted them unless he had secured himself against their destroying his school etc. by their setting up one in opposition. Fr Weld had not rejected the condition, never objected to it; but came in as it were silently accepting it. He, Fr Weld, told the Bishop that he respected it so far as that he would not have set up the school during the lifetime of [the] late Bishop. The Bishop urged that if not bound by technicality of Canon Law they were bound by honour and as between man and man to observe the condition.

The General said that they had set up a College in Limerick under some opposition, and that the Bishop established another college within three doors of the Jesuit one. The Bishop said he knew the state of feeling created in Limerick and he would not upon any account have

a similar state of things established in Manchester. It created scandal
and mischief. He urged that the system of dividing among several the
small numbers to be educated above the lower standard was to destroy
all hope of making a respectable and flourishing institution, that this
was precisely what S.J. was attempting in Manchester. The Bishop
again pointed out that S.J. had other colleges with which they should
be content.

The General urged that they desired to do good among the middle
class in Manchester. The Bishop claimed to be the judge as to what
should be done so as not to injure existing interests or to affect injuriously the Diocese. Cardinal Franchi suggested heads of a letter: 1)
Repetition of my reasons. 2) Reference to the S.J.'s rights remaining
intact and without prejudice. 3) The Bishop's declaration that he did
not exclude them forever. 4) The need of peace. 5) The wish of the
Pope that the affair should be settled by closing and in harmony. The
Bishop again urged that such a letter alone would be acceptable as gave
no rise to public misrepresentation, hence that it would not be stated
that it was closed for peace; and this all the more because the friends
of the S.J. called the Bishop a tyrant, a Bismarck etc. etc. And that
any motive which should imply that the Bishop was a disturber of the
peace would need a rejoinder from the Bishop. The Cardinal thought
that the recapitulation of the reasons assigned by me as a motive would
prevent this interpretation. The General said that that sketch would do
more or less. The Cardinal suggested that he and the Bishop should
see a sketch of the letter, and this was agreed to. Fr General said it had
been represented to him that the Bishop would yield if they set up the
college, and that he had been deceived in this fact, and that under the
circumstances a mistake had been made and it would have been better
to have acted otherwise. The Bishop added that this probably proceeded
from the Bishop's known friendly disposition to the Society, which had
been abused (he might have added, but did not, that this was an example
of the bullying with which the S.J. pursues its ends when it thinks it
can do so successfully and with impunity). The General said that the
Pope had called him to Rome to settle this matter and that he would
not therefore go away till it was settled, that the Pope had told him to
combinare [cooperate] with the Bishop, and he understood this to mean
that both were to yield something, and he did not think the Bishop was
yielding anything.

The Bishop said he wished to treat the Society with all kindness,
to use their services etc. etc. and to forget this past incident, but could
yield no power of discretion or judgement as to which might be for the
good of his Diocese at any future time. He thought the letter had better
be short, and the school closed in acquiescence with the request of the
Bishop and because the Pope desired it, and then no reason or motive

would be left out for public interpretations. The General wished for his own consolation to bring in 'the desire of the Pope.' The Cardinal and Bishop quite agreed.

As to closing, the Bishop said that the College had not yet been closed; the General said he would give [the] order to have it closed, but wished to do so at the mid-summer vacations. The Bishop urged that it be closed at once, said he had suggested the Pentecost holidays last Monday to Fr General; that it would keep the wound open; that he knew what expedients might be resorted to; that it became the more necessary on account of the tongues at work etc. Cardinal Franchi said he had received that morning a letter from Glasgow saying there was room for seven colleges in Manchester. The General urged that his difficulty arose from there being boys in the school who had been at Protestant schools before; that none had been at Catholic schools etc. The Cardinal suggested that the Bishop might undertake to provide for them. The Bishop said that Fr Birch might introduce them to the Xaverian Brothers' school or send them to one of the S.J.s many colleges. The General said he did not believe they could be sent to one of the colleges. The Bishop said the reason was not a valid one; that at the vacation it would still exist and that it was a mere pretext for delay, and would be understood as such. They could make their vacations begin on the 1st of June – next week, as well as in August. The General said if a thing had to be done it had better be done with generosity and that therefore he would write to have it closed immediately. He would get his letter to me as soon as possible. During the conversation, when the Bishop referred to his own goodwill to S.J., the General said he had also given proof of goodwill at Baltimore. The Bishop said it were better not to introduce that question as he should have some very hard things to say about it, if broached. The Cardinal thought it was not to the point, and the General did not urge it. The Bishop also referred to the immense mischief the S.J. had done in Manchester and elsewhere – by their conduct in this matter and by their talk and that of friends. The General said it was impossible to stop tongues and *de gustibus non est disputandum*. He, the General, also said that their colleges would provide vocations for secular clergy; the Bishop replied that at Liverpool the Bishop was only able to get good or clever or the better sort out of their college by chance or artifice; that it was notorious that S.J. took all the best and left the remnant to the Bishop or anyone else. In an earlier part of the conversation the General said how could it be decided what was a middle school and what was not, how could the distinction be correctly drawn? The Bishop replied that every mission is bound to have a poor school; that the Bishop and School Inspectors could clearly distinguish between the two. (The idea I suspect is to introduce a middle school in connection with the poor school and to carry their point by a side way in spite of the Bishop and any decision that may be given.) In another part of the conversation the Bishop said he was judge as to what was injurious to the welfare or organisation of his diocese. The General interposed with his privilege as not coming under the Bishop's jurisdiction. The Bishop said that the Religious could have recourse to the Holy See in such an event. The General objected to this. Then, replied the Bishop, the privileges must be clearly defined and agreed on; and still the Bishop is judge (and the Holy See) as to what is for the good, if any, to the prejudice of his Diocese and of invested [*sic*] interests.

[The] General said that some are maintaining that any person can open schools anywhere and did not know why they should not exercise the same right. The Bishop asked whether he claimed the right to open a college anywhere irrespective of the permission of the Ordinary. Cardinal Franchi interposed that this would only be where they had a canonical erection. The General turned off the subject.

During the same conversation when the Bishop represented that he had bought land etc. etc. even before the S.J. had made known their wish to have a college, the General replied that they, S.J., had bought land round the church during the life time of [the] late Bishop and that consequently they were before the Bishop in creating a vested interest. The Bishop replied that this had not been announced. (He might have added, but did not, that it is this subterraneous way of acting, undermining and encroaching without notice, even upon the plans of the Ordinary and unknown to him and against his will, that fills people with distrust of the Society. You never know where or when you are not going to be taken in and circumvented, when their interests or ends are at stake.)

26 May
Cardinal Franchi.

Called on Cardinal Franchi to say that I had heard S.J. were circulating a printed document on the Salford question among the Cardinals.[13] He had not heard of it. (Howard had seen it in Oreglia's hands). The Cardinal was a little disturbed at Cardinal Manning's long letter and showed it to me. I was able to testify to having heard all the facts before I had left England; to 1) G[allwey's] character; to the vile reports; to the report that Cardinal M[anning] had been admonished in Rome to be fair to the Religious Orders. I told him of Fr G[allwey's] conduct at the Synod and of his letter of apology written to me; of the display people had made on his nomination as Provincial. He asked whether the General had power to remove him, I said I thought he had and that it would be the best thing to do. He promised to ask General that evening

---

13 *Facts and Documents.*

to remove him.[14] The Cardinal then read me the draft of General S.J.'s letter. Agnozzi had read it to the Pope, who was "perfectly satisfied" with it. Franchi said it quite satisfied him 1) because it did not place the closing on the motive of peace; 2) because it left the initiative in employing S.J. to the Bishop, entirely recognising his authority to call or not as he might judge best for the public good etc; 3) because it suggested that the Pope had given them an admonition. He said *si sono avviliti più che io pensavo possibile* [they are more down-hearted than I thought possible.]

Franchi and Agnozzi again and again urged that from the Bishop's point of view the letter was all that could be desired. He had expected S.J. would place himself on an equality with Bishop (using his two fingers to illustrate) on the matter of education – but had left the Bishop entirely master. Having read over the letter several times I accepted it taken in conjunction with my letter and with the memo of the *abboccamento* [preliminary meeting] between the General and myself to be left in the hands of Cardinal Prefect for future reference.

The Cardinal spoke to me about the S.J. effort to regain property in Canada; saying they would continue to pay the Bishops what they now receive from Government in compensation of the confiscation of such property. I pointed out the exceptional position of Canada in regard to Church encroachment by State, and that a very little imprudent agitation might cause the forfeiture of everything; that there is a party anxious to conform the practice of Canada in respect to Church establishment to that of United States, Ireland and the colonies. The Cardinal agreed and thought it was very imprudent, adding the Bishops would rather trust the Government then the S.J. to pay them. That a Catholic Secretary of the Government had also thought it imprudent to agitate the question.

26 May
Mgr Rinaldini.

Walked with Rinaldini. He said Trent had cut down Regular privileges; that the Bishops and clergy at that time were not what they now were, and that at Vatican Council there would be made another great change in the direction of Episcopal authority. The circumstances which had called for the extraordinary privileges had passed away owing to the reform of Bishops and secular clergy. Providence was facilitating much legislation by breaking up the power of the Orders, lessening the number of their members and allowing their suppression. That a *schema*

---

[14] Gallwey ceased to be Provincial in the following year. He had only served three years; usually the Provincial's term of office is six years. See Oliver P. Rafferty, 'The Jesuit College, Manchester, 1875,' *Recusant History* 20 (2) (1990), p. 300.

is prepared, but that it will create a great discussion; that the Pope will not therefore solve the question himself but will only give such local instruction and such *norma* to the Orders in their relations with the Episcopate as shall tend in that, and preserve the authority of the Episcopate. Rinaldini held that Bishop has power to impose own obligation of Masses on a church in favour of a person who gives money for its erection. Very strong against Government knowing anything of the Church funds; S.J. since its return in 1850 (or 49) to Rome had invested everything in private names. They have now been turned out of Rome but beyond their residences have not lost a penny. He thought that the [? illegible] law, requiring registration of property had been a real injury to the Church in Rome.

27 May

Fr Weld called and said: 1) I should regret my exclusion of the S.J. college; that it would have been for good of the Diocese; that Archbishop Eyre and many others had put their seminaries under S.J; that it was a remarkable fact that a Bishop had been forced to spend six weeks in Rome to prevent the establishment of a [Jesuit] college; when a French bishop and clergy had petitioned by a deputation to Fiesole for a Jesuit college, with orders to go in to Rome if the General did not accede to the request; that the only good point he has seen in my programme was the desire to raise the standard of the clergy; that the absence of Religious from all the great towns of the Diocese was injurious; that the "native" part of the Salford clergy was inferior etc. 2) The Bishop replied that under other circumstances I might also petition for a Jesuit College, but not under the present; that the example he gave me of secular vocations from [the] Liverpool College was worth nothing; that the Bishop did not attribute to it any advantages in the increase of good vocations to secular clergy; that it was notorious that when S.J. had the Roman Seminary the students became Jesuits and the secular clergy diminished most seriously, so that the Pope removed them etc. (This he said he knew nothing about.) He did not admit the inferiority of his clergy; nor did he think S.J. would raise them; Fr Weld said they were much inferior to that of Liverpool. 3) Fr Weld asked for my pamphlets – on condition of receiving his.

He said there was only the little one of the correspondence with a few observations and I should have it. I said yes – provided I may tell Mgr Rinaldini to let me have his *ponenza*[15] – he shall have mine. He thought there was not much in Propaganda and finally agreed. 4) He complained that an expression of his – "that what is good for the Society

---

15   This refers to the Jesuit pamphlet *Facts and Documents*.

is for the good of the Church" – was unfairly interpreted; said that [he] had used it once he thought to Archbishop Manning; I said I believed he had used it in London in speaking to me, he thought not (I might have added and with Fr Gordon); I said the expression should have been "for the good of the Diocese *not* Church." He thought the expression implied arrogance, as I had represented it by identifying the interests of Diocese or Church and Society. I replied that that was precisely my view of it, and said that the whole of his conversation since he had come into my room justified my interpretation of his dictum and I referred to the foregoing complaints and warnings. He took a different view; and we remained in our divergence. 5) He complained that Cardinal Franchi had promised that he should have had a *congresso* [a formal meeting] with him at Propaganda, and have fought out our case on each side; that I had refused to meet him in that way. I replied that I did not know what the Cardinal had said to him, he had given me no instruction to meet him; that I had come all this way to Rome not to discuss the matter with him, but to appeal to Propaganda and the Pope; that he had made his statements and I mine, that all was fair but that I must decline to recognise his competency in the matter. He replied that if the matter had been settled by reason, it would have been differently settled, but that the Pope had taken it up and wished it settled one way and therefore, etc. I said I have appealed from the acts of the Society to the Pope, and the Pope has examined the matter and settled it against you. 6) He referred to the question of the condition or agreement with Dr Turner – denied it – said the Bishop told him afterwards wanted no school – that he should not have founded one in Bishop's lifetime and would not have accepted the church on the condition of no school. Bishop replied that giving him credit for speaking what he believed to be true, he must prefer the statement of Benoit who had been their chief friend (which Weld admitted, but said his memo was six years after [the] date); that it was notorious the late Bishop would not have let them in to destroy his school; (but said Weld, there was no written document to prove any agreement, and laughed at the idea of an agreement of the informal kind I referred to.)[16] I urged that as there had been no written agreement not to have a church when S.J. left Manchester because a college without a church would not pay, but an understanding had answered the Bishop's

---

[16]   In his first pamphlet, *The Claim*, Vaughan stated that the agreement between the Jesuits and Turner, "was not drawn up in writing, – the Bishop trusted to a verbal arrangement, for it was not his habit or the practice of his time to act with the same official precision, and with the same use of forms such as are becoming customary now that the Church in this country is gradually assuming its normal condition." p. 11. In his Summary sent to Rome, Vaughan had written: "… the Bishop thought he could trust to verbal conditions, and he was a good and simple man." *ibid.*, p . 26.

purpose and S.J. had acted on it, so in the second case the Bishop might well have trusted to the same sense of honour and the same of acting; Weld urged that such an agreement would not be canonical, I said that might be, but you never raised an objection to the Bishop's prohibition; in honour and before men who are straight forward it would have been satisfactory. It shows the need of caution in acting with S.J.

27 May

Cardinal Franchi at dinner at Irish College said that General had been to him and said Weld was quite pleased with his letter, because it would have been impossible to have got on with such a Bishop – they had now come to know him. The Cardinal assured me he *had never made* Fr Weld any promise of a *congresso* with me, that his statement to that effect was quite false.

30 May

Cardinal Franchi.

Told the Cardinal I had reason to fear the use that might be made of General's letter of 25th to me if it went uncorrected. 1) It made me say what I had not said. 2) Placed in the position of less freedom than other Bishops because it referred to a kind of promise to recall S.J., which I had not made. 3) The sentences might be represented as so many declarations or promises extracted from me in virtue of which the General gave up the school. 4) That I had written a correction, which if they were in good faith they would not object to and if they were not would become necessary. That this was necessary for truth's sake and for peace sake; I must foresee and provide against petition etc. at home from friends of S.J., which they would base upon General's letter if left uncorrected. 5) That the General by his letter had bound himself to nothing but to close for the present and had tried to bind me to call them in to reopen etc. etc. The Cardinal suggested and dictated a different beginning to my letter and passed the rest on quite satisfactory. I sent the letter that evening to General S.J. I remarked to Cardinal that, if S.J. complained of my reverting to the letter, which I had seen before it was sent, S.J. did precisely the same with regard to my letter; that if they complained of my delay of three or four days they had delayed 9 or 10 days in answering mine; that they had time to telegraph to England to keep the school open, if my letter should be taken as a pretext to re-open the whole subject.

31 May

Fr Weld called again. I again referred to his famous dictum;[17] said he had used it to Fr Gordon also; he was calmer. Said Fr General was

---

[17] "Whatever is good for the Society is good for the Diocese."

beautiful; his only thought was "charity". He said that he had not played any tricks, had been to Cardinal Franchi and reminded him of what had happened, and that the Cardinal who did not remember perhaps was quite satisfied. I replied that that I still held in preference to the Cardinal's version [*sic*]. I asked for an explanation of the telegram which empowered school to continue. He said Cardinal Franchi wished Fr Armellini in Low Week to stop the school *pendente lite* and Armellini wrote to Fiesole. They telegraphed to Fr Gallwey to close. Gallwey said it had been reopened three days or so before, what was he to do. They, S.J., took counsel with General and agreed to let it go on and wrote an explanation to Cardinal Franchi. This was done. (The Pope on hearing of it said it will be worse for them if they have to close later than if they closed now.)

His explanation of the telegram, cancelling promise and re-empowering Gallwey to re-open – i.e. the telegram of 18 March, was Weld's – sent without permission of Propaganda – saying continue in *statu quo*; this was another of Weld's tricks. The Cardinal said Weld pressed him very hard to let *him* send the telegraph (the Cardinal was dining at the Irish College, 17 March) but would not, saying to me he did not intend to trust to any other etc. Judge by his indignation when Weld also telegraphed giving Gallwey instruction to go on.

2 June

Sacconi tells me General most absolute: blames Weld; says it is a great lesson. De Luca says the evidence of an agreement or condition between Weld and late Bishop is unanswerable – a great lesson, *lezione solenne*. Cataldi says the Pope speaks of it as a *vera bricconata* [a real trick/a bit of mischief]. Fr [illegible] said to me (3 June) that he liked the monition of censure etc. as showing clearly the Bishop's will; that the Jesuits must have been mad; that Weld is a fool to draw distinction between a decision on reason and authority; as though the right were not the power, if they exist, and as though Pope had not good reason. On receiving telegram saying school not closed went off to General said I was going to Cardinal Franchi and Pope next day to say farewell, but should not leave till school closed. He promised to telegraph next day.

3 June

Cardinal Cullen entered into his Jesuit affair at Dublin, and the way they had tried to humbug him. Said he would make laws in next Synod to keep them and Orders under; Orders too numerous in Dublin, living on the people too much. Promised to speak to Cardinal Franchi about a letter to S.J. Saw Cardinal Franchi, read him my paper of [*sic*] reason for writing the General to prevent his people acting against will of the Bishops. He quite agreed, said it taught him much he had not clearly seen before etc., promised to write to say they must act in harmony and refer to Propaganda if need be, but never without Propaganda act against Bishops. He was very angry with Weld's speech that the decision was given not by reason but by authority.

3 June
> Audience with Holy Father 8.00 p.m. I thanked the Pope for his decision. He said blows from Gladstone do no harm, but from religious or priests they are painful. I must have patience, we all human [*sic*]. I told him I should ask S.J. to give our retreat to clergy; he was most pleased. Said we must have "regard" for S.J. because they have got influence, "not that they have it with me though people say so – they do not come to me. I give *rimprovero* [reprimand] to all, Jesuits Religious and all when needed". He added, "*C'è stato troppo caldo nei capi in Inghilterra*" [there has been too much hot headedness in England]. I said, "yes". "Perhaps we may have other trouble with S.J. *hanno prepotenza* [they are arrogant] – i.e. some of them are. In England and Scotland the Presbyterian heresy affects some of the clergy and *i Gesuiti non dicono ogni mattina posuit Deus Episcopos* [*sic*], *S.J. regna Ecclesiam Dei* [*sic*]. [The Jesuits do not say every morning God has set up the Bishops; the S.J. rules the Church of God]. The Pope laughed and said "that he had told them that even if Vooughan – or Von or whatever you call yourself – I always call you Voughan – *col g* [with g] – should be exaggerated or unreasonable or some such word – though I said you were good – and not wish for Jesuits or a religious institution in the Diocese, the Bishop must be respected in his own Diocese". He said try and act in harmony with all, and if there is any great difficulty *bisogna venire qui* [you must come here]. He was very gracious and kind.

February 1876[18]

7 February Visit to General S.J. at Fiesole
Sunday called on F[ather] Beckx and F. Weld at Fiesole. Very civil. Weld jocularly alluded to bad blood – next day called on me and asked me at Railway Station to withdraw my *ponenza* from Propaganda "lest it should ever be said that the Bp. of Salford was an enemy of ours"! He referred to what he had said about bad blood, I asked him if he would like some of my pills for his blood! And the matter ended.

Rome 10 February
Cardinal Franchi said that 4 or 5 weeks ago Duke Salviati sent the

---

[18] Later return to Rome.

Manchester petition, which was poorly signed and badly drawn up, dated July; that the Duke did not bring it in person, and made no allusion to it when he called afterwards; that the Cardinal shut it up in the Archives at once; will give it no answer. That the affair is over; that his policy of *temperamento* [? moderation] had been wise etc. etc. I told him of my conciliatory conduct; of Fr General's intention to answer my pamphlets. He said that Armellini had some months ago sent in an answer to certain charges of mine apparently against the Society; and that this also he had shut up in the Archives. I repeated that they still claim to establish Colleges *ubilibet sine alterius licentia* [wherever they like without anyone else's permission.] He replied that this is mere *sfogo* [an outburst] – that if they had ever that power they have it not now – that Propaganda will not allow anything against the Secular clergy; that S.J. cannot so act in England; that they have learnt a lesson and that they will not repeal the pact. I hear elsewhere that S.J. is much distrusted at Propaganda and that they cannot get anything as formerly.

It is current in Rome that Pius VIII used to say of S.J. 1) they are very good but necessary to keep under; 2) they form a fine picture but the frame is required!

APPENDIX ONE

Extract from the Bishop's Pastoral Letter published 30 November, 1872, announcing his intention to organise a Catholic Commercial College for Manchester.[1]

There is perhaps no Diocese in England better provided in respect to its parochial schools than that of Salford. Suitable provision has yet to be made for the education of a higher class, so that the next Diocesan undertaking, after the work of the Seminary, must be to carry on to completion the work of the Grammar School, prudently and wisely begun by my predecessor. He laid its beginnings humbly in Bethlehem, and they are in Bethlehem still. It has already, I am glad to say, borne valuable fruits, and is destined, I trust, in the future to meet the urgent need. This great commercial Metropolis ought to possess a Catholic Commercial College, worthy of itself and the Catholic name. We have excellent Classical Colleges in the Diocese and elsewhere, and they have proved by test to have reached a high state of proficiency; but we have no Commercial School, that I know of, coming up to the standard which I think we are bound to attain. Our position and the requirement of the day demand this of us. We are a commercial people, and there is no reason why the Catholic Church should not supply as highly a commercial education in Manchester as she does a liberal and classical elsewhere. She is fully equal to the task. She is a friend to commerce and industry, and to all the honourable pursuits of men. We have peculiar advantages at our disposal in Manchester, and I desire to utilise them as soon as possible. I have already taken certain preliminary steps; but the time for public action has not yet arrived.

[1] *The Claim*, p. 18.

APPENDIX TWO

Memorandum of the Late Bishop's Secretary and Confidential Adviser as to the agreement between Bishop Turner and the Provincial S.J.[1]

October 11, 1873.

I beg to state that on the Jesuit Fathers coming to Manchester, Dr. Turner told me that it was distinctly agreed upon between himself and the Provincial that the Fathers were never to establish any school, beyond the parochial school for the children of the poorer class of their congregation. This he repeated on several occasions afterwards. One day a gentleman told me that Father Jackson, if I remember right, had said to him that adjoining to their residence to be erected near the Church, the Fathers intended to have a middle school. As this seemed to me in direct opposition to the agreement made by the Bishop and the Provincial, I mentioned the report to the Bishop. His Lordship repeated more emphatically than before, that this would be contrary to their first agreement, and that he was quite sure that the Fathers would never break the agreement, and that he could not conscientiously allow the agreement to be broken, inasmuch as there were already two middle-class schools in full operation in Manchester.

As your Lordship's inquiry bears only on the education question, I take it for granted that there is no need of giving you any details of the circumstances under which the Fathers came to Manchester.

I have the honour to remain,
Your Lordship's servant in Christ,
P. Benoit.

---

[1] *The Claim*, pp. 28–29.

APPENDIX THREE

Summary of the Bishop of Salford's Case, sent to his Agent in Rome[1]

Bishop's House,
Salford,
20 December 1874.

1. I had not been consecrated a month before I published a Pastoral undertaking to do two things, (1) to form a Seminary, (2) to establish in Manchester a Catholic Commercial College. I send this Pastoral by post – please refer to pp.11 and 12.

2. The Seminary is now roofed in and will be opened in the summer. Almost within a year of the date of that pastoral, I was able to purchase a most suitable piece of land and a Protestant Chapel adjoining the Xaverian Brothers' Middle School with a view to the said Commercial College. The site is one of the best in Manchester, is ten minutes' walk from the Jesuit Church, and is just outside their parish.

3. The first I heard from the Jesuits of their desire to establish a College in Manchester, (after their educational failure of some years ago and voluntary retirement, throwing the remains of their undertaking upon the late Bishop), was from F. Gallwey, at the Synod at Old Hall, after my published intention to found a College, and after my purchase of a site for it. I told him it could not be, and thought the matter ended. But in August last the correspondence of which I send you a copy took place. I have given my reasons very briefly, each deserves to be pondered separately. You will see an indication of the treatment I have received in consequence of my decision from at least one Jesuit returning from Rome.

4. I have this month received another letter from F. Gallwey, showing how actively they have been endeavouring to obtain from Propaganda a permission – or even a command – while they admit I have many reasons, characterised by F. Gallwey as "very valid," not to grant the permission. F. Gallwey says that the Card. Prefect names Manchester as a place where he desires the Jesuits to establish a Middle School – and tells me that as the Society has got a church in Manchester, it has the right, independent of the Bishop, from the Holy See to open a College. The intimation is, that this will be done in spite of me, if I do not

1   *The Claim*, pp. 25–28.

consent, upon the strength of the Card. Prefect of Propaganda's desire, and in virtue of their own privileges.

5. Now, I say it is impossible for me to grant them this permission, and it is my duty to submit to the Holy See the grave reasons founded on *justice, expediency* and the *greater good of religion*, for which I must decline to grant the permission; and in behalf of which I must ask the support of Propaganda.

I will indicate the reasons in as few words as possible. Some of them are contained in the accompanying correspondence, and some are not. They each would carry greater force if developed; but it would make my letter too long to do so, unless required.

(a) A few years ago the S.J. endeavoured to establish a College in Manchester – they told the late Bishop they had £5,000 in hand for that purpose; on this undertaking, he gave them leave. They failed (without having spent the £5,000) voluntarily retired, and gave up the undertaking. The Bishop then, in order to prevent a scandal to religion, took it up; worked the school with his own priests, and introduced the Congregation of Xaverian Brothers to carry it on. These Brothers are doing so to this day; their College is within ten minutes' walk of the Jesuit Church – and I have bought land next to them in the hope of making a first rate College, probably in conjunction with them.

The Xaverian Brothers have *their* vested interests, and the Bishop and the Diocese have also *theirs*. All these would be sacrificed if the Jesuits were now to come forward and start a College. No one knowing Manchester would say that there is room for two first-rate Catholic Colleges. They would be mutually destructive; and nothing but scandal would come of the scramble for students and for support.

(b) The Jesuits, a few years ago, got leave to come to Manchester again – after they had given up their College and had retired – and build a Church. The late Bishop was told by them that they had been left a very large sum of money, and that this would be spent in building a splendid Church in the town. He gave them leave to do so: they chose out for themselves the richest and best locality in Manchester, and built one of the finest and most attractive churches we have. But the permission was coupled with a condition, *viz:* that they should never undertake to establish other than a *poor school*. F. Weld, who was then Provincial, tells F. Gallwey – and I learn this from F. Gallwey's letter received this morning – that "no compact whatever between him and your Lordship's predecessor on the subject of a School or College was entered into, but merely an intimation from the Bishop that he did not want us to open a School."

Now against this, I have a written memorandum made by Canon Benoit, the late Bishop's Secretary, that it was only upon the condition of their opening no College that the late Bishop let them into Manchester again. Canon Benoit is ready to substantiate this on oath: and the Vicar-

General and another canon to whom the late Bishop spoke, tell me precisely the same thing. That no *written* compact was made is true – for the Bishop thought he could trust to verbal conditions, and he was a good and simple man: but F. Weld's admission that the Bishop actually gave him "*the intimation*" he speaks of, is quite sufficient proof, if taken in conjunction with the testimony of the Vicar-General and of the Secretary and Canon, that such a condition was actually made the basis of their return to Manchester.

(c) I do not consider it *expedient* that the Jesuits should have a second College in this locally small Diocese. Locally, though not in population, this is the smallest Diocese in England. The Jesuits have their finest College, in this Diocese, at Stonyhurst. I consider they ought to be satisfied with this proportion of educational power and influence. I was myself educated at Stonyhurst, I have shown myself most friendly to this College, sending students to it and recommending it to parents. I go there whensoever invited, and oftener, and I make a point of preaching for the Jesuits, whether in Manchester or elsewhere, whenever I can. I have endeavoured to prove myself a friend to them, and have on more than one occasion publicly defended the Society. Also I ask them to give all our clergy retreats and the retreats of nearly all our Convents. But I think a due proportion should be observed, and that the Society ought not to be allowed to monopolize – for it would be nothing less than this, – the better education of the Diocese. It is only fair that the Bishop should have one good lay College in the Diocese, and that he should not be prevented from placing it in Manchester, because the S.J. desire to found a second College in the Diocese.

Nor are the Jesuits so popular in Manchester (except among a very small number of their personal friends,) as that any public reason of popular feeling can come into consideration. Indeed, I may say that the opinion has been frequently expressed by the clergy and laity that it would be an unfortunate thing if the Jesuits were to found a school which should injure what already exists and destroy the possibility of that which is in prospect, – and which has been publicly announced as to be accomplished.

F. Gallwey has urged upon me as one of his reasons for wishing to found a College in Manchester, that it would produce many vocations, – that the Society needs vocations on account of the foreign as well as of the home missions which it has to supply. And he assures me that their College would be able to supply many vocations to the secular priesthood of the Diocese. To this I reply that the Bishop has the same object in view in what *he* proposes: he too hopes to obtain many vocations both for the Diocese and for foreign missions, and will make no objection whatever to any young men or boys joining the Society, who being educated at his College have a vocation to become Jesuits.

(d) I do not consider it to be *for the greater good of religion* that the Middle-class or Commercial College of Manchester should be in the hands of the Jesuits. I have the greatest respect for the Society, and thoroughly appreciate its classical and traditional system of education for the higher classes. But this is not the system required in this great commercial metropolis – it is not the system suited or acceptable to the commercial classes, for whom a full and perfect provision should be made. The system required is not one based upon the dead languages and the classics, but upon the living language, upon certain branches of science, Catholic history and commercial methods. You will see by referring to pp. 11 and 12 of my "Seminary Pastoral", to what I am referring. I venture to think that the Church would make a serious blunder if in this centre of commerce we set down a College founded upon the system of 300 years ago, or if we provided for the commercial and industrial classes the classical education which they do not want, and the system of study and learning which belongs to the higher classes. I have my plans ready laid for bringing in to operation the system which in my belief is the better one, and the one needed. I have conferred with some of our principal Clergy and laity upon it, and it has met with their approval. Now I will venture to say this much further, I do not believe the Society would or could carry out such a system as I have alluded to. They have a large College in Liverpool 45 minutes by train from Manchester. It is a very successful College, but is not carried upon this system; and though it has deservedly many friends, there are many who hold very strongly that it is not the system needed for the commercial classes. We have moreover this experience from the Jesuit College in Liverpool, *viz*: that no other can exist by its side. F. Nugent's middle school had to be closed in consequence of it; and the Bishop has had in like manner to turn his Grammar School into a Seminary. No school can exist by the side of a Jesuit College in our small Catholic populations, unless by pursuing a system of severe competition, and making a very large expenditure of money on both sides – in order to carry on the competition. And this would be a course neither edifying nor prudent.

(e) To prove that I have nothing but goodwill towards the Society, I may here remind you that I have already promised to offer the Jesuits a certain share in carrying on the College I have engaged to establish, though I cannot offer them the entire management and control of it.

(f) Lastly, if as the English Provincial says, middle-class education is a part of their Institute, and that they do not wish to conduct their Church in Manchester without attaching to it a College, though I shall regret to lose their services I shall be willing to receive their resignation of their Church and Mission, to undertake the debt actually upon it, and to offer it to another religious body, who will work the Mission and the Church without insisting upon establishing a College also.

APPENDIX FOUR

Resolution passed by the Salford Chapter[1]

1st April, 1875.

1. It is highly desirable, and necessary for the due educational organization of the Diocese, that the course indicated by the Bishop to the Chapter, at the Capitular meeting convened in his Lordship's house, December 2nd, 1872, and then approved of by the Chapter, should be carried out to its full extent as speedily as possible. The Canons support the Bishop's course of action *re* the seminary.

2. The Chapter begs leave to offer its respectful congratulation to the Bishop on the approaching completion of the building of the Diocesan seminary, and is of the opinion that a College for commercial education should now be commenced.

3. The Chapter has a decided conviction that there is not room for more than one such institution in Manchester.

4. The Chapter has with painful surprise and regret learned of the recent action of the Jesuit Fathers in the establishment of an upper class school, in direct opposition to the expressed will of the Ordinary of the Diocese, and subversive of his plans, already publicly and officially announced.

5. It is recorded that the senior members of the Chapter have a distinct recollection that the late Bishop assured them that it was arranged with him by the Provincial S.J., on the occasion of the second coming of the Jesuit Fathers into Manchester, that though they were to have a church, they were to establish no school but an ordinary parochial school, when practical and convenient.

Croskell, Provost.

---

[1] *The Claim*, p. 29.

APPENDIX FIVE

The Provincial's Memorial to the Bishops[1]

111, Mount Street,
London.
7th April 1875

I shall be able to spare their Lordships' time, and to make my memorial much shorter than I originally intended, as the Bishop of Birmingham has kindly told me that the correspondence that has recently passed between the Bishop of Salford and myself is already before their Lordships.

I think it highly desirable that the Bishops should see the whole of that correspondence, as in one or other of the letters which I wrote will be found, I think, almost everything of importance that I would desire to lay before them, both as regards the act of Father General, and the suspension threatened by his Lordship.

It would suit my own inclinations very well to pour out all my thoughts to their Lordships – but in the first place the task would be a very long one; secondly, in order to clear up matters in a satisfactory way, I should require to have before me the statements made by the Bishop of Salford; and thirdly, to introduce occasionally [sic]

Add to this that the legal question must necessarily be now settled in Rome, and therefore I need not enter into that portion of the subject.

The points on which I wish to make a brief comment are these – 1) The Bishop states in his monition of suspension that I had admitted his reasons in refusing us a College to be very valid, etc. 2) In a recent letter he expresses his opinion that I violated a promise made to him on the 17th March.

1. It is true then that in my reply to the Bishop's letter of August 17th, 1874, I made use of the expression that some of his reasons for refusing us permission to establish a College were "very valid."

I will explain these words –

Of the reasons alleged by his Lordship two seemed to me at the time to carry weight.

a) The compact which the Bishop asserted to exist.

b) The respect due to vested interests.

---

[1] *The Case*, pp. 128–131. A handwritten draft of this is at ABSI, RX/5.

In both cases I assumed the facts alleged to be correct, when I called the reasons valid, and I should still consider them valid if the facts could be established.

1a) With regard to the compact said to exist between the late Bishop and the Society, I had never heard of it till I found this mention of it in the Bishop's letter, and when I saw the statement, it seemed to me that our case was at an end, and I certainly would not subsequently have taken any part in the establishment of a school, had not Father Weld, who was Provincial at the time, assured me that he knew of no contract or engagement binding the Society not to open a College. He fully admitted that Bishop Turner had forbidden him to establish a College, but this prohibition Father Weld never considered to be a compact by which he had bound himself. Furthermore, he assured me that for the security of his own conscience he laid fully before the Cardinal Prefect of Propaganda all that passed between Bishop Turner and himself, and that the Cardinal declared that on this score there was no difficulty. It is true that the Bishop of Salford told me recently that a memorandum exists, and that some of the Canons can bear witness to a compact. Whether the memorandum and the evidence of these Canons can establish more than the fact that the Bishop laid an injunction on Father Weld, I have no means of ascertaining. I can only say that if sufficient evidence can be produced that the Society is bound by a real compact, that compact must of course be respected, and I am quite sure that Father General would at once direct me to repair any wrong done by closing our school without delay.

1b) As to the vested interests of the Xaverian Brothers, if the good Brothers had by perseverance brought their school to a great state of efficiency, and that the people of Manchester were well contented with the education which they offer, I should consider this is a valid reason why we should not be allowed to do grievous damage to this existing Institution. But to say nothing of the statistics of the school, of the testimony of the Brothers themselves, or the voice of the public – when I find that his Lordship himself, because he considers this school quite inadequate to existing wants, publicly declares his intention of absorbing it into his proposed College, and that in his letter of August 17th he asks me to pledge myself that the Society shall help him to form staff of the said College, it seems to me clear that his Lordship agrees with the common view that the vested interest of the Brothers is but a very small one, and must not stand in the way of the souls that are in danger, though it might be quite reasonable to compensate them for any loss which they might sustain.

I am still more confirmed in my present opinion that the vested interest of the Xaverian Brothers is not a valid reason for excluding us from a work especially allotted to us by the Holy See, by the fact that his

Lordship has more than once quite recently stated to me and to others that he fully intended to allow us to have a College a little later, when his own College had been established, and that he was on the point of coming to an agreement with me when I suddenly took action. These assurances took me quite by surprise, as I had before my mind the words he wrote to me in August, "I must beg of you entirely to dismiss the idea that it is permitted for the Society to establish another house of education in Manchester," which seemed to me quite final.

Still more did our exclusion seem final when he made known to me last Passion week that the site which he had purchased on the borders of our district, and very near to our church, was not, as I then supposed, for a new church, but for his future College, and when he went on to say that he considered our system of teaching was one not at all suited to the needs of his people, and, in fact, that we were not wanted in Manchester. Probably had not our conversation been a hurried one, all these statements would have been modified so as to harmonise better. Meanwhile I think some of them go to show that the vested interest of the Brothers is no serious obstacle to the establishment of another College in Manchester.

2. I will only add a few words respecting the promise made by me on the 17th of March, and which the Bishop considers me to have broken. On that day I went to his Lordship at his request, to see if some means could not be devised of preventing the scandal that would ensue if the suspension were to be enforced on the following morning. I begged for time to consult Father General, as I had been acting under an order given by him, after long deliberation and communication with Rome. I did not think it right to close the school without instruction from him. The Bishop feared that if we continued to keep the school open the number of scholars might increase, whereby the difficulty of closing would be made greater. He however at last consented to my request, and allowed me four days. I on my part promised three things –

I. To write without delay to Father General, and I did so that night.

II. Not to allow the number of scholars to be increased during the short interval allowed me, and this was faithfully observed.

III. To close the school for the holidays on the following Monday. This was also done.

I made no other promise than these.

On the following morning I received Father General's telegram from Rome, which informed me that one had been sent to the Bishop, staying his proceedings against the Society. I hereupon went back to his Lordship to tell him of the arrival of this telegram. To me it seemed to meet all agreements of the previous evening. I however told the Bishop that as we had come to an amicable arrangement I would stand by the terms of it, and close the school on Monday for the holidays. This I accordingly did.

In conclusion, I hope that I have not, either in this paper, or in any part of my correspondence with his Lordship, used any word that is either disrespectful or unkind, and as I do not in any way complain of his Lordship for upholding what he thinks to be his Episcopal rights, or protecting what he conceives to be the interests of his flock, so on the other hand I hope that neither his Lordship of Salford, nor any of their Lordships, will take it amiss that we strive by all lawful means to preserve our rights to take part in education, which is as essential to our Institute as the choir duties are to cloistered Orders.

P. Gallwey

APPENDIX SIX

Memoranda of a few points made during the conference between the Bishop of Salford and the Most Reverend Father Beckx, General of the Society of Jesus, at Propaganda in the presence of the Cardinal Prefect on 24th of May 1875.[1]

1. Father General said that the Bishop's letter of the 16th Day of Pentecost, regarding Manchester, seemed to him to be a permanent exclusion of the Society from ever teaching again in that city.

The Bishop answered that he did not intend, when with that letter he addressed the education of middle classes in Manchester, to issue a decree excluding forever the Society or any other teaching community – that even if he had had the will to issue such a decree he would not have had the faculty to do it.

Meanwhile he could not promise anything – and he wanted to allow himself, and his successors, full freedom without compromising in any way the right to determine according to circumstances what would be most advantageous for the education of his flock.

2. The General said that they had the right or privilege of opening colleges, and added *obiter* that it was asserted that for others the permission of the Ordinary to open schools is not requested.

He then cited a passage from the Bull *Sollicitudo Omnium* of Pope Pius VII, which restored the Society,

"That by this agreement members gathered in a religious community may be free to work to imbue the young with religion and the good arts, to direct Seminaries and Colleges and, with the approval and consent of the Local Ordinaries, to hear confessions, proclaim the Word of God and administer the sacraments."

From this passage the General deduced the right of the Society to establish a college etc. as in Manchester.

To this, the Bishop of Salford replied that in his letter in answer to the General, who had declared it a sacred right to establish Colleges without the consent of the Bishop, he claimed it would be the duty of the Bishop to appeal to the Holy See for a judgment on the issue, because the Bishop and others claimed that, despite the fact that Pius VII had

[1]   APF, Anglia 20, 1875–1877.

restored the Society according to the constitution approved by Paul III, he did not thereby restore all the extraordinary privileges, among which would be that of establishing colleges in spite of the Bishop.

He then indicated the wording *regere* (to rule over) *seminaria et collegia* and not *stabilire* (establish), which would mean that the Fathers were indeed allowed to take upon themselves the task of teaching in seminaries and colleges, but not to establish them against the Bishop's wishes.

Furthermore, he added that the privileges cannot be exercised so as to cause detriment to others, as for example another teaching community, or even to the detriment of the good of the diocese. The actual circumstances are quite different compared to those of two or three hundred years ago, and account must be taken of the new set of circumstances and the new duties imposed on bishops.

3. The General believed that the College could be closed for reasons of peace. The Bishop could not accept this reason, which could possibly be interpreted as if the Bishop himself had disturbed the peace, and especially now that it is being declared that the Bishop is a tyrant and a Bismarck, a persecutor of Jesuits, for having opposed the desire of the Fathers of having a College in Manchester.

The true reason to close is therefore a reason of justice – that which is owed to the enterprise of the Bishop, to the Xaverian Brothers, who are highly considered by both the people and the clergy – and for the good of the Diocese in accordance with the judgment of the Bishop.

4. Father General was of the opinion that there was room in Manchester for several Colleges.

The Bishop answered that it was the unanimous opinion of the Bishop and of his Chapter, that there was room for only one good College in Manchester. With regards to the population of Manchester this peculiarity is to be noted: the middle class is not very numerous and is not wealthy; up to this point in time there is not one family in Manchester who owns a carriage and pair; that in living memory there was only ever one Catholic Church in Manchester; the immigration of poor Irish people [has] increased the population, but it would significantly decrease if any commercial disaster were to occur.

The Bishop noted, as proof of the difficulty of establishing even just one College, the fact that the Society itself having a few years ago started a College for the middle class, abandoned it because, as the Provincial had written, it risked not being advantageous to them.

The General added that they had not done well in abandoning that enterprise, but that it had not been advantageous to them because they had no public church.

To this the Bishop replied that this was simply evidence of the difficulty that exists in establishing a good College for the population of

Manchester – that this had been proven not only by the Jesuits, but also by the Bishop and the Xaverian Brothers who also do not have a church annexed to the school.

The Bishop also observed that it is unwise to establish more colleges than are necessary, and to divide and distribute among the [illegible] colleges the small number of students suggests that it is not possible to assemble a number large enough to form even one respectable establishment that is of some standing in public opinion.

5. The General said that it was put to him that, after having made some objection against the establishment of a College of the Society, the Bishop would finally give in to the fact; but the Fathers had in fact been mistaken.

The Bishop observed that it was true that he had always shown good will towards the Society, but that in this case his kindness had been taken advantage of in a rather disloyal manner.

(Attention is drawn to the principle here laid down by the General – a principle not very reassuring to the Bishops – the principle of accomplished fact.)

6. The General asked how could a distinction be made between the class of one school and another, in other words a school of the poor from a school of the middle class.

The Bishop replied that all missions have the obligation of having schools for the poor and that these are not in any way distinguishable from schools for the middle class by any characteristic. The Bishop in any case would be the judge of this.

7. The Bishop thought that the Fathers, instead of creating obstacles for others in Manchester by establishing a new College there, should be happy with the education of the higher classes at their Stonyhurst College, in the very diocese of Salford; with that of Liverpool, three quarters of an hour from Manchester by rail; and with the other one in Chesterfield, at a few hours' distance.

The General said that they also wanted to do something for the middle class in Manchester.

8. As far as closing the school in Manchester was concerned, the General said that there could be difficulties in closing this month, as had been requested by the Bishop, due to the presence of students recruited from Protestant schools.

The Bishop was of the opinion that these could be sent to Stonyhurst, or to the nearer college of the Xaverian Brothers – that there would be no greater difficulty in closing on the 1st of June – than the 1st of August. The General agreed to close on the 1st of June.

His Eminence, after having devised the general form of the letter to be written by the General, with great courtesy ended the conference.

APPENDIX SEVEN

Extracts taken from of the pamphlets of Monsignor Vaughan, now in the hands of the Propaganda.[1]

We are accused of spreading rumours regarding the hostility of the Bishop to the Society, to souls, to Religion.

The Bishop maintained that Rome had approved of his refusal to open the school.

The Bishop, seeing that neither his own authority, nor that of Propaganda, was taken into consideration with due respect, threatened censorship.

The Society lacked sincerity by demanding a school without notifying the Bishop; operating in the dark; invading, so-to-speak, the diocese.

Operating in a manner with no regard for conventions, or for the rights of others, the Fathers of the Society are looked upon with suspicion and distrust in the whole Church. This fear comes almost as a justification of much of what has been attributed to the Society by its enemies.

The Fathers of the Society by opening the school overturned the rights of the Bishop and Propaganda.

To add insult to injury and scandal, a number of laymen were informed of the open war that was being planned against the Bishop – and this not for the first time; that a system of procuring a favourable public opinion was used, both to weaken the moral strength of the Bishop, and to force him to give in; in other words to make his authority most unpopular.

The Fathers boasted of having implemented necessary reforms in London, Liverpool and Manchester between the Bishops and the secular clergy.

They disturbed the peace and the harmony that had existed before their arrival in the diocese of Manchester [*sic*].

They forced Catholic families that live far from the church to abandon their Confessors and directors.

They committed the [illegible] of collecting money and sometimes people from other parishes.

---

[1] APF, Anglia 20, 1875–1877. The document is simply a list of complaints against the Jesuits.

They attempted to turn the parishioners against the Bishop by making complaints in the homes of some laymen etc. etc.

And it is to be noted that before printing these serious accusations against the Fathers in Manchester the Bishop never made any complaint to his superiors; on the contrary he had always declared himself happy.

APPENDIX EIGHT

Names of the Manchester Catholic Laity who signed the Petition to Propaganda Fide[1]

Daniel Noble
   doctor   32, Ardwick Green
James Furniss
   J.P.   St Ann's Sq.
T. Aborry
   merchant   'Fairleigh', Hope, Eccles
T. Brotherton
   manufacturer   Stockport
P. Annacker
   merchant   152–154, Oxford St.
E. Nicholson
   architect   88, Mosley St.
T. Frild
   bank manager   52, Plymouth Gr.
P. Ross
   railway secretary   Manchester
T. Freeman
   metal worker   14, Nelson St.
W. Nairne
   public accountant   170, Upper Brook St.
Gervase Stringfellow
   flour dealer   91, Rumford St.
T.H. Sole
   printer & stationer   4, Beaufort Terr, Cecil St.
P. Heilsman
   merchant   Victoria Park
P. MacDonald
   merchant   Plymouth Gr.
Charles M. Cheetham
   manager   7, York Place, Oxford St.
Edward Wadsworth
   confidential clerk   48, Ackers St.

---

[1] APF, Anglia 20, 1875–1877. See pp. 134–137 above.

Charles Clinton
    warehouseman   Belgrave Cres., Eccles
W. E. Stutter
    journalist   15, Shakespeare St.
Richard Clayton
    silk merchant   58–60 Downing St.
? Cummins
    ?   Nicholas Croft
John Cummins
    merchant   Nicholas Croft
J Conery
    umbrella manuftc.   53, Grafton St.
John Butler
    carrier   ?
C. Marshall
    cashier   Victoria Park
W. H. Frank
    electrician   Moss Side
? McCormick
    cashier   Ducie House, Ducie Gr.
W. Farrington
    portmanteau maker 115, Market St.
A. Pont
    merchant   St. James St.
T. Knowles
    professor of Classics 15, Dryden St.
A. Tate
    printer   Stoneman's Sq.
J. MacDonogh
    merchant   Manchester
James Leming
    factory owner   15, Granville St.
W.H. Beardwood
    architect   55, Parkfield, Moss Side
John Alton
    accountant   5, Moss Grove
John Alton
    banker's clerk   5, Brunswick Terr.
Joshua Finley
    boat maker   46, King St.
A. Kenny
    correspondent   8, Breweston St.
H. Grundy
    pattern card maker 82, Coster St.

J. Schollan
   salesman   11 Dreymouth St.
W. Hetherington
   cashier   40, Dover St.
M. McManus
   tailor   23, Grafton St.
J. Corrigan
   engineer   9, Deanery St.

APPENDIX NINE

An account of the affair as reported in the Jesuits' 'Annual Letters' to the Jesuit curia in Rome, 1877 [1]

Since His Eminence the Cardinal Prefect of the Congregation for the Propagation of the Faith had indicated to the Administrator the Rev. Fr General (Fr. Beckx) that the cause of religion might be very much promoted in Manchester if a College were to be established by the Fathers of the Society, the Rev. Fr Provincial (Fr Gallwey), with the approval of the Fr General, immediately set this work in motion, and sent letters to the Rt Rev. the Bishop of Salford, Herbert Vaughan, and received replies. The Bishop of Salford judged that the (Society's) faculty of erecting a college in Manchester was in no wise to be conceded.

The Rev. Fr Provincial, in accordance with privileges granted to the Society of Jesus by Paul III and confirmed by Pius VII, and following the advice of H.E. Card. Franchi, and further relying on the express wish of the Fr General, established a College (1875), and informed the Bishop that the School had been opened. The Bishop immediately sent a letter to the Superior of the Mission, Fr Henry Birch, in which he threatened our Fathers with suspension from performing their sacred duties unless an end were put to the school within a specified time: and although the Rev. Fr Rector (the Rev. Fr Thomas Ullathorne), and the Rev. Fr Provincial had approached the Bishop and had explained to him with all due respect their position, no further progress was made.

The Bishop denied that we had the right to open a school. 'For when', he says, 'the Bishop my Predecessor received the Fathers of the Society of Jesus into the city of Manchester, it had been decided between the Bishop and the Provincial of England (Fr Weld) that the Fathers would in no wise build a College in the city.' On the other hand, the Rev. Fr Provincial (with the former Provincial Fr Alfred Weld as witness) denied outright that any such agreement had been made. Since much was in dispute, the case was referred to the Sovereign Pontiff.

In the meantime, the School, which had remained closed during Eastertide, thereafter it was opened and remained so till the first half of

---

[1]   ABSI, Litterae Annuae Provinciae Anglicanae Societatis Jesu 1865–1913, letters 1875–1876, pp. 56–57.

June. The Bishop had himself set out for Rome. Although the School had been open for three months, it was closed by order of the Administrator the Rev. Fr General, who, to avoid greater evils, preferred to follow this course of action because of the advice of the Cardinal Prefect and the request of the Bishop of Salford (our rights notwithstanding).

APPENDIX TEN

Fragment of a note by Weld[1]

Canon Benoit was present in a further part of the room connected with that in which we were sitting by (open) folding doors. After I had given the answer which has often been referred to, "that we are not going to open a school" the conversation passed to the subject of parochial schools of which the Bishop fully approved. After some time he said, "but there must never be a school." I then answered what I believe sincerely to be the truth, but without the least mention of pledging myself or binding the Society to anything and merely as stating a fact, that the Society would not open a school without the consent of the Bishop. Upon this the Bishop said, "That will do, make a note of that Canon Benoit." A little after Canon Benoit took a sheet of paper placed it on the desk and taking a pen invited me to write. As I had no intention of performing any act which would bind my successors, and was not prepared to assert in writing as an invariable fact that the Society would not open a school against the wish of the Bishop, I took the pen and wrote these words: 'The Society does not usually open a school without the consent of the Bishop.' I gave the paper to Canon Benoit and he put it into the desk, as far as I noticed without reading it, there are several things to be observed. In the first place it is certain that the Society had been already sounded in writing without any condition as to a school, and that the invitation had been at once acted on. It appears however that at the time of this conversation the Bishop really wished to exclude a school. This was therefore an after thought either of the Bishop himself or of some one near him, and there may be some who will think that what Fr Weld took for a casual conversation was really planned with the intention of adding a condition to an agreement already made. The word condition however was not used as it could not have been after the letter already written by the Bishop. It appears also that Father Weld's first answer was not understood by the Bishop to convey a promise that there should never be a school; and though his subsequent answer was understood as an assurance that there would not be a school without the consent of the Bishop, any such signification was by his written word which proved that he referred only to the ordinary practice of the Society. If the Bishop wished for any further pledge he was at liberty

---

[1] ABSI, RX/5, Weld, no date. The note was probably written in reply to Coleridge's request for information.

to ask for it. As he never did those written words stand as the result of the only intercourse he ever had with the Bishop on the subject of a school. In saying this, we take it for granted, that what was evidently intended to be a document was afterwards read, and consequently that both Canon Benoit and the Bishop know perfectly well that Father Weld had no intention of making any agreement. Had it not been read, we can hardly suppose that Canon Benoit when called on to give his evidence would have failed to second what he had heard from Father Weld's own mouth.

As it was important that these facts should not rest solely on Father Weld's word while there was another person living who could confirm them or deny them if they are inexact, Father Weld took the precaution of writing to Canon Benoit on the subject.

APPENDIX ELEVEN

Brief Summary of the Whole Case[1]

1. On taking possession of his See the Bishop found (1) that one-third of his Clergy were externs or foreigners; (2) that there were no Diocesan Seminary, and (3) no first-rate College in Manchester to feed such a Seminary or to provide the Commercial Education required by the people.

2. *Approbante Capitulo*, he publicly announced, November 30, 1872, his intention to establish both a Seminary and a College.

3. The Seminary is built, and important measures have been taken for the College, including a valuable purchase in the best position in Manchester.

4. Seven months ago the Provincial S.J. applied by letter for permission to open a College of the Society in the same quarter of Manchester. The Bishop felt obliged to decline to give leave on various grounds which he mentioned.

His grounds of positive refusal are:

(1) A *Diocesan* College in Manchester for the laity is essential, if the clergy are to be recruited from the *Diocese*.

(2) The Bishop having the first and chief responsibility in the education of his flock, has a right to choose the most suitable locality for such a College.

(3) He had pre-occupied the locality by public announcement and by outlay, and had acquired for the Diocese a vested interest in that locality.

(4) The Jesuit system has failed to satisfy the commercial classes, and is unsuitable for Manchester.

(5) The Jesuits attempted a College a few years ago in Manchester, and voluntarily abandoned it, because 'it threatened to be a losing concern.'

(6) The Bishop took up the abandoned remnants, and it is this School which his successor proposes to develop on a proportionate scale and plan to meet all requirements.

(7) The Xaverian Brothers have also acquired vested interests in this School, which would be ruined by a Jesuit College.

(8) It is *notorious* that there is not room for two first-rate Catholic Colleges in Manchester – two would be mutually destructive.

---

[1]   This is taken from Vaughan's pamphlet, *The Bishop's Reply*.

(9) The Jesuits were canonically admitted into Manchester on the condition of their establishing no such College. They have broken the condition.

(10) The Bishop's plan, while it provides all that is required by the Catholics in Manchester, does so in conjunction with the Brothers, whose interests will be largely increased and promoted. The Episcopal authority is given *ad aedificationem, non ad destructionem.*

(11) The formation of a Jesuit College, as proposed, would be disastrous to the interests of the Diocese, and destructive of the interests of the Brothers.

(12) The Jesuits ought to be well satisfied (*first*) with their already large and disproportionate share in higher education, and (*secondly*) with the great favour constantly shown them by the present Bishop; for he has publicly defended their Order, patronised their great College of Stonyhurst, recommending it and sending students to it, and taking part in the solemn distribution of the prizes; he invites them to give all his Clergy retreat, and the retreats of most of his Convents; and he has personally assisted at the services in their Church in Manchester more frequently than at those of any other Church in the Diocese, except only the Cathedral. He also invited them to take 'a certain part' in the College he is preparing to establish.

5. Upon declining to give permission for a Jesuit College, the Bishop was abused for want of zeal and lamentation made in the houses of the laity.

6. The Provincial, who has admitted that '*many of the Bishop's reasons are very valid,*' failing to obtain permission, began to assert a right and threatened to use it in spite of him, and contended that the agreement had been only 'a prohibition' on the part of the former Bishop, which might be disregarded by the Society.

7. Three tricks were played on three or four of the Cardinals – two of them on the Cardinal-Prefect.

APPENDIX TWELVE

A Précis of
The Case of the Bishop of Salford and the Society of Jesus[1]

1. Introduction

Had circumstances been different, the facts referred to in this publication "might perhaps have been left ... gradually to die away from memory."[2] However, it is necessary to publish this present paper as a response to the "incomplete and inexact accounts"[3] that have been circulated; which may give an altogether inaccurate impression both of the principles involved, the conduct of the persons concerned, and the manner in which the final settlement was brought about.[4] For reasons of clarity, the chief points of the narrative are provided.

1. The first entry of the Society into Manchester occurred in 1853, when a small school was opened. After a short period of time – within two years – it closed and the Jesuits retired from Manchester. Without being attached to a church the school was not viable. "This impediment made it impossible for the Society to develop its operations in the sphere legitimately allotted to it by its Institute."[5] The then Bishop, William Turner, could not allow a church due to the opposition of his clergy.

2. In 1866, the Society was invited to return to Manchester. On this occasion Bishop Turner did wish there to be a church, and he gave the Society the district in which the Holy Name church was built. He imposed "as a condition *sine qua non*," the need of the Society to purchase a property previously bought by Canon Toole, the rector of a neighbouring mission, for use as a chapel-of-ease to St Wilfrid's, Hulme. This condition was met. During a subsequent conversation, the Bishop stated to the Provincial, Fr Alfred Weld, that he invited them to his Diocese to build a church, not to open a school; "this desire was

---

1   Printed and published privately and anonymously in 1879; it was written and edited by Henry Coleridge SJ. See also the following letters, which were used in the drawing up of this document: Johnson to Coleridge, 8 April 1878; Harper to Coleridge, 23 April 1878; Johnson to Coleridge, 28 April 1878; Etheridge to Coleridge, 7 May 1878; Porter to Etheridge, 15 August 1878.
2   *The Case*, p. 1. All subsequent page references are to this pamphlet.
3   This refers to Vaughan's pamphlets.
4   p. 1.
5   *Ibid.*

acquiesced in by the Provincial, who did not wish at that time to undertake the two works simultaneously."[6] Bishop Vaughan, Bishop Turner's successor, asserted that his predecessor intended by this agreement "to exclude *for ever* the establishment of a College of the Society;"[7] and imposed it as a further *sine qua non* of the Jesuits being readmitted to Manchester. Bishop Vaughan believes that the Jesuits agreed to his second condition. The Society contests this interpretation on the grounds that no such pledge was ever given by the Provincial: "his undertaking referred solely to the time at which it was made."[8]

3. In 1873 and 1874, Fr Gallwey, the English Provincial, applied to Bishop Vaughan for leave to open a College in the district of the Holy Name. The Bishop refused; partly on the grounds of the "alleged agreement with Dr Turner, and on many other grounds."[9] In the autumn of 1874 the Society, encouraged by the Cardinal Prefect of Propaganda, and in accordance with the Bulls of the Institute – which had been acknowledged in Rome – resolved to open a College in Manchester, even if the Bishop should continue to withhold his consent. This course of action was based on the understanding that the Society possessed the privilege of opening a school wherever it had a church. When Bishop Vaughan learnt, by letter, of this proposal, he invited Fr Gallwey to dine with him. The invitation was delayed and so arrived late, by which time the Provincial had left Manchester. This was the only reply the Bishop made to the Provincial. Fr Gallwey again wrote to Bishop Vaughan, who in reply told him to do nothing about the opening of a College until he had heard from Propaganda Fide, and had returned from his impending journey to America. The Bishop maintained that in asking Fr Gallwey to wait there was, "either contained or implied, in a sufficiently explicit manner, a notice that he questioned the rights of the Society ... and that he 'appealed to Rome' and 'prohibited' any further steps to be taken until a decision had been arrived at there."[10] The Society holds that the Bishop did not, "with intelligible clearness," inform the Provincial of his making an appeal against the idea of a College.[11]

4. The school was opened soon after the Bishop's return, "in consequence of orders from the General of the Society." The Bishop was informed by the Superior of the district on the same morning as the school opened.[12] The Bishop responded by declaring he did not admit

[6] p. 2.
[7] *Ibid.*
[8] *Ibid.*
[9] *Ibid.*
[10] p. 3.
[11] *Ibid.*
[12] *Ibid.*

the right of the Society to act in this way, and that he would suspend the Jesuits in Manchester *a divinis* if the school was not closed within a week. The Bishop and the Provincial came to an agreement to the effect of closing the school at the beginning of the following week for the Easter holidays. A telegram sent the following day from Rome to the Bishop instructed him not to carry out his threatened proceedings against the Society, and to submit an account of what had taken place. The Provincial also received a telegram, informing him that proceedings against the Society had been stayed and that no new steps were to be taken. The Provincial honoured the agreement already made with the Bishop, "although he conceived that the news from Rome exonerated him from all obligation on that score, and it was not reopened till the time fixed by that agreement had expired, that is, until the end of the usual short Easter holidays."[13] The Bishop saw the reopening as "uncanonical" and "a violation of the promise made by the Provincial."[14] The Society maintains that the school continued after the holidays in virtue of the rights by which it had been originally established. Furthermore, the telegram the Provincial had received from Rome did not prohibit this happening; it had merely asked that "no new steps be taken". The reopening was not a new step, but a continuation of the normal course established prior to the Easter holidays. The Provincial had not promised not to reopen the school, but simply to close it early for the Easter holidays.

5. When the bishops met for their Low Week meeting in London (1875), Bishop Vaughan laid before them a statement of the case;[15] he refused to let the Provincial have sight of this document. The Provincial asked for, and was granted, permission to present to the bishops a memorial relating to the issue between the Bishop of Salford and himself. The Provincial did not accept an invitation to appear personally; he thought this imprudent, "on account of the refusal of the Bishop to allow him to know the charges made against him."[16]

The Bishop described the English Hierarchy has having been appointed by Propaganda Fide as a "higher tribunal ... to examine the whole question."[17] The Provincial maintained that he was never informed by the Bishop nor by Rome that the Hierarchy had been appointed to adjudicate in the matter. The submission of his memorial was a voluntary act; the Bishops had not asked for evidence on any particular point. When the Bishop had spoken of the matter passing

---

[13] p. 4.
[14] *Ibid.*
[15] This was in the form of his first pamphlet, *The Claim.*
[16] p. 4.
[17] p. 5.

to a "higher authority," the Provincial had assumed he was referring to Propaganda Fide. Subsequently the Bishop went to Rome and laid the case before the Holy See. "The result was that he wrote a letter to the General, in which he declared that without raising any question as to the privilege of the Society, his objections to the school on the ground of the good of his diocese were as strong as ever, and the General then, seeing that the privileges of the Society remained intact, and were not questioned by the Bishop, for the sake of peace acceded to the request, and gave orders for the closing of the school."[18]

These represent the chief facts of the case; as yet no complete statement of them has been drawn up.

Two pamphlets published by the Bishop of Salford,[19] despite being assigned "for official use," have been widely circulated among nonofficial persons, and for a long time after the school's closure. Not only has he continued to circulate them, he has failed to correct the errors they contain and has not fully explained the manner in which the matter ended. The second of the Bishop's pamphlets was largely a response to a collection of documents printed by the Provincial – *Facts and Documents* – of which only six copies were made.

2. First Entrance of the Society into Manchester

The first Jesuit school in Manchester – a middle school – opened in 1853, and "was considered only as an experiment."[20] Contrary to Bishop Vaughan's claim no "promise or intimation [was] given that the Society had a large sum of money ready which it intended to spend on the College."[21] After a reasonable trial the school closed. A large proportion of the diocesan clergy were opposed to the school, and both clergy and the Bishop were against the Society opening a church; for this reason the Society found it necessary to abandon the school. Bishop Vaughan's presentation of these facts speaks of the failure of the school in terms of a reproach,[22] and may also lead to the "insinuation that the object of the Society in coming to Manchester was to make money."[23] The Society contends that what they abandoned was an attempt which appeared sure to fail, and not the *education question* itself. The statements made by

---

[18] p. 5.
[19] *The Claim* and *The Bishop's Reply.*
[20] p. 7.
[21] *Ibid.*
[22] "But, as has been said, finding that 'the College threatened to become a losing concern,' after a short time, the Fathers voluntarily gave up *the education question* in Manchester, and entirely withdrew from the field, possibly with some loss, but without having spent their £5,000" (Pamphlet I, p. 17)." p. 8.
[23] p. 8.

the Bishop about the first entrance of the Jesuits are at variance with the actual facts; for example, that the Jesuits told the Bishop (Turner) that they had £5,000 to spend on a college, when in fact "there is no foundation whatever for the statement about the £5000."[24] The implication is that by not spending this amount the Society broke its promise.

The Bishop uses the phrase, "a losing concern" some half-dozen times. This is objectionable, for it insinuates that the Society held only pecuniary interests in coming to Manchester. The full context of the phrase – never used by the Bishop – in reference to the school, gives its true meaning: "the school, unsupported by a Church, threatened to be a losing concern."[25] Bishop Turner was very appreciative of the Society's efforts; he stated that "The experiment made has, I confess, surpassed my expectations ... I owe a debt of gratitude to yourself [the Provincial] and the Fathers of the Society."[26]

3. Second Entrance of the Society into Manchester

The Bishop, in his pamphlets, states that the Society "petitioned for leave" to build a church in Manchester and they told the Bishop they had a large sum of money for this purpose.[27] This is misrepresentative of the facts. The offer to the Society came from Bishop Turner, who wanted preachers who might handle in the pulpit the subjects of the day.[28] This fact must have been unknown to Bishop Vaughan. The only *sine qua non* imposed upon the Society by Bishop Turner at the time of the second entrance was the purchase of Canon Toole's property. This too, the Bishop seems unaware of, for in his pamphlet he claims that permission was granted on the stipulation that there was not to be a school or College of the Society, other than a poor school.

At the time when the negotiations were taking place between Bishop Turner and the Society, the Bishop was not thinking about a College or a school, nor had the Society any thoughts of immediately opening a College. It is acknowledged by both parties, "that something did pass verbally between the late Bishop and the Provincial, Father Weld, on the subject of a College."[29] Fr Weld had at first forgotten the details of his conversation with Bishop Turner. This was due to, "change of scene, the lapse of years, and the absence of any papers on the subject."[30] His conduct however, both at the time and in subsequent assertions "has

---

[24] p. 9.
[25] *Ibid.*
[26] p. 12.
[27] p. 11.
[28] See above, Harper's letter, 23 April 1878. This letter is also printed in *The Case.*
[29] p. 13.
[30] p. 14.

constantly shown his conviction that no agreement was ever entered into which could exclude the future establishment of a College."[31] Bishop Turner committed nothing in writing with reference to a school; the subject was mentioned in a casual conversation and Fr Weld has maintained that "the exclusion of a school was never proposed" as a condition of the Society entering Manchester.[32] He regarded the Bishop's wish as sufficient reason not to open a school during his, the Bishop's, lifetime; but "in the absence of any contract whatsoever it could have no effect when we had both of us passed away from office."[33] Had Bishop Turner wanted to bind the Society forever, he would have drawn up a written document. Canon Benoit was present when the conversation between the Bishop and the Provincial took place.[34] Both the Canon and the Bishop knew perfectly well that Fr Weld had no intention of making an agreement which would permanently exclude the possibility of a school or College, for he had written – in response to the Bishop saying: "but there must never be a school," – "the Society does not usually open a school without the consent of the Bishop."[35] This document is no longer available.[36] Bishop Vaughan has taken no notice of this document of Father Weld. Based on the evidence available "the supposition of an agreement must be dismissed for ever, and yet this is the subject of repeated and bitter accusation, and, strange to say, Father Weld is held up to obloquy as having been guilty of a 'trick', and of 'stating his own case' to the Cardinal Prefect."[37]

When Fr Weld became conscious that he had in actual fact said more about the school, and he now believed he had told the Bishop how the Society could not open a school without his consent, he went to speak to the Cardinal Prefect of Propaganda Fide about the matter. The Prefect assured him that this did not constitute a problem, and that there was no difficulty in this. Bishop Vaughan on the other hand accused Fr Weld of playing a "trick" on the Cardinal Prefect by concealing from him his opposition to the proposed school. The Society refutes this accusation, and holds how the occasion when Fr Weld spoke to the Cardinal, "was one on which it would not have been germane to the subject of the conversation to mention" the present bishop's objections.[38]

---

31 *Ibid.*
32 p. 14.
33 p. 15.
34 See Appendix 10.
35 p. 16.
36 See Appendix 10.
37 p. 17.
38 *Ibid.*

It is the usual aim and custom of the Society to open schools or colleges in all cities where they have churches; this custom is derived from the Institute itself, and from the object of the Society. This being so, the Provincial would not have acted in any way so contrary to these aims and customs so as to render a College in Manchester impossible, without consulting his superiors on the issue. There is no trace of such a consultation. The Fathers at the church of the Holy Name were continually looking for a piece of ground on which to build a College – this is further proof of it being commonly understood that no permanent exclusion had been entered into. During the time of Bishop Turner ground was bought specifically for this purpose.

The only proof produced by Bishop Vaughan in support of his assertions is the memorandum of Canon Benoit, and a resolution of the Chapter.[39] In neither of these is the word "petitioned" used when speaking of the Society coming to Manchester; yet it appears in the Bishop's pamphlets. Both the Canon and the Chapter speak of an "agreement", vis-à-vis about there being no school, other than a poor school; but the Bishop chooses to see it as a *sine qua non* of the Society's being re-admitted. In short, the language of these two documents is not nearly as empatic as that of the Bishop's pamphlets, and far less contradictory of Fr Weld's statements about the same matters. In the 'Summary'[40] he forwarded to Rome, and in his pamphlets, the Bishop wrote: "it was only upon the condition of their opening no College that the late Bishop let them into Manchester again."[41] This latter assertion does find support in the facts of the case, and goes beyond what can legitimately be drawn from the documents of Canon Benoit and the Chapter.

Fr Weld in his conversation had in effect assured Bishop Turner "that he need not fear a College being established against his will or that of his successor, but that this assurance was at the same time modified in writing into a statement of the usual practice of the Society."[42]

A full account of the Jesuits' second entrance into Manchester can be found in Fr Harper's letter of 23 April 1878; and Porter's letter of 15 August 1878 [both are reproduced in the *corpus* of correspondence in this present volume].

4. Reasons for and against the establishment in Manchester of a College of the Society

No one possessing knowledge of English Catholicism could fail to see that to shut the Jesuits out of Manchester would be to shut them

---

[39] See Appendices 2 and 4.
[40] See Appendix 3.
[41] p. 21.
[42] p. 23.

out of one of its very spheres of labour. In England there is need of higher and middle class education; this is especially true in Manchester, and in particular for the Catholics of this city. Education "has become the essential passport to advancement of every kind."[43] The progress of education has brought popular literature, which has experienced an enormous growth, within the reach of all who can read. The maxims and doctrines of the day are also within easy reach and can affect society in a malevolent way, leading to shipwreck being made of faith and virtue. If the position of the Catholic body in England is to be improved or even maintained there is need of middle class education. However, Catholic schools for the middle class "are commonly wanting, or ... are below the level of their Protestant neighbours."[44] For these reasons alone the Society would not abandon its work for education where this was practicable. Pius VII restored the Jesuits (1814) expressly with a view to the services they could offer to Catholic education.

In 1874 the population of Manchester and Salford was estimated at 592,164. Within a radius of 12 miles there are 26 other towns with an average population of 25,000. The total population of all these areas taken together equals one and a half million, of which between 130,000 – 140,000 are Catholics. The Catholic population of Manchester is 92,000. These statistics demonstrate the importance of education for Manchester.

To meet this need great effort has been made to develop Owens College into a "University for the North".[45] The spirit of this college is secular. One must consider therefore "how much might be gained to the faith, and how many souls might be preserved from ruin, if every means were taken to extend education, at once Christian and scientific, in a city which is acknowledged to be one of the great centres of activity and population, not only in England but in the world."[46] In the presence of such gigantic efforts in the cause of atheistic teaching, Catholics should feel the obligation to advance Christian education. In order to serve this much needed advancement it is important to set aside any desire to monopolize the field of education and that every available means should be employed to save the present generation of children of the poorer and middle classes from an education that would entail the loss of their faith.

There is no country in the world in which the hierarchy and the parish priests are considered to have the monopoly over higher and middle education, or that they can fulfil these tasks unaided; even less can this be said of England, and in particular of Manchester. The diocese of

---

[43] p. 28.
[44] *Ibid.*
[45] p. 29.
[46] p. 29.

Salford is exceptionally backward in comparison to other dioceses. A considerable portion of its clergy is made up of foreigners, and it is heavily in debt. In 1874 there were thirty-three priests in Manchester. In the face of such hardship the Bishop rejected the help of the Society to provide, at no cost, higher and middle-class education. "It is a difficulty in the treatment of the whole subject to which these remarks refer, that questions of a personal and incidental character have been so much mixed up with simple elements of the case ... But it is on all accounts desirable that the question should be at least stated as if these unfortunate ingredients had not been thrown in."[47] In order to do this the present document refers to the 'Summary of the Whole Case', which is to be found at the end of the Bishop's second pamphlet.[48]

The reasons why the Bishop refused help are as follows. [Numbers in brackets correspond to those of the 'Summary.']

(1) A *Diocesan* College in Manchester for the laity is necessary if the Clergy are to be recruited from the *Diocese*.

(2) The Bishop having the first and chief responsibility in the education of his flock has a right to choose the most suitable locality for such a College.

(3) He had pre-occupied the locality by public announcement and by outlay, and had acquired for the Diocese a vested interest in that locality.

The Society does not desire a monopoly of education, but only to be allowed to act according to its Institute and the privileges granted by the Holy See. Given that this is so, it is asked – if a diocesan College is necessary in Manchester in order to recruit clergy why are they not essential elsewhere? Such Colleges perhaps only exist in half the dioceses of the world, and certainly not in England.

The Bishop speaks in his pamphlet of a 'commercial college'; he further claims that a Jesuit education is not suitable for Manchester, as it lacks commercial character. But can such a College as the Bishop proposes prepare boys for a priestly vocation? Whilst it is true that the obligation of educating his flock falls primarily to the Bishop, it is not the doctrine of the Church that he exclude the religious Orders from assisting in this task or that the Bishop must monopolize education.

With regard to the second point, Bishop Vaughan speaks in terms of an implied right of monopoly. "The words of the Bishop may mean that if a certain neighbourhood, already occupied by a religious body, be in his judgement the best position for a diocesan College, he has a

---

[47] p. 31.
[48] *Ibid.* See Appendix 11 for a copy of the 'Summary'.

right to take that site to himself."[49] This implies an exaggerated idea of episcopal right and powers.

As for the third point, the Bishop in his plan for education stated that he intended "to complete the work of the Grammar School, prudently and wisely begun by my predecessor".[50] There are according to diocesan education statistics three Grammar Schools within Manchester and Salford, one of them is near the Cathedral – the 'Diocesan Grammar School.' When the Society entered Manchester in Bishop Turner's time, he placed them as far away as possible from the Cathedral. If Bishop Vaughan had chosen to develop the Diocesan Grammar School and allowed the Society a College in Manchester there would have been two great centres of education, without fear of collision. But instead of developing the Diocesan Grammar School the Bishop planned a new school, within fifty yards of the district of the Holy Name. After a short space of time the Bishop transferred this new school from its site near the Holy Name district, and removed it to Alexandra Park – "His own act may therefore be considered as the most conclusive refutation of his agreement as to the necessity of the site in question to the interests of the diocese." Had the Bishop wanted to make impossible two Catholic colleges in Manchester he could not have done it better than he did – by placing his new college within so short a distance of the Holy Name district. For it was natural that that district, where the Society had purchased land for the purpose, would have been the location for its own College.

Further reasons for the exclusion of the Society from education in Manchester are:

(4) The Jesuit system has failed to satisfy the commercial classes, and is unsuitable for Manchester.

(5) The Jesuits attempted a College a few years ago in Manchester, and voluntarily abandoned it, because "it threatened to be a losing concern."

(6) The Bishop took up the abandoned remnants, and it is this School which his successor proposes to develop on a proportionate scale and to meet all requirements.

With regards to the first point: assertion is not proof. The Jesuit College in Liverpool is proof that the Jesuit system does not fail the commercial classes. Bishop Vaughan himself acknowledged the success of this college when he said that he "cannot allow the Society to *absorb* education in Manchester, as it has done in Liverpool."[51] The ability of the

[49] p. 33.
[50] p. 34.
[51] p. 37.

Bishop to judge the Jesuit system is thus questioned. The Jesuit system is capable of modification to meet varied requirements and classes. If the diocesan college is to be, as the Bishop desires, a means of recruiting clergy for the diocese, will the education demanded for that end be suitable for the commercial classes? Despite the claims of unsuitability, "a considerable number" of Catholics in Manchester want a Jesuit college to be established there.

As for reasons (5) and (6): an account has already been given of the failure of the former Jesuit College in Manchester; with regard to the latter point – "The Bishop's own action in founding his College at Alexandra Park is sufficient proof of the possibility of the existence of different schools in Manchester."[52]

(7) The Xaverian Brothers have also acquired vested interests in this school, which would be ruined by a Jesuit College.

The Bishop claims that if there were a Jesuit College in Manchester the Xaverian School would be ruined. At the same time the Bishop's plan is to absorb the Xaverian College into his commercial college. Here there is a non sequitur in his argument: if the Jesuit College is unsuitable for the commercial classes it follows that it would not be a threat to a college set up to serve that need. If the Xaverian School is more satisfactory than a Jesuit College, why is there a need to develop it? Yet it is undeniable that the school of the Brothers was insufficient. Had it been sufficient, the Jesuits would never have contemplated opening their College. The success of the Xaverian has been with the children of the poor, and their middle school has maintained itself since the foundation of the Bishop's College [St. Bede's].

(8) It is notorious that there is not room for two first-rate Catholic Colleges in Manchester – two would be mutually destructive.

If this were so, and there was room for only one such college, it should be questioned whether the college should not be in "the hands of those whose Institute is specially designed for education, and who had succeeded best in it in other parts of the world, and particularly in England. It is new doctrine, that if the population can only support one College, that College should of necessity be in the hands of the Bishop."[53] It is a well founded opinion that there is room for two colleges in Manchester. If the Bishop had developed the Diocesan Grammar School, near the cathedral, and the Jesuits had been allowed to establish theirs in the district of the Holy Name, this would have become apparent.

---

[52] p. 38.
[53] p. 40.

(9) The Jesuits were canonically admitted into Manchester on the condition of their establishing no such College. They have broken the condition.

This has already been answered. "There is no evidence whatever that he [Turner] insisted on their [the Jesuits] making any promise never to open a College a condition *sine qua non*."[54]

(10) The Bishop's plan, while it provides all that is required by the Catholics of Manchester, does so in conjunction with the Brothers, whose interests will be largely increased and promoted. The Episcopal authority is given *ad aedificationem non ad destructionem*.

Despite the Bishop's plan being comprehensive, he certainly cannot provide all that is required by the Catholics of Manchester. There will always be parents who wish for their children to be educated by members of Religious Orders. Some feel that in this country an attempt is being made, even by persons in high office in the Church, to exclude Religious from the work of education. The rights of parents to have their children taught by Religious are being denied them "by the practical prohibition, on the part of the Ordinaries, of the opening of schools conducted by religious – especially by those of the Society of Jesus."[55]

What is further lacking in all probability in the Bishop's plan, is the performance and uniformity of excellent teaching; something which is rendered with comparative ease in the schools of the Religious Orders.

"With regard to the 'interests' of the Xaverian Brothers, experience would have shown, if the Bishop had not altogether changed his plans, whether those Brothers will not have been reduced to the position of teachers who take a very subordinate part indeed in an Institute in which their own school has been absorbed."[56] In the account of his project sent to Rome [see Appendix 3], the Bishop said "he meant to carry it out 'probably' in connection with the Brothers."[57]

The last two grounds of the Bishop's reasons may be taken together. They are:

(11) The formation of a Jesuit College as proposed would be disastrous to the interests of the Diocese, and destructive of the interests of the Brothers.

(12) The Jesuits ought to be well satisfied (first) with their already large and disproportionate share in higher education, and (secondly) with the great favour constantly shown them by the present Bishop; for he has publicly defended their Order, patronised their great College of Stonyhurst, recommending it and sending students to it, and taking

---

[54] p. 40.
[55] pp. 41–42.
[56] p. 42.
[57] *Ibid.*

part in the solemn distribution of the prizes; he invites them to give all his clergy retreat, and the retreats of most of his Convents, and he has personally assisted at the services of their Church in Manchester more frequently than at those of any other Church in the Diocese excepting only the Cathedral. He also invited them to take 'a certain' part in the College he is preparing to establish.

"It is certainly little less than astonishing to find that the Bishop can in the same breath enumerate all these instances of his 'favour' towards the Society, and also state that the establishment of a College of the Society would be disastrous to the interests of his Diocese, as well as destructive of those of the Xaverian Brothers."[58] The Bishop's statement that the Jesuits already have a "large and disproportionate share of higher education," begs the question – disproportionate to what? It is taken to mean that the Society has a greater portion of education than that of the bishops or the secular clergy. This seems to imply that "influence, power, connection, and perhaps even wealth, are the objects to be sought and gained by those who labour in the field of Christian education."[59] The large share which the Society enjoys is down to the fact that it has, since the times of persecution, laboured hard in England for the cause of religion and education.

The Bishop feared that a Jesuit College would mean fewer vocations for the secular priesthood, and so be injurious to the Diocese. The doctrine of the Church is that vocations come from God, it is wrong to attempt to force one who has a vocation to be a religious into a secular vocation and *vice versa*. There are two branches of the one clergy – secular and regular. These are not antagonistic one to the other. In his pamphlet the Bishop shows evidence of hostility and jealousy toward the Society, e.g. that some might wish to join the Jesuits rather than become secular priests. The Bishop mentions, in condemnatory terms, a saying attributed to a "trusted and distinguished member of the Order, that 'whatever is good for the Society is good for the Diocese.'"[60] This saying can certainly have a good sense, if one takes into consideration St Paul's teaching on mutual charity binding together the various members of the Body of Christ. It would not be difficult to make a collection of the Bishop's hostile comments about the Society, which could be taken to mean: 'whatever is good for the Society is bad for the Diocese.'[61]

---

[58]   p. 43.
[59]   p. 44.
[60]   p. 45.
[61]   *Ibid.*

In the diocese of Salford until recently "religious priests were jealously excluded from work in large cities."[62]

"From this examination of the grounds alleged by the Bishop against the establishment of a College of the Society in Manchester, it seems not unfair to conclude that there were no vital reasons against that establishment, which in itself was undoubtedly for the advancement of the great cause of Catholic education."[63] The Bishop of Salford has practically sought to abrogate the Society's privileges or to deny their existence.

5. Duties of the Society as to Education

This is not the place to draw out the conviction, held by many, "that a determination exists in the minds of some members of the English Hierarchy to impair, as far as lies in their power, the influence of the Religious Orders in this country, and especially the influence of the Society of Jesus," from the sphere of education.[64] In wanting to exercise their privileges, the Society in no way desires to override the wishes, nor defy the legitimate authority of the bishops. These rights and privileges were conferred for a purpose; the Bishop of Salford has practically recognised their existence. Yet he has continued to circulate his pamphlets in which these privileges are not recognised and virtually denied. He maintains that he did not exceed his right when he threatened to censure the Manchester Jesuits, and speaks of the reopening of the College as 'uncanonical'. His pamphlets create the impression that the settlement of the Manchester Case in Rome included a revocation or denial of the Society's privileges. "… such an impression is derogatory, not only to the Society of Jesus, but to the Holy See itself, from which the privileges of the Society proceed."[65] Opposing the exercise of rights of Religious Orders, and "to give an exaggerated impression of the omnipotence of the Bishops in their dioceses … is, in the ultimate analysis, to question the powers of the Successor St Peter."[66]

6. Circumstances which led to the opening of a College of the Society in Manchester

A College in connection with the church of the Holy Name was contemplated from the beginning. The Provincial, while maintaining his obeisance to Bishop Turner's desire, and at the same time not wishing

---

[62] p. 46.

[63] *Ibid.*

[64] p. 47. The examples given where the Society has experienced difficulty are Liverpool and London. These and other examples are evidence of an "aggressive and exclusive spirit which has caused so much grief and scandal in the country." p. 48.

[65] p. 50.

[66] *Ibid.*

himself to open a school, purchased a piece of land with a view to opening a College there in the future. However, he was unwilling to do this during the Bishop's lifetime. At the Fourth Provincial Synod of Westminster (1873), the Provincial, Fr Gallwey, approached Bishop Vaughan on the subject of a College in Manchester. This request was denied. In the August of the following year, the Provincial renewed his request; again this met with a refusal from the Bishop. Bishop Vaughan gave the reasons which have already been alluded to: the Society had already abandoned a school in Manchester; other schools had been established and vested interests had come into existence; he had made public his undertaking to develop one of the existing Grammar Schools into a commercial college.

As for the agreement between Fr Weld and the late Bishop, it is noted that it was not until 1874 – when Bishop Vaughan replied to the second request – that the Provincial became aware of any "agreement", "compact", or "condition", that barred the Jesuits from opening a College in Manchester. When the Bishop first refused permission he had not referred to the supposed agreement or to the memorandum of Canon Benoit – which had been drawn up after the late Bishop's lifetime; it was in fact written in October 1873.

The Bishop gave two further reasons: "the present backward condition of our diocesan and hierarchical organization" and the fact the Society already had Stonyhurst College, which is in the Bishop's diocese.[67] The first of these reasons supplies a very strong reason for calling upon the Religious Orders to supplement the work of the secular clergy and the Hierarchy. Where Religious Orders are prevented from working in large towns by the opposition of the Bishops the diocesan organization is "utterly inadequate".[68] The "backward condition" of the dioceses is evidence of the false principle that the interests of the Church are served by the Bishops who, when they cannot do everything themselves, will not allow others to do it for them.

With regard to the issue of Stonyhurst: this is a boarding school and therefore totally different from what was proposed by the Society for Manchester.

In reply to the Bishop the Provincial referred to a letter which he had received from the Cardinal Prefect of Propaganda, in which the General of the Society was asked to do all he could for middle class education in the large cities, especially in Manchester.[69]

---

[67] p. 35.
[68] p. 55.
[69] See above, Franchi to Beckx, 13 November 1874.

"One of the great ends for which God has established the Holy See at the head of the Church has always been acknowledged to be that individual Bishops might be supervised and overruled, if they sought what they considered a particular good or interest to the detriment of the common good and interest of the Body of Christ."[70] One way by which the Holy See exercises this principle of supervision is through religious that are "exempted by supreme authority from the authority of the Bishops and furnished with special rights from that Holy See itself."[71] The Cardinal, along with others, recognised that the Society had, according to its Institute, a privilege granted by the Holy See whereby it could open schools wherever it was canonically established. Religious Orders must not shrink from using their privileges and ought to use them for the execution of their legitimate work. The responsibility not to use their privileges only ceases when the Holy See retracts or fails to recognise them. In the light of this, the Society felt itself obliged to duly put into practice what the Holy See had granted it.

The Provincial wrote to the Bishop on 11 December 1874; he pointed out to his Lordship that the Society would be reluctant to undertake anything that might be contrary to the Bishop's wishes. At the same time he courteously intimated that the Bishop did not possess the absolute right to prohibit the Society from exercising this right and so establishing a College, but that it was desirous of exercising its privilege.

The Bishop did not reply to the Provincial's letter, other than an invitation to dine at Bishop's House, Salford. The invitation arrived late and by the time the Provincial was in receipt of it the date of the dinner had passed. The Provincial shortly afterwards heard that his Lordship was about to leave for America and would be away for three months; he therefore wrote yet again, simply to ask the Bishop's blessings on the Society's hopes for a College in Manchester. The Bishop asked that nothing be done until he returned from America. It should be noted that in his reply the Bishop did not deny the Society's rights and privileges *vis-à-vis* a College.

The correspondence between the Cardinal Prefect and the Society regarding middle class education, with special reference to Manchester, is described in the Bishop's words as "a trick" and "trickery". His claim is that three tricks were played on three or four of the Cardinals at Propaganda Fide. These tricks being: the Provincial, Fr Weld, concealing from the Cardinal Prefect the Bishop's objection to the proposed Jesuit College; on the occasion when Fr Weld laid his version of the agreement before the Cardinal, he continued to keep him in ignorance of this fact;

---

70 p. 59.
71 *Ibid.*

his consulting the opinion of three Cardinals as to the abstract right of the Society, and obtaining a favourable response. Bishop Vaughan claims that these three tricks were then used as three legal decisions against the Bishop. This was achieved by stating that a Jesuit College was "the wish of Propaganda"; that the Cardinal Prefect "had declared that on the score of the agreement there was no difficulty"; the Cardinals of Propaganda maintained that the Jesuits were "perfectly within their rights in setting up a College in spite of the Bishop."[72] In response to Bishop Vaughan's insinuation against Fr Weld – "It seems … as if there were persons – not Protestants or enemies of the Church – who do not appear to think that a member of the Society of Jesus can be trusted to state his own case of conscience fairly."[73]

The use of the word trick – "an invidious expression" – is strongly objected to by the Society in its application to Fr Weld.[74] The Bishop himself has acted in a way which merits such a description; for example when he misled the Provincial into thinking that the "higher authority" to which the school case had been passed was the Congregation of Propaganda Fide, when in actual fact it was the English Hierarchy. In this instance, as in others, the Society has not accused the Bishop of playing tricks. The same may also be said of how his Lordship refused to let the Provincial have sight of the accusations made against the Society by the Bishop. In urging his case in Rome the Bishop failed to mention that there was a more suitable Grammar School to be developed – the Diocesan Grammar School – rather than the Xaverian School. If he had chosen to develop the former, the Society would have been free to establish a College. The Jesuits have declined to describe this action as a "trick."

No trick was ever played by Fr Weld. The conversation which took place between himself and the Cardinal Prefect – during which the Bishop claims that the tricks were played – did not relate to the particular case of Manchester "except as far as it was involved in the abstract question" of privileges and the opening of schools.[75]

[At this point, *The Case* refers to some of the correspondence relating to the dispute.][76]

---

[72] p. 67.
[73] p. 74.
[74] p. 70.
[75] p. 76.
[76] See above for the following letters: Gallwey to Rome, 7 August 1874; Vaughan to Gallwey, 17 August 1874; Gallwey to Vaughan, 20 August 1874; Gallwey to Vaughan, 11 December 1874; Gallwey to Vaughan, 19 December 1874; Gallwey to Vaughan, New Year's day, 1875; Vaughan to Gallwey, 2 January 1875; 'Summary of the Bishop of Salford's Case, sent to his Agent in Rome', Appendix 3; 'Memorandum of the late Bishop's Secretary and Confidential Adviser as to the Agreement between Bishop Turner and the provincial S.J.', Appendix 2; 'Resolution of the Salford Chapter', Appendix 4.

7. Facts as to the opening of the College

According to the account given by the Bishop in his first pamphlet the facts of the opening are these: "Then came a trick, a threat, and the assertion of a *right*, and the ignoring of the condition and agreement. When appeal was carried to the highest tribunal of law, without waiting for the answer, the invasion was made in the night, unknown to the Bishop and in spite of him, accompanied, no doubt by the plaudits of a few. The result, the establishment of a College, was then announced to the Bishop as a *'fait accompli,'* which he was invited to bless, while prophecies were uttered and brought to him that he would soon find the invasion and occupation of the Educational position would tend to the glory of God and the good of the Diocese, and that he had better quietly yield to circumstances."

The 'trick' was the alleged concealment practised by Fr Weld on the Cardinals of Propaganda. The 'threat' was the intimation of Fr Gallwey that the Society held privileges from the Holy See to open colleges without the Bishop's permission, and despite of not having it. The Society rejects these accusations. Nor did the Society acknowledge the existence of an 'agreement' about their not having a College. The Bishop never informed the Society that he had made an appeal to Rome against their privileges or that he denied the existence of such. Nor in the statement which he sent to his agent in Rome does the Bishop question the rights of the Society.[77] In effect his 'appeal' to Rome was in fact a request for the support of Propaganda, in order that the rights of the Society may not be exercised. The Provincial understood the privileges to be notorious; he therefore acted upon them and in doing so felt that he need not consult the Bishop further. The College was opened; on the same day the Bishop was informed by letter.[78] This action the Bishop refers to "as an invasion in the night." The Society contends that if it had wanted to 'invade' the Diocese, it would have done so during the Bishop's absence. Nothing the Society did was contrary to established law.

Shortly after receiving his letter, the Bishop threatened to suspend the Manchester Jesuits if the school was not closed.[79] The Bishop and the Provincial came to an agreement that the College would close somewhat early for the Easter vacations; this did not imply that it should close indefinitely. The Bishop however drew this conclusion and then accused the Provincial of breaking his promise when the College was reopened after the holidays. In his second pamphlet the reopening is described by Bishop Vaughan as "uncanonical".

---

[77] See Appendix 3.
[78] See above, Ullathorne to Vaughan, 13 March 1875.
[79] See above, Vaughan to Birch, 16 March 1875.

Despite the repeated assertions by the Bishop of Salford, there is no strong evidence to support the belief that the English Hierarchy was ever given the powers of a "tribunal" to examine the College question. Neither is it known that they were furnished with powers as a Commission.

[At this point, *The Case* refers to the remaining parts of the correspondence, and documents related to the dispute.[80]]

8. Facts as to the final closing of the College

"It is quite certain that it was not because of any action of the English Hierarchy or of the Congregation of Propaganda itself that the College of the Society in Manchester was closed."[81] The Cardinal Prefect and other Cardinals had previously recognised the Society's right to open schools where they had a church. The Cardinal Prefect had stayed the Bishop's hand and so prevented him executing his threat of suspension of the Manchester Fathers. "It is clearly impossible to represent the closing of the College on the consequences of any decision whatever on the points of rights raised by the Bishop of Salford."[82] The College was closed by the authority of the General of the Society after having received the Bishop's letter, which he wrote on Pentecost Sunday 1875.[83]

The Bishop's pamphlets do not make clear the matter of how the College was finally closed. It is publicly known that the College is closed, but it is not publicly known how it came to close. Even after the closure, the Bishop continued to distribute his pamphlets.

It has never been admitted or decided by any authority that the Jesuits, in opening the college, were acting against the law of the Church. The Bishop, when he asked the Jesuit General to close the College, did not call into question the Society's privileges. The College was closed by the same authority that ordered its opening – that of Father General.

---

[80] See above, Gallwey to Vaughan, 13 March 1875; Vaughan to Birch, 16 March 1875; Gallwey to Vaughan, 17 March 1875; Birch to Gallwey, 22 March 1875; Gallwey to Vaughan, 23 March 1875; Vaughan to Gallwey, 24 March 1875; Vaughan to Birch, 4 April 1875; Birch to Vaughan, 4 April 1875; Vaughan to Gallwey, 4 April 1875; Gallwey to Vaughan, 7 April 1875; The Provincial's Memorial to the Bishops, Appendix 5.

[81] p. 131.

[82] p. 132.

[83] See above, letter from Vaughan to Beckx, Pentecost Sunday, 1875; Beckx to Vaughan, 25 May 1875.

SELECT BIBLIOGRAPHY

Primary Sources

MSS sources

London, *Archivum Britannicum Societatis Iesu*
    Epistolae Generalium III, Peter Beckx 1873–1884
    BN/6, Weld Letters
    C/3, A. Weld Letters as assistant
    CL/5, Jurisdiction Question, Cardinal Herbert Vaughan (Bp. of Salford)
    Letters from Bishops and Cardinals, 1753–1835 (bound volume)
    Letters to Bishops and Cardinals, 1840–1891 (bound volume)
    Litterae Annuae Provincae Anglicanae Soc. Jesu
    RX/4-5-6, Manchester School Question, 1875–81
    RY/2/1, Letters from Snead-Cox to Pollen
    RY/2/2, Manchester Jurisdiction Question
    Purcell's Suppressed Chapter

Rome, Archives of Propaganda Fide
    Anglia 19, 1871–1874
    Anglia 20, 1875–1877

Rome, *Archivum Romanum Societatis Jesu*
    Prov. Angliae 1/14–IV.4
    Prov. Angliae 1005
    Prov. Angliae 1015a

Archives of the Archbishop of Westminster
    V.I/30, Vaughan Diaries
    V.I/7, Vaughan Correspondence

Salford Diocesan Archives
    Box 179, Vaughan-Casartelli Correspondence
    Casartelli Diaries 1875
    Chapter Minutes 1872

Printed sources

Anon., *The Case of the Bishop of Salford and the Society of Jesus* (Manresa Press, 1879)

Anon., *Facts and Documents relating to the College of the Society of Jesus in Manchester* (1875)

Guy, Robert, *The Synods in English: being the text of the Four Synods of Westminster* (Stratford-upon-Avon, 1886)

Letters and Notices, vols. 22, 28 (ABSI)

Vaughan, Herbert, *The Bishop of Salford's Reply: Uncanonical Reopening of the Jesuit College and Summary of the Whole Case* (1875)

———, *The Jesuit Claim to Found a College of the Order in Manchester in Opposition to the Judgment of the Ordinary* (1875)

Secondary Sources

Newspaper and periodicals

The *Month*
The *Tablet*
The Times

Books

Abbott, Walter M., *The Documents of Vatican II* (London, 1966)

Bellenger, Dominic Aidan (ed.), *Opening the Scrolls* (Bath, 1987)

Bence-Jones, Mark, *The Catholic Families* (London, 1992)

Bossy, John, *The English Catholic Community, 1570–1850* (London, 1975)

Broadley, M. J., *Louis Charles Casartelli. A Bishop in Peace and War* (Manchester, 2006)

Butler, Cuthbert, *The Life and Times of Bishop Ullathorne* (2 vols., London, 1926)

———, *The Vatican Council* (2 vols., London, 1930)

Chadwick, Owen, *A History of the Popes 1830–1914* (Oxford, 1998)

Champ, Judith, *William Bernard Ullathorne* (Leominster, 2006)

Connell, J., *The Roman Catholic Church in England 1780–1850* (Philadelphia, 1984)

Denzinger, Enrique, *El Magisterio de la Iglesia* (Barcelona, 1963)

Furnival, John, *Children of the Second Spring: Father James Nugent and the Work of Child Care in Liverpool* (Leominster, 2005)

Gavin, M., *Memoirs of Father P. Gallwey S.J.* (London, 1913)

Küng, Hans, *Structures of the Church* (London, 1963)

Leslie, Shane, *Henry Edward Manning: His Life and Labours* (London, 1921)

———, *Letters of Herbert Cardinal Vaughan to Lady Herbert of Lea 1867 to 1903* (London, 1942)

McClelland, V. A., *Cardinal Manning: His Public Life and Influence 1865–1892* (London, 1962)

———, *English Roman Catholics and Higher Education 1830–1903* (Oxford, 1973)

——— and Michael Hodgetts (eds.), *From Without the Flaminian Gate. 150 Years of Roman Catholicism in England and Wales 1850–2000* (London, 1999)

McCoog, Thomas M. (ed.), *Promising Hope* (Rome, 2003)

Norman, Edward, *The English Catholic Church in the Nineteenth Century* (Oxford, 1984)

O'Dea, J., *The Story of the Old Faith in Manchester* (London, 1910)

O'Neil, Robert, *Cardinal Herbert Vaughan* (Tunbridge Wells, 1995)

Purcell, E. S., *Life of Cardinal Manning, Archbishop of Westminster* (2 vols., London, 1896)

Questier, Michael C., *Newsletters from the Archpresbyterate of George Birkhead*, Camden Society Fifth Series, vol. 12 (Cambridge, 1998)

Rahner, Karl (ed.), *Sacramentum Mundi: An Encyclopedia of Theology*, vol. 1, *Absolute and Contingent to Constantinian Era* (London, 1968)

Snead-Cox, J. G., *The Life of Cardinal Vaughan* (2 vols., London, 1910)

Taunton, E. L., *The History of the Jesuits in England, 1580–1773* (London, 1901)

Vidmar, J., *English Catholic Historians and the English Reformation, 1585–1954* (Brighton, 2005)

Ward, Bernard, *The Sequel to Catholic Emancipation* (2 vols., London, 1915)

Articles

Gooch, Leo, 'Henry O'Callaghan: Manning's Reluctant Episcopal Protégé,' in Sheridan Gilley (ed.), *Victorian Churches and Churchmen: Essays presented to Vincent Alan McClelland* (Woodbridge, 2005)

Plunkett, Bro., 'Historical Sketch of the English Province', in *The Ryken Quarterly* (1964)

Rafferty, Oliver P., 'The Jesuit College in Manchester, 1875,' *Recusant History* 20 (2) (1990), pp. 291–304

Whitehead, Maurice, 'The English Jesuits and Episcopal Authority: The Liverpool Test Case, 1840–43,' *Recusant History* 18 (1986), pp. 197–219

Unpublished theses

Connelly, G. P., 'Catholicism in Manchester and Salford, 1770–1850' (Ph.D. thesis, University of Manchester, 1980)

Lannon, D., 'Bishop Turner and Educational Provision within the Salford Diocesan Area, 1840–1870' (M.Phil. thesis, University of Hull, 1994)

L'Estrange, P., 'The Nineteenth-Century British Jesuits, with special reference to Their Relations with the Vicars Apostolic and the Bishops' (D.Phil. thesis, University of Oxford, 1990)

Whitehead, M., 'The Contribution of the Society of Jesus to Secondary Education in Liverpool: The History of the Development of St Francis Xavier's College, c. 1840–1902' (Ph.D. thesis, University of Hull, 1984)

INDEX

Italic page numbers indicate material in the appendices. Page spans may indicate repeated mentions rather than single entries. Letters are listed by names of senders, then recipients; the contents of letters are not itemised in the index.